STUDY GUIDE
CHAPTERS 12-26

Ann DeCapite
Coastal Carolina Community College

ACCOUNTING
Sixth Edition

Charles T. Horngren
Walter T. Harrison
Linda S. Bamber

PEARSON

Prentice Hall

Upper Saddle River, New Jersey 07458

VP/Editorial Director: Jeff Shelstad
Assistant Editor: Sam Goffinet
Manager, Print Production: Christy Mahon
Production Editor & Buyer: Wanda Rockwell
Printer/Binder: Courier, Bookmart Press

Pearson Prentice Hall™ is a trademark of Pearson Education, Inc.

10 9 8 7 6 5 4 3 2 1
ISBN 0-13-144586-3

Contents

Chapter 12 - Partnerships

CHAPTER OVERVIEW

In Chapter 1 you were introduced to the three legal forms of business organizations: sole proprietorships, partnerships, and corporation. Since then, the focus has been on either sole proprietorships or corporations. We now turn our attention to the third type, partnerships. The differences in accounting for partnerships compared to sole proprietorships and corporations lies in the accounting for the creation of the business, how profits and losses are divided among the partners, and how the admission or withdrawal of partners is accounted for. Basically, all other business transactions are accounted for exactly the same as all other forms of business organizations. The learning objectives for this chapter are to

1. Identify the characteristics of a partnership.
2. Account for partner's investments in a partnership.
3. Allocate profits and losses to the partners.
4. Account for the admission of a new partner.
5. Account for the withdrawal of a partner from the firm.
6. Account for the liquidation of a partnership.
7. Prepare partnership financial statements.

CHAPTER REVIEW

Objective 1 - Identify the characteristics of a partnership.

A **partnership** is an association of two or more persons who are co-owners of a business for profit. Partners frequently draw up a **partnership agreement**, also called **articles of partnership**. This agreement is a written contract between the partners that sets forth the duties and rights of each partner.

The characteristics of a partnership are:

1. **Limited life**. The addition or withdrawal of a partner dissolves the partnership.
2. **Mutual agency**. Every partner has the authority to obligate the business to contracts within the scope of regular business operations.
3. **Unlimited liability**. If the partnership cannot pay its debts, the partners are personally responsible for payment.
4. **Co-ownership**. Assets of the business become the joint property of the partnership.
5. **No partnership income taxes**. The net income of a partnership is divided among the partners, who individually pay income taxes on their portions of the partnership's income.
6. **Partners' owner's equity accounts**. Separate owner's equity accounts will be set up for each partner, both a Capital account and Drawing account.

Exhibit 12-2 in your text summarizes the advantages and disadvantages of partnerships.

There are two basic types of partnerships:

- **General partnership.** Each partner is an owner of the business and shares 100% of the benefits and risks of ownership.
- **Limited partnership.** Two classes of partners exist: general partners and limited partners. The general partner(s) assumes the majority of the risk of ownership. There must be at least one general partner. The limited partners are so-called because their liability for partnership obligations is limited in some way—usually to the amount of their investment in the partnership. Because their risk is limited, so is their share of potential profits. Most of the large accounting firms are organized as **limited liability partnership (LLPs).** In an LLP, the individual partner's liability for the firm's debts is restricted in some way.

An **S Corporation** is treated similar to a partnership for tax purposes. This means that the partnership pays no income taxes on its income; rather, the individual shareholders pay taxes on the distributions they receive during the year. There are restrictions to forming S Corporations and their popularity fluctuates with changes in the legislation affecting them.

Objective 2 - Account for partner's investments in a partnership.

Partners may invest assets and liabilities in a business. The simplest investment to account for is cash:

Cash	XX	
Partner's Name, Capital		XX

Assets other than cash are recorded at their current market value. Suppose Woodard, an individual, invests land that he owns outright in a partnership. The land cost him $60,000 several years ago and now has a current market value of $95,000. The correct entry on the partnership's books is:

Land	95,000	
Woodard, Capital		95,000

Suppose Woodard still owed $10,000 on the land. The entry to record the initial capital investment by Woodard would be:

Land	95,000	
Note Payable		10,000
Woodard, Capital		85,000

Objective 3 - Allocate profits and losses to the partners.

If there is no partnership agreement, or the agreement does not specify how profits and losses are to be divided, then the partners share profits and losses equally. If the agreement specifies a method for sharing profits, but not losses, then losses are shared in the same manner as profits.

Several methods exist to allocate profits and losses. Partners may share profits and losses according to a stated fraction or percentage. If the partnership agreement allocates 2/3 of the profits and losses to Taylor, and 1/3 to Simpson, then the entry to record the allocation of $60,000 of income is:

```
Income Summary                          60,000
    Taylor, Capital (60,000 x 2/3)                  40,000
    Simpson, Capital (60,000 x 1/3)                 20,000
```

Suppose Taylor and Simpson have the capital balances listed below:

```
Taylor, Capital                         240,000
Simpson, Capital                        160,000
Total Capital balances                  400,000
```

Sharing of profits and losses may also be allocated based on a combination of capital contributions and service to the business. The important point to remember is to follow the exact order of allocation specified by the partnership agreement. Assume that Taylor and Simpson's partnership agreement specifies that the first $20,000 will be divided according to each partner's capital contribution, the next $30,000 will be based on service with Taylor receiving $22,000 and Simpson receiving $8,000, and any remaining amount will be divided equally. The allocation of the $60,000 net income will be determined as follows:

	Taylor	Simpson	Total
Total net income			$60,000
Sharing of first $20,000 of net income based on capital contributions *:			
Taylor (240,000 / 400,000) x 20,000	$12,000		
Simpson (160,000 / 400,000) x 20,000		$8,000	20,000
Net income remaining for allocation			40,000
Sharing of next $30,000 based on service:			
Taylor	22,000		
Simpson		8,000	30,000
Net income remaining for allocation			10,000
Taylor	5,000		
Simpson		5,000	10,000
Net income remaining for allocation			$ 0
Net income allocated to the partners	$ 39,000	$ 21,000	$ 60,000

* To allocate income (loss) in proportion to the partner's capital contributions to the business, use this formula:

$$\text{Income allocated to a partner} = \frac{\text{Partner's capital}}{\text{Total capital}} \times \text{Net income (loss)}$$

Then, the entry to record the allocation of $60,000 of income is:

```
Income Summary                          60,000
    Taylor, Capital                                39,000
    Simpson, Capital                               21,000
```

When a loss occurs, the process does not change. Simply follow the terms of the agreement (or divide the loss equally in the absence of an agreement) in the order specified.

Partners generally make periodic withdrawals of cash from a partnership. If Simpson withdraws $5,000 from the partnership, the entry is:

Simpson, Drawing	5,000	
Cash		5,000

Just like in a sole proprietorship, the drawing accounts must be closed to the capital accounts at the end of the period. If Simpson's $5,000 withdrawal is the only withdrawal during the period, the closing entry is:

Simpson, Capital	5,000	
Simpson, Drawing		5,000

Objective 4 - Account for the admission of a new partner.

Remember that a partnership is dissolved when a new partner is added or an existing partner withdraws. Often a new partnership is immediately formed to replace the old partnership. CPA firms and law firms often admit new partners and have existing partners retire during the course of a year. All the current partners must approve the new partner in order for the new partner to participate in the business.

A new partner may be admitted into an existing partnership by either:
1. purchasing a present partner's interest, or
2. by investing in the partnership.

When **purchasing a partnership interest**, the new partner pays the old partner directly, according to the terms of the purchase agreement. Thus, the partnership receives no cash. The only entry the partnership will make is to close the old partner's capital account and open the new partner's capital account:

Old Partner, Capital	XX	
New Partner, Capital		XX

A person may also be admitted to a partnership by directly **investing in the partnership**. This investment can be a simple investment, and is recorded as:

Cash and Other assets	XX	
New Partner, Capital		XX

The new partner's interest in the business will equal:

$$\text{New partner's interest} \quad = \quad \frac{\text{New partner's capital}}{\text{Total capital}}$$

Note: The sharing of profits and losses is determined by the new partnership agreement, and not by the partnership interest allotted to the new partner.

Successful partnerships frequently require incoming partners to pay a **bonus** to existing partners. In this situation, the incoming partner will pay more for a portion of the partnership interest than the amount of capital he receives. The difference, which is a bonus to the existing partners, is computed by a three-step calculation:

1) Total capital before new partner's investment
    + New partner's investment
    = Total capital after new partner's investment

2) New partner's capital balance = Total capital after new partner's investment multiplied by the new partner's interest in the partnership

3) Bonus to existing partners = New partner's investment - New partner's capital

The entry on the partnership books to record the transaction is:

Cash	XX	
New Partner, Capital		XX
Old Partner #1, Capital (Bonus)		XX
Old Partner #2, Capital (Bonus)		XX

Note: The bonus paid by the new partner is credited to the old partners' Capital accounts. The allocation of the bonus to existing partners is based on the partnership agreement of the existing partners profit-loss sharing ratio.

In some cases, a potential new partner may bring substantial future benefits to a partnership. In this situation, the existing partners may offer the newcomer a partnership share that includes a bonus. The calculation is similar to the calculation for a bonus to the existing partners:

1) Total capital before new partner's investment
    + New partner's investment
    = Total capital after new partner's investment

2) New partner's capital balance = Total capital after new partner's investment multiplied by the new partner's interest in the partnership

3) Bonus to new partner = New partner's capital - New partner's investment

The entry on the partnership's books to record the transaction is:

Cash and Other Assets	XX	
Old Partner #1, Capital (Bonus)	XX	
Old Partner #2, Capital (Bonus)	XX	
New Partner, Capital		XX

Note: The bonus given to the new partner is debited to the old partners' Capital accounts. The allocation of the bonus to the existing partners is based on the partnership agreement of the existing partners profit-loss sharing ratio.

Objective 5 - Account for a partner's withdrawal from the firm.

Partners may **withdraw from a partnership** due to retirement, partnership disputes, or other reasons. The withdrawing partner may sell his or her interest or may receive the appropriate portion of the business directly from the partnership in the form of cash, other partnership assets, or notes.

The first step is to determine whether the partnership's assets are to be valued at book value or market value. If assets are to be valued at market value, an independent appraisal will be used to revalue the assets. Increases in asset values are debited to asset accounts and credited to the partners' capital accounts according to the profit-and-loss sharing ratio. Decreases in asset values are debited to the partners' capital accounts and credited to asset accounts according to the profit-and-loss sharing ratio. After recording the revaluation of the assets, the market value becomes the new book value of the assets.

A partner may withdraw from a partnership at book value, at less than book value, or at more than book value. (Remember that book value may or may not be equal to current market value, depending upon whether the assets have been revalued or not.) A partner willing to withdraw at less than book value may be eager to leave the partnership. A partner withdrawing at more than book value may be collecting a bonus from the remaining partners, who may be eager to have the partner withdraw.

Withdrawal at book value is recorded as:

Withdrawing Partner, Capital	XX	
Cash, Other Assets, or Note Payable		XX

Withdrawal at less than book value is recorded by:

Withdrawing Partner, Capital	XX	
Cash, Other Assets, or Note Payable		XX
Remaining Partners, Capital		XX

When a partner withdraws at less than book value, the difference between the withdrawing partner's capital and the payment to the withdrawing partner is allocated to the remaining partners based on the new profit-and-loss ratio.

Withdrawal at more than book value is recorded by:

Withdrawing Partner, Capital	XX	
Remaining Partners, Capital	XX	
Cash, Other Assets, or Note Payable		XX

When a partner withdraws at more than book value, the difference between the payment to the withdrawing partner and the withdrawing partner's capital is allocated to the remaining partners based on the new profit-and-loss ratio.

The death of a partner also dissolves the partnership. The books are closed to determine the deceased partner's capital balance on the date of death. Settlement with the partner's estate is made according to the partnership agreement.

Objective 6 - Account for the liquidation of a partnership.

Liquidation is the process of going out of business and involves three basic steps:

1. Selling the partnership's assets and allocating any gains or losses to the partners' capital accounts based on the profit-and-loss ratio.
2. Paying the partnership's liabilities.
3. Distributing the remaining cash to the partners based on their remaining capital balances.

When selling assets, gains result in credits (increases) to partners' capital accounts. Losses result in debits (decreases) to partners' capital accounts. Gains and losses are allocated between the partners according to their respective profit and loss sharing ratios.

The general worksheet for liquidation of a partnership is:

	Cash	+	Noncash Assets	=	Liabilities	+	Capital	
Balances before sale of assets	XX		XX		XX		XX	
Sale of assets and sharing of							XX	if gain, or
gains and (losses)	XX		(XX)				(XX)	if loss
Balances after sale of assets	XX		-0-				XX	
Payment of liabilities	(XX)				(XX)			
Balances after payment of liabilities	XX		-0-		-0-		XX	
Disbursement of cash to partners	(XX)						(XX)	
Ending balances	-0-		-0-		-0-		-0-	

Occasionally, allocation of losses on the sale of assets results in a capital deficiency for one or more partners. The deficient partner should contribute personal assets to eliminate the deficiency. If not, the deficiency must be allocated to the remaining partners.

Objective 7 - Prepare partnership financial statements.

Partnership financial statements are similar to the financial statements of a proprietorship. The exceptions are that a partnership income statement includes a section showing the division of net income to the partners, and the owners' equity section of the balance sheet includes accounts for each partner.

TEST YOURSELF

All the self-testing materials in this chapter focus on information and procedures that your instructor is likely to test in quizzes and examinations.

I. Matching   *Match each numbered term with its lettered definition.*

_____ 1. Articles of partnership
_____ 2. Capital deficiency
_____ 3. Unlimited personal liability
_____ 4. Dissolution
_____ 5. Liquidation
_____ 6. Mutual agency
_____ 7. Bonus
_____ 8. Limited partnership
_____ 9. General partnership
_____10. S Corporation

A. A debit balance in a partner's capital account that requires the additional investment of assets by the deficient partner or distribution to remaining partners.
B. Ending of a partnership
C. A business organization with shareholders that is treated as a partnership for tax purposes.
D. The ability of every partner to bind the business to a contract within the scope of the partnership's regular business operations
E. The process of going out of business
F. Type of partnership with at least one general partner who has unlimited liability and at least one limited partner whose liability is limited to their investment in the business.
G. When a partnership (or a proprietorship) cannot pay its debts with business assets, the partners (or the proprietor) must use personal assets to meet the debt
H. A contract among partners specifying such things as the name, location, and nature of the business; the name, capital investment, and the duties of each partner; and the method of sharing profits and losses by the partners
I. Results when assets contributed (or withdrawn) do not equal the amount credited (or debited) to a partner's capital account
J. Type of partnership in which each partner shares all the privileges and risks of ownership.

II. Multiple Choice   *Circle the best answer.*

1. If the partnership agreement does not stipulate how profits and losses will be divided, then by law, partners must share profits and losses:

   A. equally
   B. in the ratio of their capital balances.
   C. based on a ratio of time devoted to the business.
   D. in the same proportion as their initial investments.

2. Whitney invests cash of $20,000 and a building with a cost of $250,000 and accumulated depreciation to date of $95,000 in the Whitney and Becker Partnership. The building has a current market value of $345,000. A mortgage note payable of $105,000 is outstanding on the building and will be assumed by the partnership. Whitney's capital account would be credited for:

A. $365,000.   C. $260,000.
B. $175,000.   D. $165,000.

3. A partnership income statement includes:

A. a listing of all of the partners' capital account balances.
B. a listing of all of the partners' drawing account balances.
C. a section showing the division of net income to the partners.
D. both a and b are correct.

4. All of the following are characteristics of a general partnership except:

A. mutual agency.   C. limited life.
B. limited liability.   D. co-ownership of property.

5. When a partner takes money out of the partnership, the partner's:

A. drawing is credited.   C. capital is debited.
B. drawing is debited.   D. capital is credited.

6. A new partner may be admitted to a partnership:

A. only by investing in the partnership
B. only by purchasing a partner's interest
C. by purchasing common stock of the partnership
D. either by investing in the partnership or by purchasing a partner's interest

7. In a partnership liquidation, a gain from the sale of assets is allocated to the:

A. payment of partnership liabilities.
B. partners based on their profit-and-loss ratio.
C. partner with the lowest capital balance.
D. partners based on their capital balances.

8. If a partner has a debit balance in his capital account and is personally insolvent, then the other partners:

A. absorb the deficiency based on their personal wealth.
B. absorb the deficiency based on their capital balances.
C. absorb the deficiency based on their profit-and-loss ratio.
D. sue the insolvent partner's spouse.

9. ABC partnership shares profits and losses in a 2:4:4 ratio respectively. This means:

A. partner A receives 20% of the profits.
B. partner A receives 50% of the profits.
C. partner B receives 60% of the profits.
D. partner C receives 20% of the profits.

10. In a general partnership, which of the following is true?

9

A. there must be more than one limited partner   C. all partners have unlimited liability
B. there must be at least one general partner   D. some partners have limited liability

III. Completion   *Complete each of the following statements.*

1. If the partnership agreement specifies how profits will be shared, but does not specify how losses will be shared, then the losses are allocated _____.
2. The five characteristics of a partnership are: 1) _____,
   2) _____, 3) _____,
   4) _____, and 5) _____.
3. The difference between a partnership and sole proprietorship is that a partnership has _____
   _____ owners, while a sole proprietorship has _____owner.
4. _____ refers to the ability of any partner to contract on behalf of the partnership.
5. A _____ occurs when a new partner is admitted or an existing partner leaves a partnership.
6. A partnership undergoes _____ when it ceases operations and settles all its affairs.
7. A debit balance in a partner's capital account is called _____.
8. The steps in liquidating a partnership are:
   a)_____
   b)_____
   c)_____
   d)_____
9. A partner with limited liability is called a _____.
10. When liquidating, cash is distributed to the partners according to the _____.

IV. Daily Exercises

1. Two sole proprietors, Wells Co. and Bank Co., decide to form a partnership called Wells Bank. Wells will contribute the following to the proprietorship:

	Book value	Market Value
Cash	8,000	8,000
Inventory	7,200	7,600
Equipment	11,700	9,000
Liabilities	6,100	6,100

   Record the journal entry to reflect Wells' investment.

Date	Accounts and Explanation	PR	Debit	Credit

2. The X, Y & Z partnership reported $45,000 net income its first year of operations If the partners neglected to agree on the distribution of profits, how much should partners A, C, and E receive?

10

3. Refer to the information in Daily Exercise #2 above, but assume the partners agreed to a $12,000 per partner salary allowance, with any balance divided 3:2:1 among X, Y, and Z. Calculate the amount owed to each partner.

4. Review the information in Daily Exercises #3 above, but assume the first year resulted in net income of $6,000. Calculate the amount X, Y, and Z should receive.

5. Review the information in Daily Exercises #3 above, but assume the first year resulted in net loss of $10,000. Calculate the amount X, Y, and Z should receive.

6. Record the journal entry for Daily Exercise #4 above.

Date	Accounts and Explanation	PR	Debit	Credit

7. A partnership has decided to liquidate. After selling the assets and paying the debts, $9,000 in liabilities remains outstanding. To whom should the creditors look for payment?

8. Assume the same information in Daily Exercise #7, except the partnership is a limited partnership. How would your answer change?

V. Exercises

1. Frank Lord and Joseph Taylor formed a partnership. Lord contributed cash of $25,000 and land with a fair market value of $65,000 that cost $34,000. The partnership also assumed Lord's note payable on the land of $24,000. Taylor contributed $50,000 in cash, equipment with a fair market value of $62,000 and a book value of $26,000, and the partnership assumed his accounts receivable of $8,500.

Make journal entries to show each partner's contribution to the business.

Date	Accounts and Explanation	PR	Debit	Credit

2. Gapp and Kidd formed a partnership. Gapp invested $102,000 and Kidd invested $68,000. Gapp devotes most of his time on the road developing the business, while Kidd devotes some of his time to managing the home office and the rest of his time is spent at his second job. They have agreed to share profits as follows:

- The first $50,000 of profits is allocated based on the partner's capital contribution.
- The next $50,000 of profits is allocated $40,000 to Gapp and $10,000 to Kidd based on their service to the partnership.
- Any remaining amount is allocated 3:1.

A. If the partnership profits are $150,000, how much will be allocated to Kidd, and how much will be allocated to Gapp?
B. If the partnership has a loss of $80,000, how much will be allocated to Gapp, and how   much will be allocated to Kidd?
C. If the partnership profits are $42,000, how much will be allocated to Gapp, and how much will be allocated to Kidd?

12

A.

	Gapp	Kidd	Total

B.

	Gapp	Kidd	Total

C.

	Gapp	Kidd	Total

3. Keith and Vince are partners in a landscaping business. Their capital balances are $24,000 and $16,000 respectively. They share profits and losses equally. They admit Amy to a one-fourth interest with a cash investment of $8,000. Make the journal entry to show the admission of Amy to the partnership.

Date	Accounts and Explanation	PR	Debit	Credit

4. Anne, Barbara, and Cathy are partners with capital balances of $15,000, $45,000, and $30,000 respectively. They share profits and losses equally. Barbara decides to retire.

A. Make the journal entry to show Barbara's retirement if she is allowed to withdraw $25,000 in cash.

Date	Accounts and Explanation	PR	Debit	Credit

14

B. Make the journal entry to show Barbara's retirement if she is allowed to withdraw $45,000 in cash.

Date	Accounts and Explanation	PR	Debit	Credit

C. Make the journal entry to show Barbara's retirement if she is allowed to withdraw $55,000 in cash.

Date	Accounts and Explanation	PR	Debit	Credit

5. The following balance sheet information is given for DJ's Tunes For Hire:

Cash	$ 16,000	Liabilities	$ 28,000
Noncash assets	56,000	Doug, Capital	6,000
		James, Capital	24,000
		Jerome, Capital	14,000
Total assets	$ 72,000	Total liabilities and capital	$ 72,000

Doug, James, and Jerome use a profit and loss ratio of 3:4:1, respectively. Assume that any partner with a deficit in his or her capital account is insolvent. Prepare the journal entries for liquidation assuming the noncash assets are sold for $20,000.

Date	Accounts and Explanation	PR	Debit	Credit

VI. Beyond the Numbers

Review the information in Exercises 5. Assume all information is the same except Doug is a limited partner. Prepare journal entries to record the liquidation.

Date	Accounts and Explanation	PR	Debit	Credit

VII. Demonstration Problems

Demonstration Problem #1

The partnership of Ben and Jerry is considering admitting Waldo as a partner on April 1, 20X6. The partnership general ledger includes the following balances on that date:

Cash	$ 40,000	Total liabilities	$ 50,000
Other assets	85,000	Ben, Capital	25,000
		Jerry, Capital	50,000
Total assets	$ 125,000	Total liabilities and capital	$ 125,000

Ben's share of profits and losses is 1/3 and Jerry's share is 2/3.

Required:

1. Assume that Waldo pays Jerry $75,000 to acquire Jerry's interest of the business, and that Ben has approved Waldo as a new partner.

   a. Prepare the journal entries for the transfer of partner's equity on the partnership books.
   b. Prepare the partnership balance sheet immediately after Waldo is admitted as a partner.

2. Suppose Waldo becomes a partner by investing $75,000 cash to acquire a one-fourth interest in the business.

   a. Prepare a schedule to compute Waldo's capital balance. Record Waldo's investment in the business.
   b. Prepare the partnership balance sheet immediately after Waldo is admitted as a partner.

3. Suppose Waldo becomes a partner by investing $20,000 cash to acquire a one-fourth interest in the business.

    a. Prepare a schedule to compute Waldo's capital balance. Record Waldo's investment in the business.

    b. Prepare the partnership balance sheet immediately after Waldo is admitted as a partner.

Requirement 1

a.

Date	Accounts and Explanation	PR	Debit	Credit

b.

Ben and Waldo
Balance Sheet
April 1, 20X6

Requirement 2

a. Computation of Waldo's capital balance:

Date	Accounts and Explanation	PR	Debit	Credit

b.

Ben, Jerry, and Waldo
Balance Sheet
April 1, 20X6

Requirement 3

a. Computation of Waldo's capital balance:

Date	Accounts and Explanation	PR	Debit	Credit

b.

Ben, Jerry, and Waldo
Balance Sheet
April 1, 20X6

Demonstration Problem #2

The partnership of B, T, and U is liquidating. The partnership agreement allocated profits to the partners in the ratio of 3:2:1. In liquidation, the noncash assets were sold in a single transaction for $120,000 on August 31, 20X8. The partnership paid the liabilities the same day. The partnership accounts are presented at the top of the liquidation schedule that follows.

1. Complete the schedule summarizing the liquidation transactions. See the format on the next page. You may wish to refer to the partnership liquidation exhibits in the text. Assume that U invests cash of $4,000 in the partnership in partial settlement of any capital account deficiency. This cash is distributed to the other partners. The other partners must absorb the remainder of the capital deficiency.
2. Journalize the liquidation transactions.
3. Post the liquidation entries.

Requirement 1 (Summary of liquidation transactions)

	Cash	+	Noncash Assets	=	Liabilities	+	Capital B (1/2)	+	T (1/3)	+	U (1/6)
Balance before sale of assets	30,000		240,000		120,000		90,000		50,000		10,000
a) Sale of assets and sharing of loss											
Balances											
b) Payment of liabilities											
Balances											
c) U's investment of cash to share part of his deficiency											
Balances											
d) Sharing of deficiency by remaining partners in ratio of 3/5 to 2/5											
Balances											
e) Distribution of cash to partners											
Balances											

Requirement 2 (Journal entries to record the liquidation transactions)

a.

Date	Accounts and Explanation	PR	Debit	Credit

b.

Date	Accounts and Explanation	PR	Debit	Credit

c.

Date	Accounts and Explanation	PR	Debit	Credit

d.

Date	Accounts and Explanation	PR	Debit	Credit

e.

Date	Accounts and Explanation	PR	Debit	Credit

Requirement 3 (Post the liquidation transactions)

Cash	
30,000	

Noncash Assets	
240,000	

Liabilities	
	120,000

B, Capital	
	90,000

T, Capital	
	50,000

U, Capital	
	10,000

SOLUTIONS

I. Matching

1. H	5. E	9. J
2. A	6. D	10. C
3. G	7. I	
4. B	8. F	

II. Multiple Choice

1. **A** If the partnership agreement does not stipulate how profits and losses will be divided, then the partners must share profits and losses equally.

2. **C** Partners in a new business will contribute assets and liabilities. Assets and liabilities are recorded at their fair market value. To determine a partner's capital account balance, add the fair market values of the assets contributed and subtract the fair market value of any liabilities. Whitney invests cash, $20,000; a building with a fair market value of $345,000, and a mortgage note payable of $105,000. Therefore, Whitney's capital balance is $20,000 + $345,000 - $105,000 = $260,000.

3. **C** The only difference between a sole proprietorship income statement and a partnership income statement is that the partnership income statement includes a section that shows the allocation of net income among the partners.

4. **B** Limited liability is a characteristic of a limited partnership. Partners in a general partnership, just like a sole proprietorship have unlimited liability for the debts of the business.

5. **B** Withdrawing money from the partnership requires a credit to cash that is balanced with a debit to the partner's Drawing account. The balance of the partner's Drawing account will be closed to his Capital account at the end of the period.

6. **D** Of the items listed, answer C "purchasing common stock of the partnership" is inappropriate since partnerships do not have stock; answers A and B are incorrect because of the use of the word "only" in the answers.

7. **B** Gains and losses incurred in liquidation are allocated based on the partners' profit-loss sharing ratios specified in the partnership agreement.

8. **C** The deficiency in a partner's capital account balance is allocated as if it were a loss based on the partners' profit-and-loss sharing ratios specified in the partnership agreement.

9. **A** To determine a partner's fractional share, create a denominator by summing the integers (2 + 4 + 4 = 10) and use the partner's ratio as the numerator. Thus, A receives 2/10 or 20%; B receives 4/10 or 40%; and C receives 4/10 or 40%.

10. **C** A general partnership has no limited partners. All partners in a general partnership have unlimited liability for the debts of the business.

III. Completion

1. in the same way as profits.
2. limited life, mutual agency, unlimited liability, co-ownership of property, no partnership income taxes
3. two or more, one
4. mutual agency
5. dissolution
6. liquidation
7. deficit
8. adjust and close the books, sell the assets, pay the debts, distribute any remaining cash to the partners (order is important)
9. limited partner
10. the balance in the capital accounts (*not* the profit/loss ratio)

IV. Daily Exercises

1.

Cash	8,000	
Inventory	7,600	
Equipment	9,000	
Liabilities		6,100
Wells, Capital		18,500

Assets contributed are recorded at their current market value. Well's net investment is $18,500, the difference between the fair market value of the assets ($8,000 + $7,600 + $9,000) less the liabilities.

2. Each partner receives an equal share, or $15,000. When the partnership agreement fails to specify how profits and losses will be shared among the partners, the distribution of profits (and losses) is always equal.

3.

	Partners			Amount
	X	Y	Z	45,000
Salary Allowance	12,000	12,000	12,000	(36,000)
Balance				9,000
3:2:1	4,500	3,000	1,500	(9,000)
	16,500	15,000	13,500	0
Proof:	$16,500 + $15,000 + $13,500 = $45,000			

Study Tip: After the calculating, always verify the individual amounts sum back to the original amount.

4.

	X	Y	Z	Amount
		Partners		
	X	Y	Z	6,000
Salary Allowance	12,000	12,000	12,000	(36,000)
Balance				(30,000)
3:2:1	(15,000)	(10,000)	(5,000)	(30,000)
	(3,000)	2,000	7,000	0

Proof: $-3,000 + $2,000 + $7,000 = $6,000 ←

5.

	X	Y	Z	Amount
		Partners		
	X	Y	Z	(10,000)
Salary Allowance	12,000	12,000	12,000	(36,000)
Balance				(46,000)
3:2:1	(23,000)	(15,333)	(7,667)	(46,000)
	(11,000)	(3,333)	4,333	0

Proof: $-11,000 + $-3,333 + $4,333 = $-10,000 ←

6.

X, Capital	3,000	
Income Summary	6,000	
Y, Capital		2,000
Z, Capital		7,000

7. The partnership's creditors can look to any of the partners for payment. In a general partnership, each partner has unlimited personal liability for partnership's debts. Creditors would be wise to enforce their claims against the partner with the largest net worth.

8. In a limited partnership, two classes of partners exist—general and limited. The liability of a limited partner extends only to the amount invested. The fact that liabilities remain after all the assets have been sold and the cash proceeds distributed to creditors indicates the limited partners' obligations have been met. Therefore, the creditors can look only to the general partner(s) for payment.

V. Exercises

1.

GENERAL JOURNAL

Date	Accounts and Explanation	PR	Debit	Credit
	Cash		25,000	
	Land		65,000	
	Notes Payable			24,000
	Lord, Capital			66,000
	Cash		50,000	
	Equipment		62,000	
	Account Receivable		8,500	
	Taylor, Capital			120,500

2.

A.

	Gapp	Kidd	Total
Total net income			150,000
Sharing of first $50,000 of net income, based on capital contribution:			
Gapp (102,000/170,000 × 50,000)	30,000		
Kidd (68,000/170,000 × 50,000)		20,000	
Total			50,000
Net income remaining for allocation			60,000
Sharing of the next $50,000 based on service:			
Gapp	40,000		
Kidd		10,000	
Total			50,000
Net income remaining for allocation			10,000
Remainder shared equally:			
Gapp (3/4 × 10,000)	7,500		
Kidd (1/4 × 10,000)		2,500	
Total			10,000
Net income remaining for allocation			-0-
Net income allocated to the partners	77,500	32,500	110,000

B.

	Gapp	Kidd	Total
Total net income (loss)			(80,000)
Sharing of first $50,000 of net income (loss), based on capital contribution:			
Gapp (102,000/170,000 × 50,000)	30,000		
Kidd (68,000/170,000 × 50,000)		20,000	
Total			(50,000)
Net income (loss) remaining for allocation			(130,000)
Sharing of the remainder based on service:			
Gapp	40,000		
Kidd		10,000	
Total			(50,000)
Net income (loss) remaining for allocation			(180,000)
Remainder shared equally:			
Gapp (3/4 × 180,000)	(135,000)		
Kidd (1/4 × 180,000)		(45,000)	
Total			70,000
Net income (loss) remaining for allocation			-0-
Net income (loss) allocated to the partners	(65,000)	(15,000)	(80,000)

C.

	Gapp	Kidd	Total
Total net income			42,000
Sharing of first $50,000 of net income, based on capital contribution:			
Gapp (102,000/170,000 × 50,000)	30,000		
Kidd (68,000/170,000 × 50,000)		20,000	
Total			(50,000)
Net income remaining for allocation			(8,000)
Sharing of the remainder based on service:			
Gapp	40,000		
Kidd		10,000	
Total			(50,000)
Remainder shared equally:			(58,000)
Gapp (3/4 × 58,000)	(43,500)		
Kidd (1/4 × 58,000)		(14,500)	
Total			58,000
Net income remaining for allocation			-0-
Net income allocated to the partners	26,500	15,500	42,000

27

3. Total new partnerships equity is $48,000 ($24,000 + $16,000 + $8,000). One fourth of $48,000 is $12,000.

Date	Accounts and Explanation	PR	Debit	Credit
	Cash		8,000	
	Keith, Capital [1/2 × (12,000 - 8,000)]		2,000	
	Vince, Capital		2,000	
	Amy, Capital [1/4 × (24,000 + 16,000 + 8,000)]			12,000

4.

A.

Date	Accounts and Explanation	PR	Debit	Credit
	Barbara, Capital		45,000	
	Cash			25,000
	Anne, Capital			10,000
	Cathy, Capital			10,000

B.

Date	Accounts and Explanation	PR	Debit	Credit
	Barbara, Capital		45,000	
	Cash			45,000

C.

Date	Accounts and Explanation	PR	Debit	Credit
	Barbara, Capital		45,000	
	Anne, Capital		5,000	
	Cathy, Capital		5,000	
	Cash			55,000

5.

Date	Accounts and Explanation	PR	Debit	Credit
	Cash		20,000	
	Doug, Capital		13,500	
	James, Capital		18,000	
	Jerome, Capital		4,500	
	Noncash assets			56,000
	Sale of noncash assets at $36,000 loss			

Loss on sale = 36,000 (56,000 - 20,000). Therefore,

Doug = 36,000 × 3/8 = 13,500

James = 36,000 × 4/8 = 18,000

Jerome = 36,000 × 1/8 = 4,500

Date	Accounts and Explanation	PR	Debit	Credit
	Liabilities		28,000	
	Cash			28,000
	Paid liabilities			
	James, Capital		6,000	
	Jerome, Capital		1,500	
	Doug, Capital			7,500
	Allocated Doug's deficit to remaining partners			

Doug's deficit = 7,500 (6,000 - 13,500)

James   = 4/5 × 7,500 = 6,000

Jerome = 1/5 × 7,500 = 1,500

	Jerome, Capital		8,000	
	Cash			8,000
	Distributed remaining cash to Jerome based on remaining capital balance			
	James's balance = 0 (24,000 - 18,000 - 6,000 = 0)			

VI. Beyond the Numbers

Date	Accounts and Explanation	PR	Debit	Credit
	Cash		20,000	
	Doug, Capital		6,000	*
	James, Capital		24,000	**
	Jerome, Capital		6,000	
	Noncash Assets			56,000

*   Because Doug is a limited partner, the amount of loss he must absorb is limited to the balance in his capital account.

**   After debiting Doug's account for $6,000, the remaining loss is distributed between James and Jerome, as follows:

James   = 30,000 × 4/5 = 24,000

Jerome = 30,000 × 1/5 =   6,000

	Liabilities		28,000	
	Cash			28,000
	Jerome, Capital		8,000	
	Cash			8,000

VII. Demonstration Problems

Demonstration Problem #1 Solved and Explained

Requirement 1

a. Apr 1   Jerry, Capital   50,000   Debit closes Jerry's account
                 Waldo, Capital   50,000 Credit opens Waldo's account
           To transfer Jerry's equity in the partnership to Waldo.

Note that the book value of Jerry's capital account ($50,000) is transferred, not the price Waldo paid ($75,000) to buy into the business. Since the partnership received no cash from the transaction, the entry would be the same no matter what Waldo paid Jerry for the interest.

b.

Ben and Waldo
Balance Sheet
April 1, 20X6

Cash	40,000	Total liabilities	50,000
Other assets	85,000	Ben, Capital	25,000
		Waldo, Capital	50,000
Total assets	$125,000	Total liabilities and capital	$125,000

Requirement 2

a. Computation of Waldo's capital balance:
   Partnership capital before Waldo is admitted
        (25,000 + 50,000) $ 75,000
   Waldo's investment in the partnership   75,000
   Partnership capital after Waldo is admitted $150,000
   Waldo's capital in the partnership
        (150,000 1/4) $ 37,500

Date	Accounts and Explanation	PR	Debit	Credit
April 1	Cash		75,000	
	Waldo, Capital			37,500
	Ben, Capital (1/3 of $37,500)			12,500
	Jerry, Capital (2/3 of $37,500)			25,000
	To admit Waldo as a partner with a one-fourth interest in the business.			

Note that Ben's capital account increased by $12,500 and Jerry's capital account increased by $25,000. These amounts represent Ben and Jerry's proportionate share of the $37,500 amount by which Waldo's $75,000 payment exceeded his $37,500 capital account credit. When a partner is admitted by investment in the partnership, often the investment exceeds the new partner's capital account credit, and the original partners share proportionately in the difference.

b.

Ben, Jerry, and Waldo
Balance Sheet
April 1, 20X6

Cash (40,000 + 75,000)	$115,000	Total liabilities	$ 50,000
Other assets	85,000	Ben, Capital	37,500
		Jerry, Capital	75,000
		Waldo, Capital	37,500
Total assets	$200,000	Total liabilities and capital	$200,000

Requirement 3

a. Computation of Waldo's capital balance:

Partnership capital before Waldo is admitted (25,000 + 50,000)	$ 75,000
Waldo's investment in the partnership	20,000
Partnership capital after Waldo is admitted	$95,000
Waldo's capital in the partnership (95,000 × 1/4)	$ 23,750

Date	Accounts and Explanation	PR	Debit	Credit
April 1	Cash		20,000	
	Ben, Capital (1/3 of $3,750)		1,250	
	Jerry, Capital (2/3 of $3,750)		2,500	
	Waldo, Capital			23,750
	To admit Waldo as a partner with a one-fourth interest in the business.			

Note that Ben's capital account decreased by $1,250 and Jerry's capital account decreased by $2,500. These amounts represent Ben and Jerry's proportionate share of the $3,750 amount by which Waldo's capital account balance of $23,750 exceeded his $20,000 payment. When a partner is admitted by investment in the partnership, often the partnership interest received exceeds the new partner's cash investment, and the original partners share proportionately in the difference.

b.

Ben, Jerry, and Waldo
Balance Sheet
April 1, 20X6

Cash (40,000 + 20,000)	$60,000	Total liabilities	$ 50,000
Other assets	85,000	Ben, Capital	23,750
		Jerry, Capital	47,500
		Waldo, Capital	23,750
Total assets	$145,000	Total liabilities and capital	$145,000

<u>Points to Remember</u>

1. Partners may specify any profit or loss sharing method they desire. Common arrangements include:

    a. Sharing equally - unless the partners agree otherwise, profits and losses are required by law to be divided equally
    b. Sharing based on a stated fraction
    c. Sharing based on capital contributions
    d. Sharing based on salaries and interest
    e. Sharing based on a combination of the above and/or other factors

> **Study Tip:** Be alert to problems requiring an allocation of profits and losses when the capital account balances are given for each partner, but nothing is specified about the sharing method. When the sharing method is not specified, each partner receives an equal share.

2. New partners are often admitted to established partnerships. Technically, a new partnership is formed to carry on the former partnership's business, and the old partnership ceases to exist (it is dissolved). Although the old partnership dissolves, the business is not normally terminated, nor are the assets liquidated.

> **Study Tip:** Be sure you can distinguish between the admission of a partner by purchase of a partner's interest (Requirement 1) and admission by making a direct investment in the partnership (Requirements 2 & 3).

Demonstration Problem #2 Solved and Explained

Requirement 1 (Summary of liquidation transactions)

	Cash	+	Noncash Assets	=	Liabilities	+	B (1/2)	+	Capital T (1/3)	+	U (1/6)
Balance before sale of assets	30,000		240,000		120,000		90,000		50,000		10,000
a) Sale of assets and sharing of loss	120,000		(240,000)				(60,000)		(40,000)		(20,000)
Balances	150,000		-0-		120,000		30,000		10,000		(10,000)
b) Payment of liabilities	(120,000)				(120,000)						
Balances	30,000		-0-		-0-		30,000		10,000		(10,000)
c) U's investment of cash to share part of his deficiency	4,000										4,000
Balances	34,000		-0-		-0-		30,000		10,000		(6,000)
d) Sharing of deficiency by remaining partners in ratio of 3/5 to 2/5							(3,600)		(2,400)		6,000
Balances	34,000		-0-		-0-		26,400		7,600		-0-
e) Distribution of cash to partners	(34,000)						(26,400)		(7,600)		
Balances	-0-		-0-		-0-		-0-		-0-		-0-

33

Requirement 2 (Journal entries to record the liquidation transactions)

a.

Date	Accounts and Explanation	PR	Debit	Credit
	Cash		120,000	
	B, Capital [(240,000 – 120,000) × 3/6]		60,000	
	T, Capital [(240,000 – 120,000) × 2/6]		40,000	
	U, Capital [(200,000 – 120,000) × 1/6]		20,000	
	Noncash Assets			240,000
	To record the sale of noncash assets in liquidation, and to distribute loss to partners.			

b.

Date	Accounts and Explanation	PR	Debit	Credit
	Liabilities		120,000	
	Cash			120,000
	To pay liabilities in liquidation.			

c.

Date	Accounts and Explanation	PR	Debit	Credit
	Cash		4,000	
	U, Capital			4,000
	U's contribution to pay part of the capital deficiency in liquidation.			

After posting the entries above, U's capital account reveals a $6,000 deficiency, indicated by its debit balance:

U, Capital

Loss on sale	20,000	Bal.	10,000
		Investment	4,000
Bal.	6,000		

d.

Date	Accounts and Explanation	PR	Debit	Credit
	B, Capital ($6,000 3/5)		3,600	
	T, Capital ($6,000 2/5)		2,400	
	U, Capital			6,000
	To allocate U's capital deficiency to the other partners in their profit and loss ratios.			

Prior to U's withdrawal from the partnership, the partners shared profits and losses as follows:

Ratio: B   3 = 1/2
              T   2 = 1/3
              U   1 = 1/6

The remaining partners are required to absorb the deficiency left by a partner who is unable to contribute sufficient capital to cover the deficiency. After a $4,000 contribution, U's deficiency was reduced to $6,000. Note that between B and T, profits and losses are shared in the ratio of 3 to 2 (or 60% and 40%). As a result, U's uncovered deficiency is allocated to B and T by reducing their capital accounts by $3,600 ($6,000 × 60%) and $2,400 ($6,000 × 40%), respectively.

e.

Date	Accounts and Explanation	PR	Debit	Credit
	B, Capital		26,400	
	T, Capital		7,600	
	Cash			34,000
	To distribute cash to partners on liquidation of partnership.			

Requirement 3 (Post the liquidation transactions)

Cash

Bal.	30,000	Payment of liabilities	120,000 (b)
(a) Sale of assets	120,000		
(c) U's contribution	4,000		
Bal.	34,000	Final distribution	34,000 (e)
Bal.	0		

Noncash Assets

Bal. 240,000	240,000 (a)		

Liabilities

(b) 120,000	Bal. 120,000		

B, Capital

(a) Loss on sale	60,000	Bal.	90,000
(d) Deficit from U	3,600		
(e) Final distribution	26,400	Bal.	26,400
		Bal.	0

T, Capital

(a) Loss on sale	40,000	Bal.	50,000
(d) Deficit from U	2,400		
(e) Final distribution	7,600	Bal.	7,600
		Bal.	0

U, Capital

(a) Loss on sale	20,000	Bal.	10,000
		Investment	4,000 (c)
Bal.	6,000	Allocate U's deficit	6,000 (d)
		Bal.	0

35

Chapter 13 – Corporations: Paid-In Capital and the Balance Sheet

CHAPTER OVERVIEW

In Chapter 12 you learned about the partnership form of organization. In this chapter, we begin an in-depth discussion of the corporate form of organization. Because the corporate form is more complex than either sole proprietorships or partnerships, our discussion of corporations continues in Chapter 14, 15, and 16. Therefore, an understanding of the topics in this chapter is important before continuing to the next chapter. The learning objectives for this chapter are to

1. Identify the characteristics of a corporation.
2. Record the issuance of stock.
3. Prepare the stockholders' equity section of a corporation balance sheet.
4. Account for cash dividends.
5. Use different stock values in decision making.
6. Evaluate return on assets and return on stockholders' equity.
7. Account for the income tax of a corporation.

CHAPTER REVIEW

Objective 1 - Identify the characteristics of a corporation.

1. A corporation is a **separate legal entity** chartered and regulated under the laws of a particular state. The owners' equity of a corporation is evidenced by shares of stock held by stockholders, and is referred to as stockholders' or shareholders' equity.
2. A corporation has **continuous life**. A change in ownership of the stock does not affect the life of the corporation.
3. **Mutual agency of owners is not present** in corporations. A stockholder cannot commit a corporation to a binding contract (unless that stockholder is also an officer of the corporation).
4. Stockholders have **limited liability**. That is, they have no personal obligation for the debts of the corporation. A stockholder's risk of loss is limited to the individual stockholder's investment in the corporation.
5. **Ownership and management are separated**. Every corporation is controlled by a board of directors who appoint officers to manage the day-to-day operations of the business. It is the stockholders who elect the board of directors. Thus, stockholders are not obligated to manage the business; ownership is separate from management.
6. **Corporate taxes** include state franchise taxes and federal and state income taxes. Corporations pay dividends to stockholders who then pay personal income taxes on the dividends they receive. This is considered double taxation of corporate earnings.

How do corporations compare to partnerships and sole proprietorships? Let's take a look:

	Corporation	Partnership	Sole Proprietorship
Separate legal entity	Yes	No	No
Continuous life	Yes	No	No
Ease of transferability of ownership	Yes	No	No
Mutual agency	No	Yes	Yes
Limited liability	Yes	No-General Yes-Limited	No
Separation of ownership and management	Yes	No	No
Taxable entity	Yes	No	No

Exhibit 13-1 in your text summarizes the advantages and disadvantages of a corporation.

Corporations come into existence when a **charter** is obtained from that state. The charter authorizes the corporations to issue (sell) a certain number of shares of stock. The **bylaws**, or the constitution governing the corporation, are then adopted. The stockholders elect a **board of directors**, who appoint the officers of the corporation. (Review Exhibit 13-2 in your text.)

Owners receive **stock certificates** when they invest in the business. The basic unit of investment is a **share**. A corporation's outstanding stock is the number of shares of its stock that are held by stockholders and represents 100% of the ownership of the corporation. Stockholders' equity is reported differently than owners' equity of a proprietorship or a partnership because corporations must report the sources of their capital.

Corporations have two primary sources of capital:

- **Paid-in capital or contributed capital** represents amounts received from the stockholders from the sale of stock. Generally, paid-in capital cannot be used for dividends.
- **Retained earnings**. Retained Earnings is the account that at any time is the sum of earnings (net income) accumulated since incorporation, minus any losses, and minus all dividends distributed to stockholders. Similar to partnerships and sole proprietorships, revenues and expenses are closed into Income Summary during the closing process. However, in a corporation Income Summary is closed to the Retained Earnings account, not the Capital account(s).

Stockholders have four basic rights, unless specifically withheld by contract:

1. Voting rights
2. Right to share in dividends
3. Right to receive proportionate share of any assets remaining upon liquidation of the corporation.
4. Preemptive right to maintain their proportionate ownership in the corporation.

There are different types of stock that a corporation can issue with rights that are specific to each type of stock. Stock may be **common** or **preferred.** Common stock is the basic form of capital stock. Every corporation must have common stock. A corporation may also issue preferred stock that provides its owners with certain "preferences" over common stock. Typically, preferred stock provides a fixed dividend that is paid to the preferred stockholders before any dividends are paid to the common stockholders.

Stock may also be issued with a **par value** or **no-par value.** Par value is an arbitrary value that a corporation assigns to a share of stock that is used to set the corporation's legal capital. If a corporation issues no-par stock, it may assign a **stated value** to establish the legal capital of the corporation. For accounting purposes, par value and stated value are accounted for in the same way.

A corporation may also issue different classes of common or preferred stock. Each class provides different rights to the respective owners. Each class of common or preferred stock is recorded in a separate general ledger account. Preferred stockholders receive their dividends before common stockholders and take priority over common stockholders in the receipt of assets if the corporation liquidates.

Objective 2 - Record the issuance of stock.

If a corporation issues common stock at a price that equals the par value, the entry to record the transaction is:

Cash (# of shares × issue price)	XX	
Common Stock (# of shares × par value)		XX

Par value is usually set low enough so that stock will not be sold below par. A corporation usually sells its common stock at an issue price above par value. The portion of the issue price that exceeds the par value is referred to as a premium. The amount of the premium also increases paid-in capital, but is recorded in a separate account called **Paid-In Capital in Excess of Par.** A premium is not a gain, income, or profit to the corporation. A corporation cannot earn a profit or incur a loss by buying or selling its own stock. The entry to record stock issued at a price in excess of par value is:

Cash (# of shares x issue price)	XX	
Common Stock (# of shares × par value)		XX
Paid-in Capital in Excess of Par - Common (# of shares × premium)		XX

- If no-par common stock is issued with no stated value, the entry is the same as when stock is issued where the issue price is equal to par value (above), except the credit to the common stock account is equal to the number of shares multiplied by the issue price (because no par value exists).
- Accounting for no-par common stock with a **stated value** is the same as the accounting for par-value stock, except the account that is used to capture the premium above the stated value is called **Paid-in Capital in Excess of Stated Value.**
- A corporation may issue stock and receive assets other than cash. When this occurs, the corporation records the assets at their current market value.

Accounting for preferred stock follows the same pattern as accounting for common stock. The difference is that instead of the word "Common," the word "Preferred" will appear in the titles of the general ledger accounts.

Objective 3 - Prepare the stockholders' equity section of a corporation balance sheet.

Preferred stock always appears before common stock in the stockholders' equity section of the balance sheet.

The format of the stockholders' equity section of the balance sheet is:

Stockholders' Equity

Paid-in Capital:	
Preferred Stock, $ par, number of shares authorized, number of shares issued	$ XX
Common Stock, $ par, number of shares authorized, number of shares issued	XX
Paid-in Capital in Excess of Par - Common	XX
Total Paid-in Capital	XX
Retained Earnings	XX
Total Stockholders' Equity	$ XX

Study Tip: Review the Decision Guidelines *Stockholders' Equity of a Corporation* in your text.

A **cash dividend** is a distribution of cash to the stockholders of a corporation. A corporation must have sufficient Retained Earnings in order to declare a dividend; meaning the declaration of the dividend cannot result in a negative balance in Retained Earnings. The company must also have sufficient cash to pay the dividend. (However, keep in mind that Retained Earnings and Cash are not the same.) Only the board of directors can declare a dividend. And, the board of directors must declare a dividend before the corporation can pay it. Once a dividend has been declared, it is a legal liability of the corporation.

There are three important dates related to dividends:
1. On the **date of declaration** the board announces its intent to pay a dividend to stockholders in the future; thus, a liability is created.
2. Stockholders owning shares of stock on the **date of record** will receive the dividend.
3. The **payment date** is the date the dividends are actually mailed.

Objective 4 - Account for cash dividends.

When a dividend is declared, the basic entry to record the transaction is:

Retained Earnings	XX	
Dividends Payable		XX

Dividends Payable is a current liability.

The date of record falls between the declaration date and the payment date and requires no journal entry. The dividend is usually paid several weeks after it is declared. When it is paid, this entry is recorded:

Dividends Payable   XX

    Cash   XX

When a corporation has issued both common and preferred stock, dividends must be split between the two types of stock. As we have mentioned, preferred stockholders have priority over common stockholders for receipt of dividends. In other words, common stockholders do not receive dividends unless the total dividend declared is large enough to pay the preferred stockholders first and then still have some amount left over to pay to the common stockholders.

The amount of the fixed dividend for preferred stock can be stated as a percentage of par or a dollar amount per share. Preferred stock may be "5% preferred" which means that each share of preferred stock will receive an annual dividend of 5% of the par value of the stock. Thus, if preferred stock is issued with a $50 par value per share, and is "5% preferred", stockholders will receive a $2.50 ($50 × 5%) annual dividend per share. Stockholders holding "$3 preferred" stock would receive a $3 annual cash dividend per share regardless of the par value of the stock. Once the dividend that will be paid to the preferred stockholders is determined, then, the dividend to common stockholders, if any, will be calculated as follows:

Common dividend = Total dividend - Preferred dividend,
where total dividend > preferred dividend

A dividend is passed when a corporation fails to pay an annual dividend to preferred stockholders. Whether a corporation has an obligation to make up a passed dividend depends on whether the preferred stock is issued as *cumulative or noncumulative.* When **cumulative preferred stock** is issued, any passed dividends are said to be in arrears. If multiple dividends are not paid, then cumulative preferred stock continues to accumulate annual dividends until the dividends are paid. *Therefore, a corporation must pay all dividends in arrears plus the current year's dividend to the preferred stockholders before it can pay dividends to the common stockholders.*

Dividends in arrears are not liabilities. Keep in mind that a dividend does not become a liability until a dividend is declared. Dividends in arrears have not been declared; therefore, they cannot be a liability to the corporation. However, dividends in arrears are disclosed in notes to the financial statements. Preferred stock is considered cumulative unless it is specifically labeled as noncumulative. Noncumulative preferred stock does not accumulate dividends in arrears.

The following table summarizes the effects of the stockholders' equity transactions discussed in this chapter:

| Transactions: | Effects on Accounting Equation: | | | | |
| | | | Stockholders' Equity | | |
	Assets	Liabilities	Paid-in Capital	Retained Earnings	Total
Issuance of stock	Increase	No effect	Increase	No effect	Increase
Declaration of a cash dividend	No effect	Increase	No effect	Decrease	Decrease
Payment of a cash dividend	Decrease	Decrease	No effect	No effect	No effect

Objective 5 - Use different stock values in decision making.

Market value (market price) is the price at which a person could buy or sell a share of stock. Daily newspapers report the market price of many publicly traded stocks. In addition, many Internet sites provide up-to-the-minute stock prices.

Book value is the amount of stockholders' equity per share of stock. If only common stock is outstanding:

$$\text{Book value} = \frac{\text{Total stockholders' equity}}{\text{Number of shares outstanding}}$$

If both preferred and common stock are outstanding, preferred stockholders' equity must be calculated first. Preferred equity is equal to the liquidation value of preferred stock plus any dividends in arrears. The book value per share of preferred stock is equal to its liquidation value plus any cumulative dividends in arrears divided by the number of preferred shares outstanding.

$$\text{Preferred book value} = \frac{\text{Liquidation value of preferred stock + Dividends in arrears}}{\text{Number of preferred shares outstanding}}$$

Once the book value of the preferred stock is calculated, to determine the book value of the common stock, subtract the preferred equity from the total equity and divide by the number of common shares outstanding.

$$\text{Common book value} = \frac{\text{Total equity - (Liquidation value of preferred stock+ Dividends in arrears)}}{\text{Number of common shares outstanding}}$$

Objective 6 - Evaluate return on assets and return on stockholders' equity.

1. **Rate of return on total assets** $= \dfrac{\textbf{Net income + Interest expense}}{\textbf{Average total assets}}$
   (return on assets)

The return on total assets measures how successfully the company used its (average) assets to generate income for those financing the business. The net income and interest expense in the numerator represent the return to the two groups that have financed the corporation: stockholders and creditors, respectively.

2. **Rate of return on common stockholders' equity** $= \dfrac{\textbf{Net income - Preferred dividends}}{\textbf{Average common stockholders' equity}}$
   (return on equity)

The denominator, average common stockholders' equity, is equal to total stockholders' equity minus preferred equity as you saw above in the calculation of common book value.

The rate of return on common stockholders' equity also measures the profitability of the company. The return on equity should always be higher than the return on assets. This is a sign of financial strength that shows that the corporation is generating a greater return with the money invested by stockholders than it is paying out in interest expense.

Objective 7 - Account for the income tax of a corporation.

Because corporations have a distinct legal identity (they have the right to contract, to sue, and be sued-- just as individuals have these rights), their income is subject to federal income tax. However, unlike individuals, the amount of tax actually paid will differ from the expense recognized for the period (for individuals, these amounts are generally the same). The difference results from the following:

- **Income tax expense** is calculated by multiplying the applicable tax rate by the amount of income before taxes from the income statement.
- **Income tax payable** is calculated by multiplying the applicable tax rate by the amount of taxable income reported on the corporate tax return filed with the Internal Revenue Service.

Because these results will differ, a third account, **Deferred Tax Liability**, is used to reconcile the entry, as follows:

Income Tax Expense	XX	
Income Tax Payable		XX
Deferred Tax Liability		XX

The deferred tax liability account is a long-term liability account.

TEST YOURSELF

All the self-testing materials in this chapter focus on information and procedures that your instructor is likely to test in quizzes and examinations.

Matching *Match each numbered term with its lettered definition.*

_____ 1. Authorized stock
_____ 2. Book value
_____ 3. Convertible preferred stock
_____ 4. Cumulative stock
_____ 5. Legal capital
_____ 6. Market value
_____ 7. Outstanding stock
_____ 8. Stated value
_____ 9. Preferred stock
_____ 10. Stockholders' equity
_____ 11. Retained earnings
_____ 12. Deferred income tax

_____ 13. Board of directors
_____ 14. Bylaws
_____ 15. Common stock
_____ 16. Dividends
_____ 17. Paid-in capital
_____ 18. Par value
_____ 19. Preemptive right
_____ 20. Premium on stock
_____ 21. Contributed capital
_____ 22. Income tax expense
_____ 23. Income tax payable

A. An account which reconciles the difference between income tax expense and income tax payable
B. A corporation's capital that is earned through profitable operation of the business
C. A corporation's capital from investments by the stockholders
D. A group elected by the stockholders to set policy for a corporation and to appoint its officers
E. Another term for paid-in capital
F. A stockholder's right to maintain a proportionate ownership in a corporation
G. An arbitrary amount assigned to a share of stock
H. The portion of stockholders' equity that cannot be used for dividends
I. Distributions by a corporation to its stockholders
J. Owners' equity of a corporation
K. Similar to par value
L. Preferred stock that may be exchanged by the stockholders, if they choose, for another class of stock in the corporation
M. Preferred stock whose owners must receive all dividends in arrears before the corporation pays dividends to the common stockholders
N. Pre-tax accounting income multiplied by the tax rate
O. Shares of stock in the hands of stockholders
P. Stock that gives its owners certain advantages such as the priority to receive dividends and the priority to receive assets if the corporation liquidates
Q. The amount of owners' equity on the company's books for each share of its stock
R. Taxable income multiplied by the tax rate
S. The constitution for governing a corporation
T. The excess of the issue price of stock over its par value
U. The most basic form of capital stock
V. The price for which a person could buy or sell a share of stock
W. The maximum number of shares of stock a corporation may issue

II. Multiple Choice   *Circle the best answer.*

1. The board of directors for a corporation is:

   A. appointed by the state
   B. elected by management
   C. elected by the stockholders
   D. appointed by corporate officers

2. A stockholder has no personal obligation for corporation liabilities. This is called:

   A. mutual agency
   B. limited agency
   C. transferability of ownership
   D. limited liability

3. An owner's investment of cash in a corporation increases:

   A. assets and decreases liabilities
   B. one asset and decreases another asset
   C. liabilities and decreases stockholders' equity
   D. assets and increases stockholders' equity

4. A stock certificate shows all of the following except:

   A. additional paid-in capital
   B. stockholder name
   C. par value
   D. company name

5. The ownership of stock entitles common stockholders to all of the following rights except:

   A. right to receive guaranteed dividends
   B. voting right
   C. preemptive right
   D. right to receive a proportionate share of assets in a liquidation

6. When a corporation declares a cash dividend:

   A. liabilities increase, paid-in capital decreases
   B. liabilities increase, retained earnings decrease
   C. no effect on paid-in capital
   D. both B. and C.

7. When a corporation pays a cash dividend:

   A. liabilities decrease, assets increase
   B. assets decrease, retained earnings decreases
   C. liabilities decrease, assets decrease
   D. retained earnings decrease, liabilities increase

8. When a company issues stock in exchange for assets other than cash, the assets are recorded at:

A. market value   C. book value
B. original cost   D. replacement cost

9. Dividends Payable is a(n):

A. expense   C. paid-in capital account
B. current liability   D. stockholders' equity account

10. Dividends in arrears on preferred stock are reported:

A. as a liability on the balance sheet   C. on the income statement as expense
B. as a reduction of retained earnings   D. as a footnote to the financial statements

III. Completion   *Complete each of the following.*

1. Every corporation issues _____ stock.
2. The corporation's constitution is called the _____.
3. Preferred stockholders have preference over common stockholders in _____ _____ and _____.
4. Dividends are declared by _____.
5. Taxable income multiplied by the applicable tax rate equals _____.
6. Stockholders' equity minus preferred equity equals _____.
7. The date of _____ determines who receives the dividend.
8. The date of _____ establishes the liability to pay a dividend.
9. The price at which a share of stock is bought or sold is called the _____ value.
10. Corporations come into existence when a _____ is approved by the _____ government.

IV. Daily Exercises

1. The following selected list of accounts with their normal balances was taken from the general ledger of Dayton Corporation as of December 31, 20X6:

Cash	173,500
Common stock, $1 par	190,000
Retained earnings	131,500
Preferred stock, $100 par	500,000
Paid-in capital in excess of par-common	380,000

    a. Prepare the stockholders' equity section of the balance sheet at December 31, 20X6.

    b. How many shares of common stock have been issued? _____

    c. How many shares of preferred stock have been issued? _____

2. Einstein Corporation has 20,000 shares of noncumulative, 5%, $100 par, preferred stock outstanding as well as 100,000 shares of $3 par common stock. The board of directors has passed dividends for the past three years, not counting the current year. The board of directors wants to give the common stockholders a $1.25 dividend per share. The total dividends to be declared must be:

3. A company issues 40,000 shares of common stock for $30 per share. Record this transaction (omit explanation) assuming each independent situation below:

   a. the stock had a par value of $1 per share
   b. the stock had no par value, but a stated value of $1 per share
   c. the stock had no par or stated value

Date	Accounts and Explanation	PR	Debit	Credit

4. On September 10, the board of directors declares an annual dividend of $30,000 payable on October 30 to stockholders of record on September 30. Make the journal entries that would be recorded on the following dates:

   a. the declaration date
   b. the date of record
   c. the payment date.

Date	Accounts and Explanation	PR	Debit	Credit

5. Refer to the information in Daily Exercise #4 and assume the company has 4,000 shares of $50 par, 4% preferred stock issued and 10,000 shares of $1 par common stock. The preferred stock is non-cumulative and the corporation has no dividends in arrears. Make the journal entries that would be recorded on the following dates:

   a. the declaration date
   b. the date of record
   c. the payment date.

Date	Accounts and Explanation	PR	Debit	Credit

6. Refer to the information in Daily Exercise #5, but assume the preferred stock is cumulative and the company has two years of dividends in arrears. Calculate the amount due each class of shareholder.

V. Exercises

1. The charter of Berger Corporation authorizes the issuance of 25,000 shares of preferred stock and 300,000 shares of common stock. During the first year of operation, Berger Corporation completed the following transactions:

March 1   Issued 40,000 shares of $1 par common stock for cash of $15 per share.

March 10   Issued 5,000 shares of 6%, no-par preferred stock with stated value of $50 per share. The issue price was $50 per share.

March 28   Received inventory valued at $25,000 and equipment with a market value of $60,000 in exchange for 2,000 shares of $1 par common stock.

Prepare the journal entries for each transaction.

Date	Accounts and Explanation	PR	Debit	Credit

2. Review the information in Exercise #1 and assume retained earnings has a balance of $95,000. Prepare the stockholders' equity section of the Berger Corporation's balance sheet at the end of the first year.

3. The Hot Springs Corporation has 3,000 shares of $100 par, cumulative, 8% preferred stock outstanding. There were no dividends in arrears at the end of 20X3, and no dividends have been paid for 20X4, 20X5 & 20X6. Hot Springs has 20,000 shares of $2.50 par common stock outstanding.

   a. How much will each class of stockholders receive if Hot Springs declares an $80,000 dividend at the end of 20X6?

   b. How much will each class of stockholders receive if Hot Springs declares a $50,000 dividend at the end of 20X6?

4. Natural Fibers Corporation reported income before taxes of $242,000 on their income statement and $186,000 taxable income on their tax return. Assuming a corporate tax rate of 45%, present the journal entry to record Natural Fibers taxes for the year.

Date	Accounts and Explanation	PR	Debit	Credit

VI. Beyond the Numbers

Using the information in Daily Exercises #5 and #6, analyze the effect (increase, decrease, no effect) of the dividend payment, as of 12/31 on the return on assets and return on stockholders' equity.

VII. Demonstration Problems

Demonstration Problem #1

On January 1, 20X5, the state of Vermont approved Video Productions, Inc. corporate charter which authorized the corporation to issue 100,000 shares of 6%, $25 par preferred stock and 1,000,000 shares of common stock with a $1 par value. During January, the corporation completed the following transactions:

Jan 10 Sold 50,000 shares of common stock at $15 per share.
    11 Issued 6,000 shares of preferred stock for cash at $25 per share.
    17 Issued 20,000 shares of common stock in exchange for land valued at $420,000.
    27 Sold 2,000 shares of preferred stock at $25 a share.
    31 Earned a small profit for January and closed the $3,800 credit balance of Income Summary into the Retained Earnings account.

Required

1. Record the transactions in the general journal.
2. Post the journal entries into the equity accounts provided.
3. Prepare the stockholders' equity section of Video Productions, Inc. balance sheet at Jan. 31, 20X5.

Requirement 1 (journal entries)

Date	Accounts and Explanation	PR	Debit	Credit

Requirement 2 (postings)

Common Stock	Paid-in Capital in Excess of Par-Common

Preferred Stock	Retained Earnings

Requirements 3 (Stockholders' equity section)

Video Productions, Inc.
Balance Sheet - Stockholders' Equity Section
January 31, 20X5

Demonstration Problem #2

Wilcox Corporation has the following capital structure: 5,000 shares of $25 par, 4% preferred stock authorized and outstanding, and 100,000 authorized shares of $2 par common stock, 20,000 shares issued. During years X1 through X6, the corporation declared the following dividends:

X1	$0
X2	2,000
X3	40,000
X4	120,000
X5	0
X6	20,000

A. Assume the preferred stock is noncumulative; calculate the amount of dividends per share for each year.

Year	Dividend Amount	Preferred	Common

B. Assume the preferred stock is cumulative; calculate the amount of dividends per share each year.

Year	Dividend Amount	Preferred	Common

SOLUTIONS

I. Matching

1. W	5. H	9. P	13. D	17. C	21. E
2. Q	6. V	10. J	14. S	18. G	22. N
3. L	7. O	11. B	15. U	19. F	23. R
4. M	8. K	12. A	16. I	20. T	

II. Multiple Choice

1. C The common stockholders of the corporation elect the board of directors. Each share of common stock usually gives the stockholder one vote.

2. D Recall that mutual agency is a characteristic of partnerships not present in corporations. Transferability of ownership is a characteristic that the corporate form of organization simplifies as compared with partnerships. Limited agency has no meaning.

3. D When cash is invested in a corporation, assets increase and stockholders' equity, specifically, paid-in capital increases.

4. A Additional paid-in capital is the excess of the price paid to the corporation over the par value of the stock. It is an amount that is calculated to account for the sale of stock, but not shown on the stock certificate.

5. A Dividends represent the distribution of the earnings of the corporation and are not guaranteed.

6. D The declaration of a dividend reduces retained earnings and increases the liability account, Dividends Payable, and has no effect on paid-in capital.

7. C The payment of a cash dividend results in cash being paid to stockholders to settle the liability created by the declaration of the dividend.

8. A When capital stock is issued in exchange for non-cash assets, the assets should be recorded at fair market value. Any excess amount over the par value will be recorded in the Paid-in Capital in Excess of Par account.

9. B The declaration of a dividend by the board of directors creates a current liability.

10. D Dividends in arrears are not a liability since a dividend must be declared to create a liability. However, dividends in arrears do impair the amount of capital available to common stockholders. Dividends in arrears are usually disclosed by a footnote.

III. Completion

1. common (Corporations may also issue preferred stock, but that is optional.)
2. bylaws
3. receiving dividends and in event of a liquidation
4. the board of directors
5. Income Tax Payable
6. common stockholders' equity
7. record
8. declaration
9. market
10. charter; state

IV. Daily Exercises

1.   a. Prepare the stockholders' equity section of the balance sheet for December 31, 20X6.

Dayton Corporation
Balance Sheet (partial)
December 31, 20X6

Paid-in Capital:	
Preferred Stock, $100 par	500,000
Common Stock, $1 par	$190,000
Paid-in capital in excess of par-common	380,000
Total paid-in capital	1,070,000
Retained earnings	131,500
Total Stockholders' Equity	$1,201,500

b. How many shares of common stock have been issued? $190,000/$1 par = 190,000 shares

c. How many shares of preferred stock have been issued? $500,000/$100 par = 5,000 shares

2.   Step 1: Calculate the fixed dividend due the preferred stockholders:
      5% x $100 par = $5.00 dividend per share of preferred stock
      $5.00 x 20,000 shares = $100,000 dividend to preferred stockholders.

Step 2: Calculate the amount of dividend desired for the common stockholders:
      100,000 shares x $1.25 dividend per share = $125,000 dividend to common stockholders

Step 3: Calculate the total dividend that needs to be declared to meet the goal of the board of directors:

Preferred dividend	$100,000
Common dividend	125,000
Total dividend required	$225,000

3.

a.	Cash (40,000 shares x $30 per share)	1,200,000	
	Common Stock (40,000 shares x $1 par)		40,000
	Paid-in Capital in Excess of Par - Common		1,160,000
b.	Cash (40,000 shares x $30 per share)	1,200,000	
	Common Stock (40,000 shares x $1 stated value)		40,000
	Paid-in Capital in Excess of Stated Value - Common		1,160,000
c.	Cash (40,000 shares x $30 per share)	1,200,000	
	Common Stock (40,000 shares x $30 per share)		1,200,000

4.

9/10	Retained Earnings	30,000	
	Dividends Payable		30,000
9/30	No entry		
10/30	Dividends Payable	30,000	
	Cash		30,000

> **Study Tip:** Remember no entry is required on the record date. This simply determines who will receive the dividend when paid.

5.

9/10	Retained Earnings	30,000	
	Dividends Payable-Preferred*		8,000
	Dividends Payable-Common**		22,000
9/30	No entry		
10/30	Dividends Payable-Preferred	8,000	
	Dividends Payable-Common	22,000	
	Cash		30,000

*Preferred: $50 × 4% = $2 per share × 4,000 shares = $8,000.
**Common: $30,000 - $8,000 = $22,000, or $2.20 per share ($22,000/10,000 shares).

Since the preferred stock is noncumulative, the preferred shareholders are only entitled to the current year's dividend ($8,000). The balance is distributed to the common stock.

6.

Preferred dividends in arrears: $8,000 per year (see above) × 2 years	$16,000
Preferred current year dividend:	8,000
Total dividend to the preferred stockholders:	$24,000
Total dividend to the common stockholders ($30,000 - $24,000)	$6,000

Since the preferred stock is cumulative, the preferred shareholders are entitled to the two years of dividends in arrears and the current year's dividend. The balance, if any, is distributed to the common stockholders.

V. Exercises

1.

3/1	Cash (40,000 shares x $15 per share)		600,000	
	Common Stock (40,000 shares x $1 par)			40,000
	Paid-in Capital in Excess of Par - Common			560,000
3/10	Cash (5,000 shares x $50 per share)		250,000	
	Preferred Stock (5,000 x $50 par)			250,000
3/28	Inventory		25,000	
	Equipment		60,000	
	Common Stock (2,000 x $1 par)			2,000
	Paid-in Capital in Excess of Par - Common			83,000

2.

Stockholders' Equity

Paid-in capital:

Preferred stock, 6%, no-par, $50 stated value, 25,000 shares authorized, 5,000 shares issued	$ 250,000
Common stock, $1 par, 300,000 shares authorized, 42,000 shares issued	42,000
Paid-in capital in excess of par – common stock	643,000
Total paid-in capital	935,000
Retained earnings	95,000
Total stockholders' equity	$ 1,030,000

3.

A. Preferred: $100 par $\times$ 8% $\times$ 3,000 shares $\times$ 3 years = $72,000
   Common: $80,000 - $72,000 = $8,000

B. Preferred: $50,000

Since $50,000 is less than the $72,000 preferred stockholders must receive before common stockholders receive anything, all $50,000 goes to the preferred stockholders. And the common stockholders receive nothing!

4.

Income Tax Expense	108,900	
Income Tax Payable		83,700
Deferred Tax Liability		25,200

Income Tax Expense = $242,000 $\times$ 45% = $108,900
Income Tax Payable = $186,000 $\times$ 45% = $83,700
Deferred Tax Liability = $108,900 - $83,700 = $25,200

VI. Beyond the Numbers

Here's the solution—see below for the explanation. This is more difficult than you might have thought.

Situation	Return on Assets	Return on Stockholders' Equity
a. preferred stock is non-cumulative	increase	decrease
b. preferred stock is cumulative	increase	decrease

The formulas are:

Rate of return on total assets $\quad = \quad \dfrac{\text{Net income + Interest expense}}{\text{Average total assets}}$

Rate of return on common stockholders' equity $\quad = \quad \dfrac{\text{Net income - Preferred dividends}}{\text{Average common stockholders' equity}}$

For the return on assets, neither net income nor interest expense change because dividends of $30,000 were paid (regardless of who got how much.) However, average total assets will decrease because of the $30,000 reduction in cash. Therefore, return on assets will increase in both situations.

For return on stockholders' equity, the numerator (net income less preferred dividends) is smaller because of the dividend payment. The denominator (average stockholders' equity) is also decreasing because the total dividends are debited to Retained Earnings. In Exercise #5, the numerator is decreasing by $8,000 while the denominator is decreasing by $30,000. In Exercise #6, the numerator is decreasing by $24,000 while the denominator is decreasing by $30,000.

VII. Demonstration Problems

Demonstration Problem #1 Solved and Explained

Requirement 1

1/10   Cash   750,000
            Common Stock (50,000 × $1 par)   50,000
            Paid-in Capital in Excess of Par - Common (50,000 × $14)   700,000
            Sold common stock at $14 per share.

The payment of cash is recorded by debiting Cash and crediting Common Stock for the number of shares times the par value of the stock (50,000 × $1). The balance is recorded in the premium account, Paid-in Capital in Excess of Par - Common Stock.

1/11   Cash (6,000 × $25)   150,000
            Preferred Stock (6,000 × $25 par)   150,000
            Issued preferred stock at par.

Preferred Stock is credited for the number of shares multiplied by the par value (6,000 × $25).

1/17   Land   420,000
            Common Stock (20,000 × $1 par)   20,000
            Paid-in Capital in Excess of Par - Common ($420,000 - $20,000)   400,000
            To issue common stock at a premium price.

When a corporation issues stock in exchange for an asset other than cash, it debits the asset received (in this case, land) for its fair market value and credits the capital accounts, the same as it would if cash were the asset received.

1/27   Cash   50,000
            Preferred Stock (2,000 × $25 par)   50,000

Preferred Stock is credited for the number of shares multiplied by the par value (2,000 × $25).

| 1/31 | Income Summary | 3,800 | |
| | Retained Earnings | | 3,800 |

To close Income Summary by transferring net income into Retained Earnings.

At the end of each month or year, the balance of the Income Summary account is transferred to Retained Earnings. Video Productions, Inc. earned a small profit in January. The closing entry will debit Income Summary (to reduce it to zero) and credit Retained Earnings (increasing stockholders' equity to reflect profitable operations for the month).

Requirement 2

Preferred Stock		Common Stock	
	1/11 150,000		1/10 50,000
	1/27 50,000		1/17 20,000
	Bal. 200,000		Bal. 70,000

		Paid-in Capital in Excess of Par – Common	
Retained Earnings			1/10 700,000
	1/31 3,800		1/17 400,000
	Bal. 3,800		Bal. 1,100,000

Requirements 3

Video Productions, Inc.
Balance Sheet - Stockholders' Equity Section
January 31, 20X5

Stockholders' equity:	
Preferred stock, 6%, $25 par, 100,000 shares authorized, 8,000 shares issued	$ 200,000
Common stock, $1 par, 1,000,000 shares authorized, 70,000 shares issued	70,000
Paid-in capital in excess of par - Common	1,100,000
Total paid-in capital	1,370,000
Retained earnings	3,800
Total stockholders' equity	$1,373,800

Demonstration Problem #2 Solved and Explained

A. Preferred stock is noncumulative.

Year	Dividend Amount	Preferred	Common
X1	$0	$0	$0
X2	$2,000	$0.40 per share ($2,000 dividend ÷ 5,000 shares)	$0
X3	$40,000	$1.00 per share 5,000 shares × $25 par × 4% = $5,000 $5,000 ÷ 5,000 shares = $1.00	$1.75 per share $40,000- $5,000 = $35,000 $35,000 ÷ 20,000 shares = $1.75
X4	$120,000	$1.00 per share 5,000 shares × $25 par × 4% = $5,000 $5,000 ÷ 5,000 shares = $1.00	$5.75 per share $120,000 - $5,000 = $115,000 $115,000 ÷ 20,000 shares = $5.75
X5	$0	$0	$0
X6	$20,000	$1.00 5,000 shares × $25 par × 4% = $5,000 $5,000 ÷ 5,000 shares = $1.00	$.75 per share $20,000 - $5,000 = $15,000 $15,000 ÷ 20,000 shares = $0.75

The preferred stock is noncumulative so the shareholders are only entitled to the current year's dividend, which is $1/share for a total of $5,000. Any (and all) excess goes to the common shareholders.

B. The preferred stock is cumulative.

Year	Dividend Amount	Preferred	Common
X1	$0	$0	$0

There are now $5,000 of preferred dividends in arrears.

Year	Dividend Amount	Preferred	Common
X2	$2,000	$0.40 per share ($2,000 ÷ 5,000 shares)	$0

There is now $8,000 of preferred dividends in arrears.

Year	Dividend Amount	Preferred	Common
X3	$40,000	$2.60 per share $8,000 in arrears + $5,000 current = $13,000 $13,000 ÷ 5,000 shares = $2.60	$1.35 per share $40,000-$13,000 = $27,000 $27,000 ÷ 20,000 shares = $1.35
X4	$120,000	$1.00 per share 5,000 shares × $25 par × 4% = $5,000 $5,000 ÷ 5,000 shares = $1.00	$5.75 $120,000 - $50,000 = $115,000 $115,000 ÷ 20,000 shares = $5.75

Preferred has no arrearage so they receive $1.00 per share with the remainder going to common.

Year	Dividend Amount	Preferred	Common
X5	$0	$0	$0

There is now $5,000 of preferred dividends in arrears.

Year	Dividend Amount	Preferred	Common
X6	$20,000	$ 2.00 per share $5,000 in arrears + $5,000 current = $10,000 $10,000 ÷ 5,000 shares = $2.00	$ .50 per share $20,000-$10,000 = $10,000 $10,000 ÷ 20,000 shares = $0.50

Study Tip: Most preferred stock is cumulative. The term has no meaning when applied to common stock.

Chapter 14 - Retained Earnings, Treasury Stock, and the Income Statement

CHAPTER OVERVIEW

In Chapter 13 you learned about capital stock, cash dividends, stock values, corporate income taxes, and other topics related to corporations. We expand those topics in this chapter to learn about stock dividends, treasury stock and a corporate income statement, among other topics. The learning objectives for this chapter are to

1. Account for stock dividends.
2. Distinguish stock splits from stock dividends.
3. Account for treasury stock.
4. Report restrictions on retained earnings.
5. Analyze a complex income statement.
6. Prepare a statement of stockholders' equity.

CHAPTER REVIEW

Retained Earnings is the account that reports all the corporation's net income less any net losses and less dividends declared, accumulated over the life of the business. Increases in Retained Earnings will only result from profitable operations (net income). Decreases in Retained Earnings typically result from net losses and the declaration of dividends. A deficit or debit balance in the Retained Earnings account may exist, but is rare. A deficit in retained earnings means that net losses have exceeded net incomes and typically leads to corporate failure and bankruptcy. It is also important to remember that Retained Earnings is not a reservoir of cash.

Objective 1 - Account for stock dividends.

In addition to the declaration of a cash dividend, which was discussed in Chapter 13, corporations may also declare **stock dividends.** A stock dividend may be declared instead of a cash dividend when the board of directors wants to 1.) conserve cash or 2.) reduce the market price per share of stock. Unlike cash dividends, stock dividends are not distributions of corporate assets. A stock dividend is a proportional distribution of the corporation's stock to its stockholders. Thus, a stock dividend affects only a corporation's stockholders' equity accounts. The result of a stock dividend is a reduction in Retained Earnings, and an increase in contributed capital; thus, total stockholders' equity stays the same.

The effect of declaring a stock dividend is to "capitalize" or transfer a portion of Retained Earnings to Paid-in Capital, specifically in the Common Stock account. If the stock dividend is a small stock dividend, then a portion of Retained Earnings is also transferred to the Paid-in Capital in Excess of Par-Common account in order to reflect the excess of market value above par of the stock dividend.

- A **small stock dividend** is one that comprises less than 20-25% of the shares issued.
- A **large stock dividend** comprises 25% or more of the shares issued. Large stock dividends are rare. Instead of declaring large stock dividends, companies will split their stock. Stock splits will be discussed later in this chapter.

Small stock dividends are accounted for at the market value of the stock on the declaration date. The entry is:

Retained Earnings	XX	
Common Stock		XX
Paid-in Capital in Excess of Par - Common		XX

Step 1: Calculate the amount of the debit to Retained Earnings:

Number of Common Shares Outstanding × Dividend % × Market Price Per Share

Step 2: Calculate the amount of the credit to Common Stock:

Number of Common Shares Outstanding × Dividend % × Par Value Per Share

Step 3: Calculate the amount of the credit to Paid-in Capital in Excess of Par - Common:

Number of Common Shares Outstanding × Dividend % × (Market Price Per Share – Par Value Per Share)

Objective 2 - Distinguish stock splits from stock dividends.

A **stock split** increases the number of authorized, issued and outstanding shares and proportionately reduces the par value of the stock. However, no account balances are affected. A corporation will split its stock when it wants to decrease the stock's market price to make it more affordable to investors.

Carefully review Exhibit 14-2 in your text for a summary of the stockholders' equity effects of cash dividends, stock dividends, and stock splits.

Objective 3 - Account for treasury stock.

Stock that a corporation issues and later reacquires is called **treasury stock**. Because the issuing corporation holds treasury stock, it does not receive dividends and has no voting rights. Corporations may want treasury stock for the following reasons:

1.) to try to increase net assets by buying low and selling high
2.) to support or raise the market price
3.) to avoid a takeover.

The entry to record the purchase of treasury stock is:

Treasury Stock, Common	XX	
Cash		XX

(# of shares repurchased × market price per share = cost of treasury stock to corporation)

Treasury Stock is a contra equity account that has a normal debit balance and reduces total stockholders' equity. Note that treasury stock is *not* an asset, and that a corporation *never* incurs a gain or loss by dealing in its own stock.

The purchase of treasury stock does not change the number of shares authorized or issued, but decreases the number of shares outstanding. To determine the number of shares outstanding, take the number of shares issued and deduct the number of shares of treasury stock. The result is the number of shares outstanding.

When treasury stock is sold, the entry to record the transaction depends on the relationship between the selling price and the cost of the Treasury Stock.

1.) The entry to record the sale of treasury stock *at cost* is:

Cash (Number of shares × Current price)	XX	
Treasury Stock, Common (Number of shares × Orig. price)		XX

2.) The entry to record the sale of Treasury Stock *above cost* is:

Cash (Number of shares × Current price)	XX	
Treasury Stock, Common (Number of shares × Orig. price)		XX
Paid-in Capital from Treasury Stock Transactions		XX

3.) The entry to record the sale of Treasury Stock *below cost* is:

Cash (Number of shares × Current price)	XX	
Paid-in Capital from Treasury Stock Transactions	XX	
(or Retained Earnings)	XX	
Treasury Stock, Common (Number of shares × Orig. price)		XX

Note: When treasury stock is sold, the Treasury Stock account is credited for the original cost of the treasury stock. Any difference between cost and selling price is recorded in the Paid-in Capital from Treasury Stock Transactions account. However, this Paid-In Capital Account cannot have a debit balance. If Treasury Stock is sold below cost, and the Paid-in Capital from Treasury Stock Transactions account does not exist or does not have a sufficient balance to absorb the difference, then the Retained Earnings account may be debited.

Review the table on the next page for a summary of the stockholders' equity transaction from Chapter 13 in addition to the effects of stock dividends, stock splits, and treasury stock transactions. It is important to be very familiar with this table to secure your understanding of these two chapters.

Transactions:	Effects on Accounting Equation:				
				Stockholders' Equity	
	Assets	**Liabilities**	**Paid-in Capital**	**Retained Earnings**	**Total**
Issuance of stock	Increase	No effect	Increase	No effect	Increase
Declaration of a cash dividend	No effect	Increase	No effect	Decrease	Decrease
Payment of a cash dividend	Decrease	Decrease	No effect	No effect	No effect
Declaration of stock dividend	No effect	No effect	Increase	Decrease	No effect
Stock split	No effect	No effect	No effect	No effect	No effect
Purchase of Treasury Stock	Decrease	No effect	No effect	No effect	Decrease
Sale of Treasury Stock at cost	Increase	No effect	No effect	No effect	Increase
Sale of Treasury Stock above cost	Increase	No effect	Increase	No effect	Increase
Sale of Treasury Stock below cost	Increase	No effect	Possible Decrease	Possible Decrease	Increase

You may also find it beneficial to review the Decision Guidelines in this chapter titled *Accounting for Retained Earnings, Dividends and Treasury Stock.*

Objective 4 - Report restrictions on retained earnings.

In addition to issuing stock, many corporations obtain financing through long-term loans. Creditors wish to ensure that funds will be available to repay these loans. Thus, loan agreements frequently **restrict** the amount of retained earnings that can be used to pay dividends and purchase treasury stock. No journal entry is required for restrictions on retained earnings. These restrictions are usually reported in notes to the financial statements.

If a corporation **appropriates** a portion of retained earnings for a specific purpose, then a formal journal entry is required:

Retained Earnings   XX
    Retained Earnings Appropriated   XX

Review Exhibit 14-4 in your text so you understand how a detailed stockholders' equity presentation can be condensed.

Objective 5 – Analyze a complex income statement.

Investors may want to examine the trend of a company's earnings and the composition of its net income. Therefore, the corporate income statement has three sections that are used to analyze the performance of the business:
1. Continuing operations
2. Special items
3. Earnings per share

See Exhibit 14-5 in your text.

1. **Continuing operations** are the results of operations that are expected to continue in the future. Income from continuing operations helps investors make predictions about future earnings. Income from continuing operations is shown both before and after income tax has been deducted.

2. There are three types of **special items**:

   - **Discontinued operations.** When a corporation sells one of its segments, the gain or loss on the sale is reported in a section of the income statement called discontinued operations. Such sales are viewed as one-time transactions, and are therefore not a future source of income. Thus, they are separated from the section labeled "continuing operations". Gains and losses resulting from discontinued operations are shown net of its related tax effect.

   - **Extraordinary gains and losses** are both unusual <u>and</u> infrequent, and, like discontinued operations, are reported net of tax. Extraordinary items are those that are unusual and not likely to occur in the future. Examples are natural disasters and expropriations of business assets by foreign governments.

   - **Changes in accounting principles.** On occasion, companies change an accounting method. When this occurs, it is difficult for financial statement users to compare consecutive years' activity unless they are informed of changes. For this reason, the cumulative (total) effect of any change in accounting principle is reported separately. This cumulative effect is also reported net of its related tax effect.

3. **Earnings per share** reports the amount of net income per share of outstanding common stock and is computed for each source of income or loss. To compute EPS, divide net income by the average number of shares of common stock outstanding.

   When preferred dividends exist, they must be subtracted from income subtotals (income from continuing operations, income before extraordinary items and cumulative effect of accounting change, and net income) in the computation of EPS. Preferred dividends are not subtracted from income or loss from discontinued operations, extraordinary gains and losses and cumulative effect of accounting change.

   Dilution must be considered if preferred stock can be converted into common stock because there is the potential for more common shares to be divided into net income. Corporations therefore provide **basic EPS** and **diluted EPS** information.

Comprehensive income refers to the changes in total stockholders' equity from all sources other than from the owners of the business (the shareholders). In addition to net income, comprehensive income includes unrealized gains/losses on certain investments and foreign currency translation adjustments (both of these are discussed in greater detail in Chapter 16). FASB Statement 130, which dictates the reporting of comprehensive income, does not require EPS calculations for these additional components.

Prior period adjustments are journal entries that are recorded to make a correction in the current accounting period that result from an error made in a previous accounting period. Prior period adjustments that decrease income from a prior period are debited to Retained Earnings:

Retained Earnings	XX	
Asset or Liability account		XX

Prior period adjustments that increase prior period income are credited to Retained Earnings:

Asset or Liability account	XX	
Retained Earnings		XX

Note that, because of the matching principle, prior period adjustments *never* affect revenue or expense accounts in the current period.

Objective 6 - Prepare a statement of stockholders' equity.

A **statement of stockholders' equity** reports the changes in all elements of stockholders' equity. Therefore, it contains the details of any changes in stock (both preferred and common), retained earnings, and treasury stock. Review Exhibit 14-8 in your text as an example.

TEST YOURSELF

All the self-testing materials in this chapter focus on information and procedures that your instructor is likely to test in quizzes and examinations.

I. Matching   *Match each numbered term with its lettered definition.*

_____ 1. Stock dividend
_____ 2. Earnings per share
_____ 3. Extraordinary item
_____ 4. Prior period adjustments
_____ 5. Small stock dividend
_____ 6. Appropriation of retained earnings
_____ 7. Date of record
_____ 8. Date of declaration

_____ 9. Other gain or loss
_____ 10. Discontinued operations
_____ 11. Stock split
_____ 12. Treasury stock
_____ 13. Deficit
_____ 14. Dilution
_____ 15. Comprehensive income

A. A correction to Retained Earnings for an error from an earlier period
B. Gain or loss that is both unusual for the company and nonrecurring (infrequent)
C. Results when a corporation sells a significant portion of its business
D. A gain or loss that is reported as part of continuing operations on the income statement.
E. A stock dividend of less than 20-25% of the corporation's issued stock
F. A proportional distribution by a corporation of its own stock that affects only the owners' equity section of the balance sheet
G. Amount of a company's net income per share of its outstanding common stock
H. An increase in the number of outstanding shares of stock coupled with a proportionate reduction in the par value of the stock
I. Date on which the board of directors announces the intention to pay a dividend
J. Date by which the stock must be owned in order to receive a dividend
K. Restriction of retained earnings that is recorded by a formal journal entry
L. The stock that a corporation issues and later reacquires
M. The change in total stockholders' equity from all sources other than from the owners of the business
N. What occurs when convertible preferred stock is converted into common stock.
O. A debit balance in Retained Earnings

II. Multiple Choice   *Circle the best answer.*

1. The correct order for the relevant dividend dates is:

   A. declaration date, record date, payment date   C. declaration date, payment date, record date
   B. record date, declaration date, payment date   D. record date, payment date, declaration date

2. Small stock dividends are recorded at:

   A. par value   C. book value
   B. market value   D. carrying value

3. The market price of a share of Moule Corporation's common stock is $60. If Moule declares a 2-for-1 stock split, the market price will adjust to approximately:

   A. $30   C. $90
   B. $12   D. $40

4. The statement that reports the changes in all categories of equity during the period is called the:

   A. statement of retained earnings and income   C. income statement
   B. statement of stockholders' equity   D. statement of retained earnings

5. The purchase of treasury stock will:

   A. decrease assets   C. increase stockholders' equity
   B. increase liabilities   D. have no effect on stockholders' equity

6. The purchase of treasury stock decreases the number of:

   A. authorized shares   C. issued shares
   B. outstanding shares   D. both B and C

7. If a company shows a loss on discontinued operations of $60,000 and is subject to a 45% tax rate, the tax effect is:

   A. a tax savings of $27,000   C. a tax savings of $33,000
   B. additional tax liability of $27,000   D. additional tax liability of $33,000

8. An appropriation of retained earnings will:

   A. decrease total retained earnings   C. not affect total retained earnings
   B. increase total retained earnings   D. increase total assets

9. All of the following would usually be reported as extraordinary items on the income statement *except:*

   A. a flood loss   C. the loss from a strike by workers
   B. the loss on assets taken by a foreign D. a tornado loss
      government

10. Prior period adjustments are found on the:

    A. balance sheet   C. statement of cash flows
    B. income statement   D. statement of retained earnings

III. Completion *Complete each of the following statements.*

1. Earnings per share is calculated by dividing _____ by _____.
2. _____ stock does not receive cash dividends.
3. Extraordinary gains and losses on the income statement are both _____ and _____.
4. What are the main sections of the income statement?

   _____

   _____

   _____
5. The change in total stockholders' equity from all sources other than from the owners of the business is called _____.
6. When a corporation changes from straight-line depreciation to double-declining-balance, this is called a(n) _____, and is reported _____ on the income statement.
7. A _____ is a distribution of cash to the owners of a corporation, where a _____ is a distribution of stock.
8. A(n) _____ occurs when a stockholder returns shares to the corporation and receives more shares in the exchange.
9. An error affecting net income in a previous accounting period is called a _____.
10. On the income statement, special items are reported _____.

IV. Daily Exercises

1. Number the following items in the order in which they should appear on the income statement. Use an asterisk (*) to indicate those categories that should be shown net of tax.

   _____ A. Discontinued Operations

   _____ B. Continuing Operations

   _____ C. Extraordinary Items

   _____ D. Cumulative Effect of Change in Accounting Principle

2. A stockholder owns 4,000 shares of Utronics, Inc., $6 par, common stock. If the company declares and issues a 15% stock dividend when the market value of the stock is $10, how many shares will the stockholder own? What will the par value be after the stock dividend?

3. Examine the information in Daily Exercise #2 above, but assume a 3-for-1 stock split. How many shares will be owned after the split? What will the par value be after the split?

4. How many shares of common stock are outstanding if a corporation has 3,000,000 shares authorized, 2,250,000 shares issued and 360,000 shares of Treasury stock?

5. Review the information in #4 above, how many shares of common stock are outstanding if the corporation sells 5,000 shares of the Treasury stock?

6. Calloway Corporation reports net income for 20X9 of $250,000. Calloway Corporation had outstanding for all of 20X9 25,000 shares of cumulative $50 par, 10% preferred stock and 175,000 shares of $10 par common stock. Calculate earnings per share.

V. Exercises

1. Indicate the effect of each of the following transactions on Assets, Liabilities, Paid-in Capital, and Retained Earnings. Use + for increase, - for decrease, and 0 for no effect.

	Assets	Liabilities	Paid-in Capital	Retained Earnings
A. Declaration of a cash dividend	_____	_____	_____	_____
B. Payment of a cash dividend	_____	_____	_____	_____
C. Declaration of a stock dividend	_____	_____	_____	_____
D. Issuance of a stock dividend	_____	_____	_____	_____
E. A stock split	_____	_____	_____	_____
F. Cash purchase of treasury stock	_____	_____	_____	_____
G. Sale of treasury stock below cost	_____	_____	_____	_____

2. Wholesome Corporation had 400,000 shares of $5 par common stock issued and outstanding on October 1. On October 14, Wholesome distributed an 18% stock dividend when the market price was $27 per share. Prepare the journal entry to record the stock dividend.

Date	Account and Explanation	PR	Debit	Credit

How many shares of common stock are issued and outstanding after the distribution of the stock dividend? _____

3. Following is the stockholders' equity section of the balance sheet of Purple Man Inc.

Paid-in capital:	
Preferred stock, 5%, cumulative $50 par, 35,000 shares authorized, 12,000 shares issued	$ 600,000
Common stock, $5 par, 140,000 shares authorized, 75,000 shares issued	375,000
Paid-in capital in excess of par-common	243,750
Total paid-in capital	1,218,750
Retained earnings	320,000
Total stockholders' equity	$ 1,538,750

The corporation has announced a 4-for-1 stock split of common stock. Prepare the stockholders' equity section of the balance sheet after the stock split.

4. Prepare journal entries for the following transactions:

Feb 10 Purchased 800 shares of $5 par treasury stock for $24 per share.
Jul   1 Sold 500 shares of treasury stock for $28 per share.
Dec 12 Sold 300 shares of treasury stock for $16 per share.

Date	Account and Explanation	PR	Debit	Credit

5. Use the following information to present the stockholders' equity section in good form:

Common Stock, $1.00 par, 2,000,000 shares authorized, 1,205,000 issued	1,205,000
Paid-in Capital in Excess of Par - Common	5,620,000
Preferred Stock, $10 par, 100,000 shares authorized, 50,000 issued	500,000
Retained Earnings	10,418,000
Treasury Stock-Common (30,000 shares)	465,000

VI. Beyond the Numbers

Review the facts in Daily Exercises 2 & 3, but assume a 3-for-2 stock split when the market price was $60 per share.

1. How many shares will be owned after the split? _____

2. To what market price will the shares approximately adjust? _____

VII. Demonstration Problems

Demonstration Problem #1:

Maxx Communications Inc., reported the following stockholders' equity:

Stockholders' Equity:	
Preferred stock, 6%, $25 par value	
Authorized - 1,000,000 shares	
Issued 175,000 shares	$4,375,000
Common stock $1 par value	
Authorized - 5,000,000 shares	
Issued - 600,000 shares	600,000
Paid-in capital in excess of par - common	3,750,000
Retained earnings	8,155,000
Less: Treasury stock, at cost (4,000 common shares)	28,000
Total stockholders' equity	$16,852,000

Required: (Work space to complete each of these questions is provided on the following pages.)

1. What was the average issue price per share of the common stock?
2. What was the average issue price per share of the preferred stock?
3. Assume that net income for the year was $1,025,000 and that issued shares of both common and preferred stock remained constant during the year. Journalize the entry to close net income to Retained Earnings. What was the amount of earnings per share?
4. Journalize the issuance of 15,000 additional shares of common stock at $23.50 per share. Use the same account titles as shown in the problem.
5. How many shares of common stock are outstanding after the 15,000 additional shares have been sold?
6. How many shares of common stock would be authorized, issued, and outstanding after the corporation split its common stock 2 for 1? What is the new par value?
7. Journalize the distribution of a 10% common stock dividend after the 2-for-1 stock split when the market price is $22.50 per share.
8. Journalize the following treasury stock transactions in the order given:
   a. Maxx Communications Inc., purchases 2,500 shares of treasury stock at $20 per share.

b. One month later, the corporation sells 1,000 shares of the same treasury stock for $25 per share (credit Paid-in Capital from Treasury Stock Transactions).

c. An additional 1,000 shares of treasury stock acquired in 8a are sold for $14 per share.

9. The board of directors has voted to appropriate $975,000 of retained earnings for future expansion of foreign operations. Prepare the journal entry to record this event.

10. Set up the beginning balances in the following T-accounts using the information provided in the Stockholders' Equity section for Maxx Communications Inc. at the beginning of the problem.

11. Post the journal entries from instructions 3, 4, 7, 8a, 8b, 8c, and 9 to the T-accounts above.

12. Prepare a current Stockholders' Equity section for Maxx Communications Inc. using the ending balances in the T-accounts in #11.

Requirement 1

Requirement 2

Requirement 3

Date	Account and Explanation	PR	Debit	Credit

Requirement 4

Date	Account and Explanation	PR	Debit	Credit

Requirement 5

Requirement 6

Requirement 7

Date	Account and Explanation	PR	Debit	Credit

Requirement 8

a.

Date	Account and Explanation	PR	Debit	Credit

b.

Date	Account and Explanation	PR	Debit	Credit

c.

Date	Account and Explanation	PR	Debit	Credit

Requirement 9

Date	Account and Explanation	PR	Debit	Credit

Requirements 10 and 11

Preferred Stock

Common Stock

Paid-in Capital in Excess of Par - Common

Retained Earnings

Treasury Stock

79

Requirement 12

Demonstration Problem #2

The following items, listed alphabetically, were taken from the records of Atlas Manufacturing, Inc., for the year ended December 31, 20X3.

Administrative Expenses	185,000
Cost of Goods Sold	2,648,000
Cumulative Effect of Change in Accounting Principle	82,000
Extraordinary Loss	(296,000)
Gain on Sale of Equipment	48,000
Income from Discontinued Operations	45,720
Sales (net)	5,014,200
Selling Expenses	305,000

Atlas Manufacturing is subjected to a combined 45% tax rate.

Required

1. Present the multiple-step income statement in good form for Atlas Manufacturing for the year ended December 31, 20X3.
2. Assume Atlas's average number of common shares outstanding is $275,000. Present earnings per share information.

Requirement 1 (income statement)

Requirement 2 (earnings per share)

SOLUTIONS

I. Matching

1. F	5. E	9. D	13. O
2. G	6. K	10. C	14. N
3. B	7. J	11. H	15. M
4. A	8. I	12. L	

II. Multiple Choice

1. A   The board of directors declares a dividend on the declaration date, to stockholders of record on the date of record that is paid on the payment date.

2. B   A small stock dividend (less than 20-25%) is accounted for at market value on the date of declaration.

3. A   If the market price for one share of stock is $60 prior to a 2-for-1 stock split, then it can be reasonably expected that the doubling of the number of shares outstanding will decrease the market price by half, or $30.

4. B   Of the choices given, only the statement of stockholders' equity reports the changes in all of the stockholders' equity accounts for a period of time.

5. A   Treasury Stock, a contra stockholders' equity account, is acquired by purchasing it; cash is decreased and stockholders' equity is decreased.

6. B   Treasury stock is authorized and issued, but it is no longer outstanding.

7. A   A loss results in an income tax savings whereas a gain results in additional income tax expense. A loss on discontinued operations is reported on the income statement net of the income tax effects. Therefore, $60,000 x .45 = $27,000 tax savings. So, the loss would be reported on the income statement as $33,000.

8. C   Appropriating retained earnings has no effect on total retained earnings. The appropriation indicates that some retained earnings are not available for dividends.

9. C   To be treated as an extraordinary item on the income statement an event must be unusual and infrequent. In today's business environment worker strikes are neither, whereas the other listed items can be considered both.

10 D   By its definition, prior period adjustments are corrections to retained earnings for errors of an earlier period.

III. Completion

1. net income less preferred dividends; average number of common shares outstanding
2. Treasury (Treasury stock is treated the same as unissued stock, which is not in the hands of stockholders, nor does it receive dividends.)
3. unusual in nature; infrequent in occurrence (Note that extraordinary items must be unusual and infrequent.)
4. continuing operations, special items, earnings per share
5. comprehensive income
6. cumulative effect of a change in accounting principle, net of tax
7. cash dividend; stock dividend
8. stock split
9. prior period adjustment
10. net of tax

IV. Daily exercise

1. A. 2*
   B. 1 (Note, however, that income from continuing operations is shown both before and after income taxes.)
   C. 3*
   D. 4*

2.
Current holdings	4,000 shares
Dividend (.15 × 4,000)	600 shares
Total	4,600 shares

Par value would remain $6, as par value is not affected by stock dividends. Total paid-in capital will increase by $6,000 or (600 shares x $10) as a result of the stock dividend. Stock dividends shift value out of retained earnings and into paid-in capital. However, total stockholders' equity does not change.

3.
Current holdings	4,000 shares
Stock split	× 3
Total	12,000 shares

Par value would decrease to $2 or ($6 x 1/3) as a result of the stock split. Notice that the total par value of the common stock is $24,000 both before and after the stock split. Therefore, total paid-in capital does not change after a stock split.

4.
2,250,000	Shares issued
- 360,000	Shares Treasury stock
1,890,000	Outstanding shares

5.
2,250,000	Shares issued
- 355,000	Shares Treasury stock
1,895,000	Outstanding shares

6. $\dfrac{\$250{,}000 \text{ net income} - \$125{,}000 \text{ preferred dividend}}{175{,}000 \text{ average number of common shares outstanding}} = \$.71$ earnings per share

V. Exercises

1.

	Assets	Liabilities	Paid-in Capital	Retained Earnings
A. Declaration of a cash dividend	0	+	0	-
B. Payment of a cash dividend	-	-	0	0
C. Declaration of a stock dividend	0	0	+	-
D. Issuance of a stock dividend	0	0	0	0
E. A stock split	0	0	0	0
F. Cash purchase of treasury stock	-	0	0*	0*
G. Sale of treasury stock below cost	+	0	-**	-**

* While a cash purchase of treasury stock does not affect Paid-in Capital or Retained Earnings, it does reduce stockholders' equity.

** The sale may reduce one or the other, or both. In addition, the sale also increases total stockholders' equity, by the amount of the credit to Treasury Stock.

2.

Date	Account and Explanation	PR	Debit	Credit
	Retained Earnings *		1,944,000	
	Common Stock (72,000 sh × $5 par)			360,000
	Paid-in Capital in Excess of Par-Common			1,584,000

*400,000 shares outstanding
   × .18
72,000 shares distributed as a dividend
   × $27 market price
$1,944,000

How many shares of common stock are issued and outstanding after the distribution of the stock dividend? <u>472,000 shares</u>

3.

Paid-in capital:	
Preferred stock, 5%, cumulative $50 par, 35,000 shares authorized, 12,000 shares issued	$ 600,000
Common stock, **$1.25 par, 560,000 shares authorized, 300,000 shares issued**	375,000
Paid-in capital in excess of par-common	243,750
Total paid-in capital	1,218,750
Retained earnings	320,000
Total stockholders' equity	$ 1,538,750

4.

Date	Account and Explanation	PR	Debit	Credit
Feb 10	Treasury Stock (800 × $24)		19,200	
	Cash			19,200
Jul 1	Cash		14,000	
	Treasury Stock (500 × $24)			12,000
	Paid-in Capital from Treasury Stock Transactions			2,000
	[($28 - 24) × 500]			
Dec 12	Cash (300 × $16)		4,800	
	Paid-in Capital from Treasury Stock Transactions		2,000	
	Retained Earnings		400	
	Treasury Stock (300 × $24)			7,200
The July 1 transaction resulted in a $2,000 balance in the Paid-in Capital from Treasury Stock Transactions account. This credit balance is not large enough to absorb the entire $2,400 difference between the Treasury Stock cost and its selling price (300 shares × $16). Therefore, the Paid-in Capital from Treasury Stock Transactions account is debited up to its credit balance ($2,000) and the excess is charged against Retained Earnings. The Paid-in Capital Treasury Stock Transactions account cannot carry a debit balance.				

5.

Paid-in Capital

Preferred Stock, $10 par, 100,000 shares authorized, 50,000 issued		$ 500,000
Common Stock, $1.00 par, 2,000,000 shares authorized, 1,205,000 issued	$ 1,205,000	
Paid-in Capital in Excess of Par - Common	5,620,000	6,825,000
Total Paid-In Capital		7,325,000
Retained Earnings		10,418,000
Subtotal		17,743,000
Less: Treasury Stock (30,000 shares common)		465,000
Total Stockholders' Equity		$17,278,000

VI. Beyond the Numbers

No journal entries are required when a company declares a stock split. The outstanding shares are returned to the company and replaced with new shares. After the split there will be 6,000 shares of common stock outstanding or (4,000 shares × 3/2). Each new share will have a par value of $4 or ($6 × 2/3). The total common stock remains at $24,000 and paid-in capital remains unchanged, however. The market price will drop proportionately to $40 per share or ($60 × 2/3). Stock splits have the same effect on market price as large stock dividends.

Demonstration Problem #1 Solved and Explained

1. Average issue price of the common stock was $7.25 per share:

Common stock at par ($1 × 600,000 shares)	$ 600,000
Paid-in capital in excess of par - common	3,750,000
Total paid in for common stock	4,350,000
÷ number of issued shares	÷ 600,000
Average issue price	$7.25

2. Average issue price of the preferred stock was $25 per share:

Preferred stock at par ($25 × 175,000 shares)	$4,375,000
Paid-in capital in excess of par - preferred	0
Total paid in for preferred stock	4,375,000
÷ number of issued shares	÷175,000
Average issue price	$25.00

3. Income Summary   1,025,000
       Retained Earnings   1,025,000

   Earnings per share is $1.286:

Net income	$1,025,000
Less: Preferred dividends (175,000 × $1.50)	262,500
Net income available to common stock	762,500
÷ average outstanding shares (600,000 issued - 4,000 treasury stock)	÷ 596,000
Earnings per share (rounded)	$1.28

4. Cash (15,000 shares × $23.50 selling price)   352,500
       Common Stock (15,000 × $1)   15,000
       Paid-in Capital in Excess of Par - Common   337,500
   To issue common stock at a premium.

5. Shares outstanding = 611,000
   600,000 shares issued plus 15,000 shares from answer 4 = 615,000 issued
   615,000 shares issued less 4,000 shares treasury stock = 611,000 shares outstanding

6. Shares *authorized* after stock split = 10,000,000
   5,000,000 shares authorized before split × 2/1 = 10,000,000 shares after the split

   Shares *issued* after stock split = 1,230,000
   615,000 shares authorized before split × 2/1 = 1,230,000 shares after the split

   Shares *outstanding* after 2-for-1 split = 1,222,000:
   611,000 shares outstanding immediately before split × 2/1 = 1,222,000 shares outstanding after the split.
   The new par value of the common stock is $0.50 ($1.00 × 1/2)

7. a. Retained Earnings (1,222,000 outstanding shares ×

10% × $22.50)	2,749,500	
Common Stock		61,100
(122,200 × $.50)		
Paid-in Capital in Excess of Par - Common		2,688,400
(122,200 shares × $22.00 premium)		

   To distribute a 10% stock dividend.

When a *small stock dividend* occurs (GAAP defines a small dividend as one for less than 25%), Retained Earnings should be capitalized for the *fair market* value of the shares to be distributed (in this case, $2,749,500). Note that 1,222,000 shares were outstanding after answer 6 above, and that the 2-for-1 stock split reduces par value to $0.50 per share. The 10% distribution was for 122,200 shares (1,222,000 × 10% = 122,200).

8. a.
Treasury Stock (2,500 × $20)	50,000	
Cash		50,000

   To purchase 2,500 shares of treasury stock at $20 per share.

   b.
Cash (1,000 × $25)	25,000	
Treasury Stock (1,000 × $20)		20,000
Paid-in Capital from Treasury Stock Transactions		5,000

   To sell 1,000 shares of treasury stock at $25 per share.

   c.
Cash (1,000 × $14)	14,000	
Paid-in Capital from Treasury Stock Transactions	5,000	
Retained Earnings	1,000	
Treasury Stock (1,000 × $20)		20,000

   To sell 1,000 shares of treasury stock at $14 per share.

A company does not earn income on the purchase and sale of its own stock. The sale of treasury stock results in an increase to paid-in capital, not income. Paid-in Capital from Treasury Stock Transactions (a paid-in capital account is *credited* for sales in excess of cost (as in answer 8b) and *debited* for a sale below cost). If the account balance is not large enough to cover a sale below cost, it may be necessary to debit Retained Earnings (as in answer 8c).

9.   Retained Earnings   975,000
            Retained Earnings Appropriated
            for Future Expansion   975,000
        To appropriate retained earnings for future expansion of foreign operations.

10 & 11.

Preferred Stock-$25 par	
	Bal. 4,375,000

Common Stock-$1 par	
	Bal. 600,000
	(4) 15,000
	(7) 61,100
	Bal. 676,100

Paid-in Capital in Excess of Par - Common	
	Bal. 3,750,000
	(4) 337,500
	(7) 2,688,400
	Bal. 6,775,900

Retained Earnings	
(7) 2,749,500	Bal. 8,155,000
(8c) 1,000	(3) 1,025,000
(9) 975,000	
	Bal. 5,454,500

Treasury Stock	
Bal. 28,000	(8b) 20,000
(8a) 50,000	(8c) 20,000
Bal. 38,000	

Paid-in Capital from Treasury Stock Transactions	
(8c) 5,000	(8b) 5,000
	Bal. 0

Retained Earnings Appropriated	
	(9) 975,000
	Bal. 975,000

12.

Stockholders' Equity:		
Preferred Stock, 6%, $25 par value		
Authorized - 1,000,000 shares		
Issued 175,000 shares	$4,375,000	
Common Stock $0.50 par value		
Authorized - 10,000,000 shares		
Issued - 1,352,200 shares	676,100	
Paid-in Capital in Excess of Par - Common	6,775,900	
Total Paid-in Capital		$11,827,000
Retained earnings		
Appropriated	975,000	
Unappropriated	5,454,500	
Total Retained Earnings		6,429,500
Total Paid-in Capital and Retained Earnings		18,256,500
Less: Treasury stock, at cost (8,500 common shares)		
		38,000
Total Stockholders' Equity		$18,218,500

Explanation:

All the amounts were taken directly from the ending T-account balances. These ending balances are the result of requirements #10 and #11. Remember, the common shares split 2 for 1, thereby reducing the par value of each from $1.00 to $.50. Therefore, the ending balance in the common stock account of $676,100 must represent 1,352,200 shares × $ .50 par. The Treasury Stock balance represents the original balance of $28,000 plus the 500 shares remaining from the transactions in entry 8. The total shares are now 8,500 because the original 4,000 shares were affected by the 2 for 1 split in #6 (4,000 × 2 = 8,000 + 500 = 8,500).

Demonstration Problem #2 Solved and Explained

Requirement 1 (income statement)

Atlas Manufacturing
Income Statement
For the Year Ended December 31, 20X3

Sales		$5,014,200
Cost of Goods Sold		2,648,000
Gross Margin		2,366,200
Less: Operating Expenses		
Selling	305,000	
Administrative	185,000	490,000
Operating Income		1,876,200
Other gains (losses)		
Gain on Sale of Equipment		48,000
Income from continuing operations before income tax		1,924,200
Income tax expense (45%)		865,890
Income from continuing operations		1,058,310
Discontinued Operations, income of $45,720, less income tax of $20,574		25,146
Income before extraordinary item and cumulative effect of change in accounting principle		1,083,456
Extraordinary Loss, $296,000, less income tax saving of $133,200		(162,800)
Cumulative Effect of Change in Accounting Principle, $82,000, less income tax of $36,900		45,100
Net Income		$ 965,756

Requirement 2 (Earnings per share)

Income from continuing operations ($1,058,310 ÷ 275,000 shares)	$3.85
Income from discontinued operations ($25,146 ÷ 275,000 shares)	0.09
Income before extraordinary loss and cumulative effect of change in accounting principle ($1,083,456 ÷ 275,000 shares)	$3.94
Extraordinary loss ((162,800) ÷ 275,000 shares)	(0.59)
Cumulative effect of change in accounting ($45,100 ÷ 275,000 shares)	0.16
Net income	$3.51

Study Tip: Proof = $965,756 ÷ 275,000 = $3.51

Chapter 15 - Long-Term Liabilities

CHAPTER OVERVIEW

In Chapters 13 and 14, you learned about topics related to stockholders' equity. You saw that paid-in capital is a major source of financing for corporations. Remember, paid-in-capital comes from the owners or stockholders of the company. The most desirable source of funds for any business is those generated from profitable operations. However, sometimes corporations may also need to obtain funds by borrowing money. In this chapter we examine long-term liabilities generated from borrowing money, specifically those transactions related to bonds. The learning objectives for the chapter are to:

1. Account for bonds payable transactions.
2. Measure interest expense by the effective-interest method.
3. Account for retirement and conversion of bonds payable.
4. Report liabilities on the balance sheet.
5. Show the advantages and disadvantages of borrowing.

Appendix to Chapter 15
Time Value of Money: Future Value and Present Value

CHAPTER REVIEW

Objective 1 - Account for bonds payable transactions

Corporations issue **bonds** to borrow large amounts of money from multiple lenders called bondholders. Bonds are long-term liabilities that appear on the balance sheet. When a bond is issued, the bondholder, or purchaser, receives a **bond certificate** as evidence of the transaction that states the following:

1) **Principal** of the bond represents the amount borrowed and is also referred to as the **maturity value** or **par value** of the bond
2) **Stated interest rate** is the interest rate stated on the bond certificate that determines the amount of the interest payments the bondholder will receive over the life of the bond. Interest payments are typically made either annually, semiannually, or quarterly and are a fixed amount over the life of the bond.
3) **Maturity date** is the date on which the principal amount of the bonds must be repaid.
4) **Interest payment date(s)** indicate the date(s) on which the bondholder will receive the fixed interest payments.

Exhibit 15-1 in your text presents a typical bond certificate.

There are several different types of bonds:

- **Term bonds** mature at the same time.
- **Serial bonds** mature in installments over a period of time.
- Unsecured bonds are called **debentures**.
- **Secured bonds** may be referred to as mortgage bonds (i.e., used to purchase a building). The owners of a secured bond have the right to take specified assets of the issuer in the event of default.

Bonds are often traded on bond markets. Bond prices are quoted as a percentage of their maturity value. For example, a $10,000 bond selling for 97 would sell for $9,700, or 97% of the maturity value (principal) of the bond. Like stock, bond prices fluctuate daily. A bond's "price" represents how much money the issuing (borrowing) corporation will receive when the bond is issued (sold). On the opposite side of the transaction, the "price" of the bond determines how much money the bondholder (creditor) will pay to the corporation on the issue date. Bonds issued at a price above the maturity value (par) are being sold at a **premium**; bonds issued at a price below maturity value (par) are being sold at a **discount**.

How is the price at which the bond will be sold determined? The relationship of the market (effective) interest rate to the stated (coupon) interest rate will determine whether the bond will be issued at par, a discount, or a premium. The market interest rate is the amount that potential investors are currently demanding to earn on their money in the marketplace. The stated interest rate is set on the bond certificate and is a fixed amount; however, the market rate fluctuates daily as a result of fluctuations in the market.

When a bond is issued, that is the moment when the company receives the cash it has borrowed. How much cash the company receives depends on the relationship of the market interest rate to the stated interest rate on the bond certificate.

- If market rate = stated rate, then the amount of cash received will be equal to the maturity value or principal of the bond. This bond will be issued at par or 100.
- If market rate > stated rate, the bond is issued at a discount. This means that the amount of cash received will be less than the maturity value of the bond. How much less? Well, you must either know the price at which the bond is quoted (e.g. 95, or something less than 100) or, if the bond quote is not provided, you must calculate the issue price of the bond by calculating the present value of the future cash flows from the bond.
- If market rate < stated rate, the bond is issued at a premium. This means that the amount of cash received is more than the maturity value of the bond. How much more? Well, you must either know the price at which the bond is quoted (e.g. 102, or something greater than 100) or, if the bond quote is not provided, you must calculate the issue price of the bond by calculating the present value of the future cash flows from the bond.

In summary, the price that an investor will be willing to pay today, in the present, is determined by the relationship between the market rate of interest and the stated rate of interest. Exhibit 15-3 in your text illustrates this relationship. The price that an investor is willing to pay today is the amount of cash that the issuing company receives. Remember, you are always analyzing and measuring transactions from the perspective of the business. So, with respect to bonds, you are concerned about accounting for the increase in cash upon issuance of the bond, and the recording of the liability. You must also account for any discount or premium that may exist.

Once the bond is issued, the company now has the obligation to begin making the periodic interest payments. The bond certificate will define when the interest payments must be made. Interest payments on bonds are typically made annually (once per year), semiannually (once every six months) or quarterly (once every three months).

The simplest transaction occurs when bonds are issued on an interest payment date and the stated rate is equal to the market rate of interest.

A basic understanding of the concept of present value is necessary to understand bond prices. When companies borrow money they have to pay interest on the debt. To the lender this represents the time value of money. Therefore a lender would not be interested in giving up $500 today only to receive $500 five years from now. If the lender wants to receive $500 years from now, the question is, how much would the lender be willing to give up today to do so? The answer to the question represents the present value of that future amount ($500). Present value is discussed in detail in the Chapter 15 Appendix.

Issuing Bonds at Maturity Value

The simplest transaction occurs when bonds are issued on an interest payment date and no difference exists between the stated rate and the market rate. Debit Cash for the cash received and credit Bonds Payable for the principal of the bond. When interest is paid, debit Interest Expense and credit Cash. When the bonds mature and are paid off, debit Bonds Payable and credit Cash.

When **bonds are issued between interest dates**, the corporation collects from the purchaser, the selling price of the bond **plus** the interest that has accrued from the last interest payment date to the date of issuance. Debit Cash, credit Bonds Payable, and credit Interest Payable.

The first interest payment is recorded with a debit to Interest Expense, a debit to Interest Payable, and a credit to Cash (for the full 6 months' interest payment).

Interest payments are not prorated based on the issue date. The interest payment to the purchaser is composed of the accrued interest collected from the purchaser plus the interest expense from the sale date to the next interest date; in other words, the full 6 months' interest.

Issuing Bonds at a Discount

If the market interest rate is higher than the stated rate of a bond issue, then the issuer will **sell the bonds at a discount** that is at an amount that is less than maturity value of the bond in order to attract buyers. The entry to record a bond issued at a discount debits Cash, debits **Discount on Bonds Payable**, and credits Bonds Payable.

Discount on Bonds Payable is a contra account to Bonds Payable. On the balance sheet, the discount balance is subtracted from Bonds Payable to equal the book value or carrying amount of the bond. Over the life of the bond, the issuer will have to make periodic interest payments and then repay the principal amount of the bonds on the maturity date. Remember, a bond issued at a discount means the issuer received an amount that was less than the maturity value of the bond. If the issuer must repay the maturity value of the bond on the maturity date, then the amount of the discount must represent additional interest expense to the issuer. Thus, the discount raises the overall interest expense on the bond to the market rate of interest.

For each accounting period over the life of the bond, the discount is accounted for as interest expense through a process called amortization. The amortization of the discount adheres to the matching principle set forth by GAAP. **Straight-line amortization** of the discount is computed by dividing the discount by the number of accounting periods over the life of the bonds. On each interest date, the entry to record interest expense debits Interest Expense, credits Cash, and credits Discount on Bonds Payable. *Therefore, the total cost to the corporation of borrowing the money is the sum of the interest payments plus the discount.*

Issuing Bonds at a Premium

If the market rate is lower than the stated rate of a bond issue, then the issuer will **sell the bonds at a premium**, that is, at an amount that is greater than the maturity value of the bond. The entry debits Cash, credits Bonds Payable and credits Premium on Bonds Payable.

Premium on Bonds Payable is an adjunct account to Bonds Payable. On the balance sheet, the premium is added to Bonds Payable to show the book value or carrying amount. Over the life of the bond, the issuer will have to make periodic interest payments and then repay the principal amount of the bonds on the maturity date. Remember, a bond issued at a premium means the issuer received an amount that was greater than the maturity value of the bond. If the issuer must repay only the maturity value of the bond on the maturity date, then the amount of the premium must represent a reduction to the interest expense of the issuer. Thus, the premium decreases the overall interest expense on the bond to the market rate of interest. *Therefore, the total cost to the corporation of borrowing the money is the sum of the interest payments minus the premium.*

Straight-line amortization of the premium is computed by dividing the premium by the number of accounting periods during the life of the bonds. On each interest date, the entry to record interest expense debits Interest Expense, debits Premium on Bonds Payable and credits Cash.

Adjusting entries are prepared to accrue interest and amortize the discount or premium for the period from the last interest date to the end of the accounting period. Debit Interest Expense, credit Interest Payable, and either debit Premium on Bonds Payable or credit Discount on Bonds Payable.

Objective 2 – Measure interest expense by the effective-interest method.

The straight-line method of amortizing the discount or premium is introduced to illustrate the allocation of the discount or premium to interest expense and to show the overall effect of both on the total interest cost of the bond. However, straight-line amortization of a discount or premium is not considered GAAP. GAAP requires that discounts and premiums be amortized using the **effective-interest method**. However, when the difference between the straight-line and effective-interest methods is not material, either method may be used.

The objective of the effective-interest method is to measure interest expense as a constant percentage of the changing carrying value of the bonds rather than as a constant amount each period (straight-line). The effective interest rate is the market rate in effect when the bonds are sold. Three steps are followed when using the effective interest method:

1. Interest expense is calculated by multiplying the effective interest rate by the carrying value of the bonds. (This amount changes each period.)

> **Study Tip:** Carrying value equals principal plus unamortized premium or minus unamortized discount.

2. The cash paid to bondholders is calculated by multiplying the stated interest rate by the principal amount of the bonds. (This amount is the same each period.)

3. The difference between the interest expense and the cash paid is the amount of discount or premium amortized.

Remember that amortization of bond discount or premium will change the carrying value of the bonds before the next calculations are made. If a premium is amortized, the carrying value of the bonds will decrease; if a discount is amortized, the carrying value will increase.

Carefully study Exhibits 15-4, 15-5, 15-6 and 15-7 in your text in order to understand the effective-interest method.

As with straight-line amortization, adjusting entries must be prepared for a partial period from the last interest date to the end of the accounting period in order to accrue interest and amortize bond discount or premium. Debit Interest Expense, credit Interest Payable, and either debit Premium on Bonds Payable or credit Discount on Bonds Payable.

Objective 3 - Account for the retirement and conversion of bonds payable.

Sometimes corporations retire bonds prior to the maturity date. **Callable bonds** may be retired at the option of the issuer, or bonds may be bought back on the open market and retired. If interest rates have dropped, the issuer may compare the book value of the bonds to the market price to decide whether to retire the bonds. When bonds are retired and the bonds were initially sold at either a premium or discount, the entry to retire the bonds must also remove the unamortized premium or discount from the books. A **gain (or loss) on retirement** results when the carrying value of the bonds is greater (or lesser for a loss) than the cash paid for the bonds. Any gain or loss on the retirement of bonds payable is an extraordinary item according to GAAP.

> **Study Tip:** Remember from Chapter 14 that extraordinary items are reported separately on the income statement, net of tax.

Bonds that can be converted into common stock are called **convertible bonds**. Investors will convert the bonds when the stock price of the issuing company increases to the point that the stock has a higher market value than the bonds. The entry transfers the bond's carrying value into stockholders' equity:

```
Bonds Payable                                    XX
    Premium on Bonds Payable (if applicable)     XX
        Discount on Bonds Payable (if applicable)          XX
        Common stock                                       XX
        Paid-in Capital in Excess of Par - Common          XX
```

Study Tip: Note both Premium and Discount cannot appear in the same entry.

There will never be a gain or loss recorded on the conversion of bonds. The credit to Paid-in Capital in Excess of Par-Common is the difference between the carrying value of the bonds (Bonds Payable + Premium on Bonds Payable – Discount on Bonds Payable) and the par value of the shares issued.

Objective 4 – Report liabilities on the balance sheet

A bond is reported on the balance sheet as a liability at its carrying or book value.

If a bond is issued at par, then the carrying value = maturity value of the bond (because there is no discount or premium)

If a bond is issued at a discount, then the carrying value = maturity value of the bond
                                        - unamortized discount on bonds payable
                                        = carrying value of bond

If a bond is issued at a premium, then the carrying value = maturity value of the bond
                                        + unamortized premium on bonds payable
                                        = carrying value of bond

Objective 5 - Show the advantages and disadvantages of borrowing.

Advantages of borrowing:

1. Borrowing does not affect ownership; bondholders are creditors, not stockholders.
2. Interest on debt is deductible for tax purposes.
3. **Trading on the equity** usually increases EPS. This means that the corporation earns a return on the borrowed funds that is greater than the cost of the borrowed funds.

Disadvantages of borrowing:

1. High interest rates
2. Interest on debt must be paid; dividends on stock are optional.

Appendix: Future Value and Present Value

FUTURE VALUE:

Compute the future value of an investment made in a single amount.

Because you can earn interest on your money over time, the value of invested funds is greater in the future than it is today. This is referred to as the **time value of money**. To determine what a **future value** will be you simply apply an interest rate to the amount of your investment and calculate the amount of interest. Add this result to your original amount and the sum becomes the future value at the end of one interest period. Repeat this process for additional interest periods, remembering to add in the interest each time. Therefore there are three factors involved in determining a future value: 1) the amount of the original investment, 2) the length of time and 3) the interest rate. Obviously the longer the time, the more calculations are involved. Fortunately mathematical tables are available to ease your task. Review Exhibit 15A-2 carefully. This is the table used to determine a future value of a single investment, again assuming time and interest rate.

Here's an example: How much will you have in 6 years if you invest $4,000 today at 8% with interest paid semiannually? Using the table in Exhibit 15A-2, find the intersection of 12 periods (6 years × 2 payments per year) and 4%. Why 4%? Because 8% is an annual rate, and if interest is paid semiannually, or twice per year, then the interest paid per period is 4% or (8% ÷ 2). The value at the intersect is 1.601. Multiply this by $4,000, and the result is $6,404. This is the future value of your $4,000 investment, given the time and rate assumed above.

Compute the future value of annuity-type investment.

Instead of investing a single amount for a specific period, you might wish to invest multiple amounts over time. This is an example of an **annuity-type investment**. In other words, you invest identical amounts for several years—what is the future value of these multiple investments? Of course, you could calculate each individually and add the results, or you can consult mathematical tables that do the multiple calculations for you. Review Exhibit 15A-3 carefully. This is the table used to determine the future value of multiple investments, again assuming time and interest rate. This table is used to answer questions like, "If I start setting aside (investing) $500 each year for the next ten years, what will it be worth at the end of the tenth year, assuming I can invest this money at 8%?" Exhibit 15A-3 shows the value 14.487 at the intersection of 10 and 8%. Multiply this value by your annual investment ($500) and the result is $7,243.50.

PRESENT VALUE:

Compute the present value of a single future amount.

Another way to look at present and future values is to begin with the future value and work backwards. In other words, in order to have a specific amount some time in the future, how much would one need to set aside today? Again assumptions need to be made about the time and the interest rate (this is always true).

As with the preceding discussions, you could calculate the result manually but the longer the period of time the more calculations you would have to complete. Once again, mathematical tables are available to use. Study Exhibit 15A-6 carefully. The value at the intersection of the appropriate period and rate is multiplied by the future amount to determine the present value.

For example, if you needed $10,000 at the end of 5 years and could invest a single amount in an account earning 6%, how much would you need to invest today? Using the table in Exhibit 15A-6, find the intersection of 5 periods and 6%. The value at the intersect is 0.747. Multiply this value by $10,000, and the result is $$7,470. Therefore, you must deposit $7,470 today in an account earning 6% to have $10,000 at the end of 5 years, given the time and rate assumed above.

Compute the present value of an annuity.

Rather than determining the present value of a single amount, you may be interested in the **present value of an annuity-type investment**. In other words, what is the present value of an investment that will give you the same fixed amount over a number of periods? As with earlier discussions, this value can be calculated manually, but it is time-consuming. Once again, tables are available to simplify the process. Study Exhibit 15A-7 carefully.

Study Tip: BEFORE PROCEEDING, BE CERTAIN YOU UNDERSTAND THE CIRCUMSTANCES IN WHICH YOU USE EACH TABLE. This is vital to understanding the topics that follow.

Chapter 15 examines long-term liabilities, primarily bonds payable. What is a bond? It is a way for a company to borrow funds. When a company issues a bond, what happens? The company promises to pay the maturity value of the bond at the maturity date AND over the life of the bond, the company also promises to pay a series of fixed interest payments. The maturity value that must be repaid at maturity is a single amount, whereas the interest payments are like an annuity, a series of fixed payments. Therefore, when a company issues bonds it needs to know what price should be asked (remember bond prices are quoted as percentages of maturity value) in order to attract investors. To calculate the issue price of a bond, you must use the appropriate tables—in this case Exhibits 15A-6 and 15A-7 in your text. Using the market rate of interest, the first table will give you the present value of a future single amount, and the second the present value of an annuity. Sum the results and you have an estimate of the market price of the bonds. The market rate of interest is used because this is the rate potential investors will demand for the use of their funds. If the market rate is higher than the stated (or coupon) rate of interest, the bonds will have to be sold at a discount to attract investors. Conversely, if the market rate is lower than the stated rate, the bonds will sell at a premium.

TEST YOURSELF

All the self-testing materials in this chapter focus on information and procedures that your instructor is likely to test in quizzes and examinations. *Questions followed by the letter "A" refer to topics in the chapter appendix.*

I. Matching   *Match each numbered term with its lettered definition.*

_____ 1. Bond discount
_____ 2. Bond premium
_____ 3. Callable bonds
_____ 4. Debentures
_____ 5. Stated interest rate
_____ 6. Market interest rate
_____ 7. Present Value

_____ 8. Bonds payable
_____ 9. Serial bonds
_____ 10. Term bonds
_____ 11. Annuity
_____ 12. Convertible bonds
_____ 13. Mortgage

A. Bonds that may be exchanged for the common stock of the issuing company at the option of the investor
B. Bonds that mature in installments over a period of time
C. Bonds that the issuer may pay off at a specified price whenever the issuer desires
D. Bonds that all mature at the same time for a particular issue
E. Borrower's promise to transfer the legal title to certain assets to the lender if the debt is not paid on schedule
F. Amount a person would invest now to receive a greater amount at a future date
G. Excess of a bond's maturity (par) value over its issue price
H. Excess of a bond's issue price over its maturity (par) value
I. Groups of notes payable issued to multiple lenders, called bondholders
J. Interest rate that investors demand in order to lend their money
K. The interest rate that determines the amount of cash interest the borrower pays
L. Unsecured bonds backed only by the good faith of the borrower
M. A fixed amount paid (or received) over a number of periods

II. Multiple Choice   *Circle the best answer.*

1. A $10,000 bond quoted at 96 5/8 has a market price of:

    A. $10,000
    B. $9,662.50

    C. $9,658.00
    D. $9,606.25

2. Amortization refers to the allocation of the bond discount or premium to

    A. Accumulated depreciation
    B. Bonds payable

    C. Interest Expense
    D. Interest Revenue

3. The present value of a future amount does not depend on the:

    A. interest rate
    B. convertibility of a bond

    C. amount of the future payment
    D. length of time until the future payment is made

4. The interest rate demanded by investors in order to lend their money is the:

    A. stated rate   C. effective rate
    B. issue rate   D. coupon rate

5. The premium on a bond payable:

    A. increases the interest expense only in the year the bonds are sold
    B. increases the interest expense over the life of the bonds
    C. reduces interest expense only in the year the bonds mature
    D. is a liability account that is amortized (to expense) over the life of the bonds

6. The book value of Bonds Payable on the balance sheet equals:

    A. Bonds Payable + Discount on Bonds Payable or + Premium on Bonds Payable
    B. Bonds Payable - Discount on Bonds Payable or - Premium on Bonds Payable
    C. Bonds Payable + Discount on Bonds Payable or - Premium on Bonds Payable
    D. Bonds Payable - Discount on Bonds Payable or + Premium on Bonds Payable

7. When bonds are issued at a premium, their carrying amount:

    A. decreases from issuance to maturity   C. remains constant over the life of the bonds
    B. increases from issuance to maturity   D. decreases when the market interest rate
                                                  increases

8. Gains and losses from the early conversion of debt to equity are:

    A. reported as operating gains and losses on the income statement
    B. reported as increases or decreases to Retained Earnings on the statement of retained earnings
    C. reported as extraordinary items on the income statement
    D. not reported

9. When a convertible bond is exchanged for common stock:

    A. stockholders' equity increases   C. revenues increase
    B. liabilities increase   D. expenses increase

10. When a bond is retired, the issuing corporation may pay the bondholders

    A. a specified call price   C. the carrying value
    B. the current market price in the open market   D. either A. or B.

III. Completion   *Complete each of the following statements.*

1. When the market interest rate is _____ than the stated rate, bonds will sell at a discount.
2. When the discount on bonds payable is reduced, the book value of bonds payable _____.
3. Gains or losses on early retirement of debt is accounted for as _____ and reported separately on the income statement.
4. A premium _____ the overall interest cost on a bond.
5. The _____ method of interest amortization results in the same amount of discount/premium amortization for identical periods of time.
6. Amortization of a bond discount or premium is an example of the _____ principle.
7. When the market interest rate is less than the stated rate, the bonds will sell at a _____.
8. Convertible bonds give the _____ the right to convert the bonds to common stock.
9. When the _____ method of amortization is used, the total amount of interest expense over the life of the bonds is a constant percentage.
10. A (n) _____ is a fixed sum of money received over a number of periods.

IV. Daily Exercises

1. Calculate the cash proceeds when a $10,000, 6% bond is sold at 98 ½ on December 15, assuming interest is paid on October 15 and April 15.

2. Refer to the facts in Daily Exercise 1 above and record the necessary journal entry on December 15.

3. On December 31, the following information appears on the balance sheet:

Bonds Payable	1,000,000	
Less: Discount on Bonds Payable	24,800	975,200

Assuming the interest has been paid through December 31, journalize the entry to convert the bonds into 180,000 shares of $0.50 par common stock.

4. Assume the same information in Daily Exercise 3, but the bonds are called at 101 ½. Record the entry to retire the bonds.

V. Exercises

1. Complex Communications issued $5,000,000 in 20-year bonds with a stated interest rate of 7%. The bonds were issued at par on April 1, 2005. Interest is paid October 1 and April 1.

   Give the journal entries for:

   A. Issuance of the bonds on April 1, 2005.
   B. Payment of interest on October 1, 2005.
   C. Maturity payment of bonds on April 1, 2025.

	Date	Account and Explanation	Debit	Credit
A.				
B.				
C.				

2. Maxwell Corporation issued $500,000 in 7-year bonds with a stated interest rate of 8%. The bonds were sold on January 1, 2007, for $474,443 to yield 9%. Interest is paid July 1 and January 1. Maxwell uses the effective interest method to amortize Discount on Bonds Payable. (Assume a December 31 year-end.)

   Record the journal entries for:
   A. Issuance of bonds on January 1, 2007.
   B. Payment of interest on July 1, 2007.
   C. Accrual of interest and related amortization on December 31, 2007 (year end)
   D. Payment of interest on January 1, 2008.
   E. Maturity payment of bonds on January 1, 2014.

Date	Account and Explanation	Debit	Credit
A.			
B.			
C.			
D.			
E.			

3. Crawford Corporation issued $500,000 in 7-year bonds with a stated interest rate of 8%. The bonds were sold on January 1, 2007, for $474,443 to yield 9%. Interest is paid July 1 and January 1. Crawford uses the straight-line method to amortize Discount on Bonds Payable. (Assume an October 31 year-end.)

Record the journal entries for:

A. Issuance of bonds on January 1, 2007.
B. Payment of interest on July 1, 2007.
C. Accrual of interest and related amortization on October 31, 2007 (year end)
D. Payment of interest on January 1, 2008
E. Maturity payment of bonds on January 1, 2014.

Date	Account and Explanation	Debit	Credit
A.			
B.			

C.			

D.			
E.			

4. Feldman Corporation issued $500,000 in 7-year bonds with a stated interest rate of 8%. The bonds were sold on January 1, 2007, for $556,480 to yield 6%. Interest is paid July 1 and January 1. Feldman uses the effective interest method to amortize Premium on Bonds Payable. (Assume a December 31 year-end.)

Record the journal entries for:

A. Issuance of bonds on January 1, 2007.
B. Payment of interest on July 1, 2007.
C. Accrual of interest and related amortization on December 31, 2007 (year-end)
D. Payment of interest on January 1, 2008
E. Maturity payment of bonds on January 1, 2014.

	Date	Account and Explanation	Debit	Credit
A.				
B.				
C.				
D.				
E.				

5. The board of directors for K. Market, Inc., has approved a financial package to raise additional capital for expansion purposes. Included in the package are 10-year debentures for $22,500,000. The interest rate for the bonds approved by the board is 7%, per annum, paid semiannually. When the bonds are issued, the market rate of interest is 8%. Determine the price at which the bonds should be sold.

VI. Beyond the Numbers

Review the information in Exercise 3 and 4 above and assume, in each case, that each $1,000 bond is convertible, at the option of the holder, into 31.25 shares of the corporation's common stock. Determine when an investor should seriously consider exercising the option to convert the bonds to stock.

_____
_____
_____
_____
_____
_____
_____
_____
_____
_____

VII. Demonstration Problems

Demonstration Problem #1

On February 1, 2006, Speed-Pak, Inc., issued $20,000,000 of 7% bonds at 97 ½. The market rate on that date was approximately 8%. The bonds mature in 10 years. Interest is paid each July 31 and January 31.

Required:

1. Record the issuance of the bonds.
2. Record the July 31, 2006, interest payment and straight-line amortization of premium or discount.
3. Accrued interest and amortize premium or discount as of December 31, 2006, the last day of the reporting year for Speed-Pak, Inc. Use straight-line amortization.
4. Show how the bonds would be reported on the balance sheet on December 31, 2006.
5. Record the payment of interest and amortization of the premium or discount on January 31, 2007. Use straight-line amortization.
6. On February 1, 2008, bondholders convert $5,000,000 of the bonds into 350,000 shares of $1 par value common stock. Record the transaction.
7. On February 1, 2009, the remaining $15,000,000 of bonds are called by the corporation at a call price of 102. Record the retirement of the bonds.

Date	Account and Explanation	Debit	Credit
1.			

2.

3.

4.

5.

Date	Accounts and Explanation	Debit	Credit

6.

7.

Demonstration Problem #2

McCall-Carlton Corporation has outstanding an issue of 10% callable bonds that mature in 2023. The bonds were dated January 1, 2008, and pay interest each July 1 and January 1. Additional bond data:

a. Fiscal year end for McCall-Carlton Corporation: September 30.
b. Maturity value of the bonds: $2,000,000.
c. Issue price: 106.
d. Market interest rate at time of issue: 9%

Required:

1. Complete the effective interest method amortization table through January 1, 2011. Round pennies to the nearest dollar. You may use the Summary Problem in Chapter 15 of the text as a guide.

2. Using the amortization table that you have completed, record the following transactions:
   a. Issuance of the bonds on January 1, 2008.
   b. Payment of interest and amortization of premium on July 1, 2008.
   c. Accrued interest and amortization of premium as of September 30, 2008.
   d. Payment of interest and amortization of premium on January 1, 2009.
   e. Retirement of the bonds on January 2, 2010. Callable price of bonds was 102. Bonds were called on January 2, 2010.

Requirement 1

Semi-annual Interest Date	A Interest Payment	B Interest Expense	C Premium Amortiza-tion	D Premium Account Balance	E Bond Carrying Value
1/1/08				120,000	2,120,000
7/1/08					
1/1/09					
7/1/09					
1/1/10					
7/1/10					
1/1/11					

Requirement 2

	Date	Account and Explanation	Debit	Credit
a.				
b.				
c.				
d.				
e.				

SOLUTIONS

I. Matching

1. G	5. K	9. B	13. E
2. H	6. J	10. D	
3. C	7. F	11. M	
4. L	8. I	12. A	

II. Multiple Choice

1. B The number 96 5/8 means 96.625% (or .96625) of the maturity value:
    $10,000 × 96.625% = $9,662.50.

2. C According to the matching principle, a bond discount or premium must be allocated to Interest Expense over the life of the bond.

3. B Interest rate, amount of payment, and length of time until payment all affect present value whether or not the bond is convertible.

4. C Effective rate of interest and market rate of interest are synonymous.

5. D Amortization of the premium on bonds payable serves to reduce the recorded amount of interest expense over the life of the bonds.

6. D The book value or carrying amount of a bond is equal to the maturity amount of the bond minus the unamortized discount or plus the unamortized premium.

7. A The carrying amount of a bond is the maturity amount of the bond plus (minus) unamortized premium (discount). Since the balance of the premium (discount) account is amortized over the life of the bond, it moves towards zero. Accordingly, the carrying amount of bonds issued at a premium (discount) decreases (increases) over time.

8. D GAAP identifies gains and losses on early retirement of debt as an extraordinary item. However, when debt is converted to equity no gain or loss results. The carrying value of the debt is converted into paid-in capital.

9. A The conversion of a bond to common stock converts a liability to paid-in capital, which increases stockholders' equity.

10. D When bonds are retired, the issuing corporation may pay a call price or simply purchase the bonds in the open market, whichever is less.

III. Completion

1. higher
2. increases (The book value or carrying value amount of a bond is equal to the maturity amount of the bond plus (minus) the unamortized premium (discount).)
3. extraordinary (Though not meeting the normal "infrequent and unusual" requirement for other extraordinary items, GAAP specifies that such gains and losses are extraordinary items.)
4. decreases (If a bond is issued at a premium, then the interest expense recognized over the life of the bond will be less than the periodic interest payment. Thus, the premium decreases the overall interest expense on the bond to the market rate of interest.)
5. straight-line (This method divides the amount of the discount/premium by the number of time periods resulting in the same figure each period.)
6. matching
7. premium (because the bondholder will receive a greater return on the loan than the market rate provides)
8. bondholder or lender (not the borrower; convertibility make the bonds more attractive to prospective lenders because of the potential for greater returns)
9. effective interest (as compared with the straight-line method where the amount of discount/premium is constant). The effective-interest method is required, although the straight-line method can be used if the difference between the two is not material.
10. annuity

IV. Daily Exercises

1. $10,000 × 98 ½ % = $9,850.00 In addition, interest must be accrued from 10/15 to 12/15 (the sale date). Interest = $10,000 × 6% × 2/12 = $100.00.
    Proceeds = $9,850.00 + 100.00 = $9,950.00

2.

12/15 Cash	9,950	
Discount on Bonds Payable	150	
Bonds Payable		10,000
Interest Payable		100

3.

Bonds Payable	1,000,000	
Discount on Bonds Payable		24,800
Common Stock		90,000
Paid-in Capital in Excess of Par - Common		885,200

On the date of conversion, the carrying value of the bonds is $975,200 ($1,000,000 principal less $24,800 discount.) The carrying value, not the principal is the amount being converted. The credit to the Common Stock account = 180,000 shares × $0.50 per share (from Chapter 13). The difference of $885,200 ($975,200 - $90,000) is credited to the paid-in capital account.

Study Tip: Gains or losses NEVER arise when debt is converted to equity.

4.

Bonds Payable	1,000,000	
Loss on Retirement of Bonds	39,800	
Discount on Bonds Payable		24,800
Cash		1,015,000

The loss of $39,800 is the difference between the cash paid to retire the bonds and the carrying value of the bonds ($1,015,000 - $975,200 = $39,800). Remember, when carrying value > call price, difference = gain; when carrying value < call price, difference = loss.

Gains or losses on retirement of bonds are accounted for as extraordinary items and reported on the income statement net of tax.

> **Study Tip:** A gain or loss on the retirement of bonds will always occur unless call price equals carrying value.

V. Exercises

1. A. Cash   5,000,000
   Bonds Payable   5,000,000

 B. Interest Expense ($5,000,000 × .07 × 6/12)   175,000
   Cash   175,000

 C. Bonds Payable   5,000,000
   Cash   5,000,000

2. A. Cash   474,443
  Discount on Bonds Payable   25,557
   Bonds Payable   500,000

 B. Interest Expense (474,443 ×.09 × 6/12)   21,350
   Cash (500,000 ×.08 × 6/12)   20,000
   Discount on Bonds Payable   1,350

  New book value of bonds = Bonds Payable - Discount on Bonds Payable = 500,000 - (25,557 − 1,350) = 475,793

 C. Interest Expense (475,793 ×.09 × 6/12)   21,411
   Interest Payable (500,000 ×.08 × 6/12)   20,000
   Discount on Bonds Payable   1,411

  New book value of bonds = Bonds Payable - Discount on Bonds Payable = 500,000 - (24,207- 1,411) = 477,204. Notice that as the Discount on Bonds Payable is amortized, the carrying value of the bond increase toward the maturity value of the bond.

D.	Interest Payable		20,000	
	Cash			20,000
E.	Bonds Payable		500,000	
	Cash			500,000

Note that after the last interest payment, the account Discount on Bonds Payable has a zero balance.

3.	A.	Cash	474,443	
		Discount on Bonds Payable	25,557	
		Bonds Payable		500,000
	B.	Interest Expense (20,000 + 1,575)	21,825.50	
		Cash (500,000 ×.08 × 6/12)		20,000.00
		Discount on Bonds Payable		1825.50
		(25,557 / 14 interest payments)		
	C.	Interest Expense (13,333 + 1,217)	14,550.00	
		Interest Payable (500,000 × .08 × 4/12)		13,333.00
		Discount on Bonds Payable (25,557/14 × 2/3)		1,217.00

Note: In this exercise, the year-end is October 31, not December 31.

	D.	Interest Expense [(20,000 - 13,333) + 608.50]	7,275.50	
		Interest Payable	13,333.00	
		Cash (500,000 × .08 × 6/12)		20,000.00
		Discount on Bonds Payable (25,557/14 × 1/3)		608.50
	E.	Bonds Payable	500,000	
		Cash		500,000
4.	A.	Cash	556,480	
		Bonds Payable		500,000
		Premium on Bonds Payable		56,480
	B.	Interest Expense (556,480 × .06 × 6/12)	16,694	
		Premium on Bonds Payable	3,306	
		Cash (500,000 × .08 × 6/12)		20,000

New book value of bonds = Bonds Payable + Premium on Bonds Payable = 500,000 + (56,480 – 3,306) = 553,174

	C.	Interest Expense (553,174 × .06 × 6/12)	16,595	
		Premium on Bonds Payable	3,405	
		Interest Payable (500,000 × .08 × 6/12)		20,000

New book value of bonds = 500,000 + (53,174 - 3,405) = 549,769. Notice as the Premium on Bonds Payable is amortized, the carrying value of the bonds decreases toward the maturity value of the bond.

D.	Interest Payable	20,000	
	Cash		20,000
E.	Bonds Payable	500,000	
	Cash		500,000

Note that after the last interest payment, the account Premium on Bonds Payable has a zero balance.

5.

To determine the selling price of the bonds (expressed as a percentage of their maturity value), two calculations are required, both using present value tables. First we calculate the present value of the bonds, using the table in Exhibit 15A-6 in your text.

PV of $22,500,000 at 4% for 20 periods = $22,500,000 × 0.456 = $10,260,000

Second, we determine the present value of the periodic interest payments over the life of the bond. Each interest payment equals $22,500,000 × 7% × 6/12 or $787,500. Remember, the interest payments are like an annuity—a fixed amount paid periodically. Therefore, we use the table in Exhibit 15A-7 in the text and find the intersection of 4% and 20 periods; 4% because the market rate of interest is 8%, but paid semiannually.

PV of $787,500 for the life of the bonds is therefore $787,500 × 13.590, or $10,702,125.

Now, sum the two results, $10,260,000 + $10,702,125 = $20,962,125

Given that the market rate of interest is higher than the stated rate, the bonds will have to be sold at a discount (i.e., less than maturity value). Other things being equal (which, of course, they never are) the selling price of the bonds should be 93.165%.

VI. Beyond the Numbers

If each $1,000 bond can be converted into 31.25 shares of common stock, then a quick calculation indicates an investor should seriously think about converting when the market price of the stock reaches $32 per share ($1,000 divided by 31.25 shares). However, this assumes the investor paid maturity value for the bonds. In Exercise 3, investors purchased the bonds at a discount of 94.89% of maturity value ($474,443 divided by $500,000) or $948.90 for each $1,000 bond. Therefore, investors in Crawford's bonds could consider converting at a lower price of approximately $30.36 per share ($948.90 divided by 31.25). In Exercise 4 the investors paid a premium for the bonds because they were purchased at 111.30% of maturity value ($556,480 divided by $500,000). These investors would not be interested in converting until the price rose to $35.62 ($1,113.00 divided by 31.25 shares).

VII. Demonstration Problems

Demonstration Problem #1 Solved and Explained

(Amounts rounded to nearest dollar)

Requirement 1

2/1/2006	Cash	19,500,000	
	Discount on Bonds Payable	500,000	
	Bonds Payable		20,000,000

(Selling price = 97 ½% × $20,000,000 = $19,500,000)

Requirement 2

7/31/2006	Interest Expense	725,000	
	Discount on Bonds Payable		25,000
	Cash		700,000

(Interest Payment = $20,000,000 × 7% × 6/12 = $700,000)

The straight-line method of interest amortization ignores the market rate of interest at the time the bonds are sold. To amortize you divide the amount of the premium (or discount) by the total number of interest payments ($500,000 / 20 = $25,000).

Requirement 3

12/31/2006	Interest Expense	604,166	
	Discount on Bonds Payable		20,833
	Interest Payable		583,333

(Interest Payable = $20,000,000 × .07 × 5/12 = $583,333)
(Discount on Bonds Payable = $500,000 / 10 × 5/12 = $20,833)

Requirement 4

| Bonds Payable | $20,000,000 | |
| Less Discount on Bonds Payable | 454,167 | 19,545,833 |

(Discount on Bonds Payable = $500,000 - $25,000 - $20,833 = $454,167)

Study Tip: When bonds are sold at a discount, their carrying value INCREASES over time; when sold at a premium, their carrying value DECREASES over time. The carrying value is always moving toward the maturity value of the bonds.

Requirement 5

1/31/2007	Interest Expense	120,834	
	Interest Payable	583,333	
	Cash		700,000
	Discount on Bonds Payable		4,167

This may seem a difficult transaction but it is not if you separate it and THINK. The bondholders are owed $700,000. This is your credit to cash ($20,000,000 × .07 × 6/12). In Requirement 3 you accrued $583,333 as Interest Payable. This is your debit to the same account. Also in Requirement 3 you recorded five months of discount amortization ($20,833). You now need to amortize one additional month, or $4,167 (six months' amortization is $25,000 - see Requirement 2; therefore, one month's amortization is $25,000 / 6 = $4,167). The debit to Interest Expense reconciles the entry.

Requirement 6

2/1/2008	Bonds Payable	5,000,000	
	Discount on Bonds Payable		100,000
	Common Stock		350,000
	Paid-in Capital in Excess of Par – Common		4,550,000

$5,000,000 equals one-fourth of the bond issue. Therefore, one-fourth of the original discount, or $125,000 ($500,000 × ¼) applies to the bonds. Two years have passed since the bonds were issued, one-fifth of the discount, or $25,000 ($125,000 × 1/5) has already been amortized. The amount of remaining discount attached to the $5,000,000 is $100,000 ($125,000 - $25,000). Therefore, the carrying value of the bonds on date of conversion is $4,900,000. This is the amount credited to the Common Stock and Paid-in Capital in Excess of Par accounts. The Common Stock account is credited for the number of shares × par value (350,000 × $1.00) while the difference is credited to the Paid-in Capital in Excess of Par-Common account.

Requirement 7

2/1/2009	Bonds Payable	15,000,000	
	Loss on Retirement Bonds Payable	562,500	
	Discount on Bonds Payable		262,500
	Cash		15,300,000

The carrying value of the bonds on the call date is $14,737,500 ($15,000,000 - $262,500). The cost of calling the bonds is $15,300,000 ($15,000,000 × 102%). Therefore, a loss of $562,500 ($15,300,000 - $14,737,500) results. Of the original $500,000 discount, three-fourths or $375,000, applies to the $15,000,000. Three years have passed since they were originally issued, so 3/10 of the discount, or $112,500 (3/10 × $375,000) has already been amortized. Therefore, $262,500 ($375,000 - $112,500) remains.

Demonstration Problem #2 Solved and Explained

Requirement 1

Semi- annual Interest Date	A Interest Payment	B Interest Expense	C Premium Amortiza- tion	D Premium Account Balance	E Bond Carrying Value
1/1/08				120,000	2,120,000
7/1/08	100,000	95,400	4,600	115,400	2,115,400
1/1/09	100,000	95,193	4,807	110,593	2,110,593
7/1/09	100,000	94,977	5,023	105,570	2,105,570
1/1/10	100,000	94,751	5,249	100,321	2,100,321
7/1/10	100,000	94,514	5,486	94,835	2,094,835
1/1/11	100,000	94,268	5,732	89,103	2,089,103

> **Study Tip:** As the premium is amortized, the carrying amount moves toward the maturity value.

Requirement 2

a. 1/1/08   Cash ($2,000,000 × 106/100)   2,120,000
                  Premium on Bonds Payable   120,000
                  Bonds Payable   2,000,000
             To issue 10%, 15-year bonds at premium.

The bonds were sold at 106, indicating that investors were willing to pay a premium of $120,000 to earn 10% of interest on $2,000,000 of principal over a 15-year period. This is to be expected because the bond is paying 10% annual interest at a time when the market rate of interest is only 9%.

b. 7/1/08   Interest Expense ($100,000 - $4,600 amortization)   95,400
             Premium on Bonds Payable   4,600
                  Cash   100,000
             To pay interest and amortize bond premium for six months.

Note that the amortization of the premium has the effect of reducing interest expense from the stated rate ($100,000) to the market rate ($95,400). If the bond is sold at a discount, the interest expense is increased from the stated rate to the market rate.

c. 9/30/08   Interest Expense ($50,000 - $2,404 amortization)   47,596
             Premium on Bonds Payable ($4,807 × 3/6)   2,404
                  Interest Payable   50,000
             To accrue three months' interest and amortize three months' premium.

d. 1/1/09   Interest Expense ($50,000 - $2,403 amortization)   47,597

            Interest Payable   50,000

            Premium on Bonds Payable ($4,807 × 3/6)   2,403

               Cash   100,000

            To pay semiannual interest, part of which was accrued, and amortize three months' premium on bonds payable.

In this entry, six months of interest is actually paid to the bondholders on January 1. Note, however, only half (three months' worth) of the interest is current accounting period expense; the remaining amount represents the payment of the September 30 accrual of three months' interest.

e. 1/2/10   Bonds Payable   2,000,000

            Premium on Bonds Payable   100,321

               Gain on Retirement of Bonds Payable   60,321

               Cash ($2,000,000 × 102/100)   2,040,000

            To record the retirement of bonds payable at 102, retired before maturity.

This entry removes the bonds payable and related premium account from the corporate records, and records the gain on retirement. The carrying value of the bonds ($2,100,321) is greater than the cost to call the bonds ($2,040,000) resulting in the $60,321 gain. Had the price paid to call the bonds been greater than the carrying value, the entry would have recorded an extraordinary loss. Extraordinary gains and losses are reported separately on the income statement net of taxes.

The interest rate stated on a debt instrument such as a corporate bond will typically differ from the actual market rate of interest when the bond is ultimately issued to the public. This occurs because of the lag in time that frequently occurs between the approval of the bond by the corporation (and regulatory agencies), its actual printings and finally, its issuance to the public. Rather than reprint the bond and potentially miss the rapidly changing market interest rate again, bonds are sold at a discount or premium. Occasionally, bonds are sold at maturity amount.

Study Tip: A bond is sold at a discount when the stated interest rate of the bond is below the current market rate. A premium is paid when the stated rate is higher than interest rates paid by comparable investments.

Premiums and discounts are, in effect, an adjustment to the interest rates. Thus, premiums and discounts should be amortized over the life of the bond. A few things should be noted:

1. A good rule to remember is that Bonds Payable are always recorded at the maturity amount of the bond. Premiums and discounts are recorded in separate accounts.

2. The actual interest paid to the bondholders at the periodic payment dates (generally semiannually) will always be the maturity value of the bond multiplied by the stated interest rate. A discount or premium will not affect these periodic cash payments.

3. The carrying amount (or book value) of a bond is conceptually similar to the book value of a fixed asset. Premiums are added to the maturity amount of bonds payable, and discounts are subtracted.

$$
\begin{array}{rl}
 & \text{Bonds Payable} \\
+ & \text{Unamortized Bond Premium or} \\
- & \underline{\text{Unamortized Bond Discount}} \\
= & \text{Carrying Value}
\end{array}
$$

Study Tip: Bonds sold at a premium will have a carrying amount greater than the maturity amount owed and discounted bonds will have a smaller value. In both cases, the carrying value will always move toward the maturity amount of the bond as the discount or premium is amortized. (Because of this, it is possible to quickly double-check your amortization entries—be sure the bond carrying value is moving in the right direction.)

Chapter 16 - Investments and International Operations

CHAPTER OVERVIEW

In Chapters 13 and 14, you learned about capital stock from the perspective of the issuing corporation. In Chapter 15 we examined long-term liabilities and how corporations account for bonds payable also from the perspective of the issuing corporation. Now, we expand these topics but change the perspective. Rather than using the perspective of the issuing corporation, we are going to evaluate how corporations account for the purchase of stocks and bonds as investments. In addition, we learn about parent and subsidiary relationships and foreign currency transactions. The learning objectives for this chapter are to

1. Account for trading investments.
2. Account for available-for-sale investments.
3. Use the equity method for investments.
4. Understand consolidated financial statements.
5. Account for long-term Investments in bonds.
6. Account for transactions stated in a foreign currency.

CHAPTER REVIEW

Stocks are traded in markets. Prices are quoted as the market price per share in dollars and cents. The owner of a stock is the investor. The corporation that issues the stock is the investee.

Stock investments are assets to the investor and may be classified as short-term or long-term on the balance sheet.
- **Short-term investments (also called marketable securities)** are 1) liquid (readily convertible to cash) and 2) the investor intends to convert the security into cash within one year.
- **Long-Term Equity-Method Investments** are 1) expected to be held for longer than one year or 2) not readily marketable.

Stock investments fall into two categories: 1) trading securities or 2) available-for-sale securities. It is important you understand the distinction between the two types!
- **Trading securities** are always classified as current assets because the investor's intent is to hold them for only a short time in the hopes of earning profits on price changes.
- **Available-for-sale securities** are stock investments other than trading securities where the intent is not to capture immediate profits from price changes.

Trading securities, by definition, are always current assets whereas available-for-sale securities could be either current or long term.

Objective 1 - Account for trading investments.

Because trading securities will be sold in the near future at their current market value, the **market-value method** is used to account for all trading investments. When acquired, trading investments are debited to a Short-Term Investment account at their cost (price per share × number of shares acquired, plus any associated costs), as follows:

Short-Term Investments	XX	
Cash		XX

As dividends are received, the transaction is

Cash	XX	
Dividend Revenue		XX

On the balance sheet date, all trading investments are reported at their current market value, which is likely to be different from their original cost. If the current market value of the investment is greater than the cost, the following adjustment is recorded:

Short-Term Investment	XX	
Gain on Trading Investment		XX

The amount of the entry is the difference between the current market value and the original cost. If the current market value is lower than the original cost, the adjustment is:

Loss on Trading Investments	XX	
Short-Term Investment		XX

Either way, the effect of the adjustment is to report the trading investment on the balance sheet at its current market value. Gains and Losses are reported on the Income Statement in the "other gains or losses" section.

When a trading investment is sold, the proceeds are compared with the current carrying value (NOT THE ORIGINAL COST) to determine whether a gain or loss results. Gains and losses on the sale of trading securities are also reported in the "other gains or losses" section of the Income Statement.

Objective 2 - Account for available-for-sale investments.

As with all assets, available-for-sale securities are recorded at cost. Thereafter, however, they are reported at their current market value. Any cash dividends received are credited to an appropriate revenue account. Stock dividends do not trigger an entry. Rather, the portfolio is updated to reflect the additional shares. At the end of the accounting period, the market value of the securities is determined and compared with the balance in the investments account. If the current market value for long-term available-for-sale investments is greater than the cost, the following adjusting entry is recorded on the balance sheet date:

Allowance to Adjust Investment to Market	XX	
Unrealized Gain on Investments		XX

When the current market value of the available-for-sale security is less than the balance in the account, the adjustment is:

Unrealized Loss on Investments   XX

     Allowance to Adjust Investment to Market   XX

The word "unrealized" means that the gain or loss resulted from a change in market value, not the actual sale of the investment. The Allowance to Adjust Investment to Market account is a companion account to the Long-Term Equity-Method Investment account. Recall that a companion account is added to (or subtracted from) a related account. With available-for-sale securities, it is the use of the Allowance account that increases/decreases the Investment account to the current market value. If the Allowance account has a debit balance the effect is to increase the Investment account. If the Allowance account has a credit balance the effect is to decrease the Investment account.

Unrealized Gains/Losses are reported in the stockholders' equity section of the balance sheet; gains are an addition to equity and losses are a reduction.

Study Tip: The Allowance to Adjust Investment to Market account is used regardless of an increase or decrease in the market value. Compare the current market value with the carrying value of the investment and adjust accordingly, always using the Allowance account.

When an available-for-sale investment is sold, a *realized* gain or loss on sale will result when the proceeds are greater than (a gain) or less than (a loss) the cost of the investment. Realized gains and losses are reported on the income statement as "other gains or losses" after the operating income.

Objective 3 - Use the equity method for investments.

The **equity method** is used when an investor holds between 20% and 50% of an investee's voting stock because the investor has the ability to exercise significant influence on the investee's business decisions.

When using the equity method, investments are initially recorded at cost. Debit Long-Term Equity-Method Investment and credit Cash.

The investor must also record its proportionate ownership of the investee's net income and dividends. For example, if the investor owns 40% of the voting stock, the investor will record 40% of the net income as revenue and will receive 40% of the dividends.
- The proportionate share of income increases the investment account and is recorded with a debit to the Long-Term Equity-Method Investment account and a credit to Equity-Method Investment Revenue. Equity-Method Investment Revenue is reported as "Other Revenue" on the income statement.
- The receipt of cash dividends reduces the investment. Therefore, the dividend is recorded with a debit to Cash and a credit to the Long-Term Equity-Method Investment account.

When the equity method is used and an investment is sold, the gain (or loss) on sale is the difference between the sale proceeds and the investment's carrying amount.

Joint ventures, regardless of the percentage owned, also use the equity method.

Objective 4 - Understand consolidated financial statements.

An investor who owns more than 50% of an investee's voting stock has a controlling (majority) interest. The investor is called the **parent company**, and the investee is called the **subsidiary**. See Exhibits 16-3 and 16-4 in your text. Parent-subsidiary relationships are very common.

Consolidation accounting combines the financial statements of two or more companies that are controlled by the same owners. The assets, liabilities, revenues, and expenses of the subsidiary are combined with the parent's accounts. The consolidated financial statements report the combined account balances and are presented in the name of the parent company as if the parent and its subsidiaries were the same.

Goodwill is an intangible asset that is recorded during the consolidation process and reported on the balance sheet of the parent company only if the parent buys the subsidiary for a price that is greater than the market value of the net assets of the subsidiary company.

A **minority interest** will appear on the consolidated balance sheet when the parent company owns more than 50% but less than 100% of the subsidiary's stock. Minority interest usually is recorded as a liability on the consolidated balance sheet.

Consolidated income is equal to the net income of the parent plus the parent's proportionate interest in the subsidiary's net income.

Objective 5 - Account for long-term investment in bonds.

Investors purchase bonds issued by corporations. The investor can purchase short-term (current asset) or long-term (Long-Term Investment) bonds.

Short-term investments in bonds are rare. More commonly, companies purchase bonds as Long-Term Investments in Bonds, known as **held-to-maturity securities**. When acquired, these held-to-maturity bonds are recorded at cost; thereafter, they are reported on the balance sheet at their **amortized cost**. This means the balance in the Long-Term Investment in Bonds account reflects both the initial cost of the bond plus or minus a portion of the discount (an addition to the account) or premium (a reduction to the account) on the bond. From the perspective of the investor, no Discount or Premium account is used. If the bonds were initially purchased at a discount, the balance in the Long-Term Investment in Bonds account increases as the bonds approach maturity. If the bonds were initially purchased at a premium, the balance in the Long-Term Investment in Bonds account decreases as the bonds approach maturity. The amortization of the bond discount would appear as follows:

Long-Term Investment in Bonds	XX	
Interest Revenue		XX

The amortization of a bond premium would be recorded as follows:

Interest Revenue	XX	
Long-Term Investment in Bonds		XX

Study Tip: From the buyer's perspective, a discount means additional interest revenue while a premium

122

Carefully review the Decision Guideline in your text. It presents an excellent summary of the rules governing stock and bond investments.

Objective 6 - Account for transactions stated in a foreign currency.

International accounting deals with business activities that cross national boundaries. Each country uses its own national currency; therefore, a step has been added to the transaction—one currency must be converted into another.

The price of one nation's currency stated in terms of another country's currency is called the **foreign currency exchange rate**. The conversion of one currency into another currency is called **translation**. Exchange rates are determined by supply and demand.

A **strong currency** is rising relative to other nations' currencies and a **weak currency** is falling relative to other currencies.

When Company A in Country A purchases goods from Company B in Country B, the transaction price may be stated in the currency of either country. If we assume the transaction is stated in Country A's currency, the transaction requires two steps:

1. The transaction price must be translated for recording in the accounting records of Company B.
2. When the payment is received, Company B may experience a foreign-currency transaction gain or loss. This gain or loss results when there is a change in the exchange rate between the date of the sale on account and the date of the subsequent receipt of cash.

Note that there will be no foreign-currency transaction gain or loss for Company A because the transaction price was stated in the currency of Country A.

The net amount of Foreign Currency Transaction Gains and Losses are combined for each accounting period and reported on the income statement as "other gains or losses".

Hedging is a means of protecting the company (Company B, in our example) from foreign currency transaction losses by purchasing a **futures contract**, the right to receive a certain amount of foreign currency on a particular date.

United States companies with foreign subsidiaries must consolidate the subsidiary's financial statements into their own for external reporting. This can cause two problems:

1. GAAP may be different in the foreign country. (See Exhibit 16-8.)
2. When the foreign subsidiary's financial statements are translated into dollars, there may be a translation adjustment.

A **foreign currency translation adjustment** arises because of changes in exchange rates over time. Assets and liabilities are translated using exchange rates as of the balance sheet date. Stockholders' equity, including revenues and expenses, are translated using the exchange rates that were in effect when those transactions were executed (this results in shareholders' equity not equaling assets minus liabilities). The adjustment necessary to bring the subsidiary's balance sheet back into balance ("translation adjustment") is reported as part of stockholders' equity on the consolidated balance sheet. The translation adjustment will be positive when the book value of the investment in the foreign subsidiary has increased. A negative amount reflects a reduction.

Unrealized gains and losses on available-for-sale investments and foreign-currency translation adjustments are two of the main elements of comprehensive income (you were introduced to comprehensive income in Chapter 14). These are reported on the income statement as "other comprehensive income" and on the balance sheet within stockholders' equity. (Review Exhibit 16-9 in your text.)

TEST YOURSELF

All the self-testing materials in this chapter focus on information and procedures that your instructor is likely to test in quizzes and examinations. Items with an *A* refer to information in the chapter appendix.

I. Matching   *Match each numbered term with its lettered definition.*

_____ 1.   Consolidated statements
_____ 2.   Joint ventures
_____ 3.   Controlling interest
_____ 4.   Held-to-maturity investments
_____ 5.   Equity method for investments
_____ 6.   Foreign currency exchange rate
_____ 7.   Short-term investments
_____ 8.   Hedging
_____ 9.   Long-Term Investment
_____ 10. Trading securities

_____ 11. Minority interest
_____ 12. Parent company
_____ 13. Available-for-sale securities
_____ 14. Strong currency
_____ 15. Subsidiary company
_____ 16. Foreign currency translation adjustment
_____ 17. Weak currency
_____ 18. Market value method

A.   A separate entity or project owned and operated by a small group of businesses
B.   The balancing figure that brings the dollar amount of the total liabilities and stockholders' equity of a foreign subsidiary into agreement with the dollar amount of total assets
C.   Stocks and bonds held for the short term with the intent of realizing profits from increases in prices
D.   Combine the balance sheets, income statements, and other financial statements of the parent with those of the majority-owned subsidiaries into an overall set as if the separate entities were one
E.   Currency whose exchange rate is rising relative to other nations' currencies
F.   Investee company in which a parent owns more than 50% of the voting stock
G.   Investor company that owns more than 50% of the voting stock of a subsidiary company
H.   Stocks and bonds not held with the intent of realizing profits from increases in prices
I.   Method used to account for investments in which the investor can significantly influence the decisions of the investee
J.   Bonds and notes that investors intend to hold to maturity
K.   Ownership of more than 50% of an investee company's voting stock
L.   An investment that is readily convertible to cash and that the investor intends to convert to cash within one year or to use to pay a current liability
M.   Separate asset category reported on the balance sheet between current assets and plant assets
N.   Strategy to avoid foreign currency transaction losses
O.   Subsidiary company's equity that is held by stockholders other than the parent company
P.   The price of one country's currency stated in terms of another country's monetary unit
Q.   Currency whose exchange rate is decreasing relative to other nations' currencies
R.   Used to account for all available-for-sale securities

II. Multiple Choice   *Circle the best answer.*

1. A stock is listed in the Wall Street Journal as having a Close of 43 1/2, and a Net Change of +1 1/4. What was the previous day's closing price?

    A. $46.50
    B. $41.75

    C. $44.75
    D. $42.25

2. Assets listed as Short-term Investments on the balance sheet are

    A. only liquid.

    B. listed on a national stock exchange.

    C. only intended to be converted to cash within one year.

    D. liquid and intended to be converted to cash within one year.

3. Available-for-sale securities are reported on the balance sheet at

    A. current cost.
    B. historical cost.

    C. lower of cost or market.
    D. market value.

4. Trading securities are reported on the balance sheet at

    A. current cost.
    B. historical cost.

    C. lower of cost or market.
    D. market value.

5. If an investor owns 20-50% of the investee's voting stock, the investment must be accounted for using the:

    A. market-value method.
    B. equity method.

    C. historical cost method.
    D. allowance method.

6. The minority interest account is usually classified as a(n)

    A. revenue.
    B. expense.

    C. liability.
    D. asset.

7. The rate at which one unit of a currency can be converted into another currency is called the foreign currency:

    A. market rate.
    B. interest rate.

    C. exchange rate.
    D. conversion rate.

8. A strong currency has an exchange rate that is

    A. inelastic with respect to other nations' currencies.
    B. inelastic with respect to its balance of trade.
    C. increasing relative to other nations' currencies.
    D. decreasing relative to other nations' currencies.

9. Available-for-sale securities are

   A. stock investments only.
   B. bond investments only.

   C. the same as held-to-maturity investments.
   D. those other than trading securities and held-to-maturity investments.

10. An unrealized gain (or loss) results from

   A. available-for-sale securities.
   B. trading securities.

   C. held-to-maturity securities.
   D. all of the above.

III. Completion   *Complete each of the following statements.*

1. The price at which stock changes hands is determined by the _____.
2. Gains and losses on trading securities are reported on the _____ in the _____.
3. Investments in stock are initially recorded at _____.
4. The _____ method is used to account for investments when the investor can significantly influence the actions of the investee.
5. A(n) _____ is ownership of at least 50% of the voting stock of a company.
6. Goodwill is a(n) _____ asset.
7. A change in the currency exchange rates between the date of purchase and the date of payment will result in a(n) _____.
8. _____ combine the balance sheet, income statements, and cash-flow statements of the parent company plus those of its majority-owned subsidiaries.
9. When a parent owns less than 100% of a subsidiary, the other owners are called the _____.
10. Unrealized gains and losses on Available-for-Sale investments are reported on the _____ in the _____ section.

IV. Daily Exercises

1. On October 20 of the current year, Miller Corporation purchases 1,000 shares of Webster Company for 18 3/8 a share, plus a broker's commission of $55. On December 15, Miller receives a cash dividend of $0.50 a share. Assuming Miller's investment does not give Miller significant influence over Webster Company, what is the balance in Miller's Investment account immediately after receipt of the cash dividend?

2. Review the information in Daily Exercise #1 and assume the Webster shares are trading at 20 ¾ on December 31, the end of Miller's fiscal year. Assuming this investment is classified as a trading security, prepare the necessary adjusting entry.

3. Review the same facts in Daily Exercise #1 and #2, but assume the shares are classified as an available-for-sale security. Prepare the necessary adjusting entry on December 31.

4. When a company purchases equity securities as an investment, what determines whether the investment is classified as a trading security or an available-for-sale security?

5. On October 1 of the current year, Long Company purchased a $100,000, 8%, 10-year bond at 98. Interest is payable on October 1 and April 1 each year. Long's intent is to hold the bond to maturity. Prepare the entry to record the purchase of the bond.

6. Review the information in Daily Exercise #5 and prepare the necessary adjusting entries on December 31, the end of Long's fiscal period.

V. Exercises

1. Polly Company purchased 85,000 shares of Cracker Corporation on January 1, 20X9, for $425,000. Cracker Corporation has 850,000 shares outstanding. Cracker earned income of $240,000 and paid dividends of $80,000 during 20X9. Cracker Corporation stock was trading at 6 1/8 on December 31, 20X9.

   A. What method should be used to account for the investment in Cracker?

   B. How much revenue will be recorded by Polly in 20X9 from the investment in Cracker?

   C. What is the balance in Polly's Investment account at the end of 20X9?

2. King Company purchased 40% of Prince Corporation on January 1, 20X7, for $6,750,000. Prince Corporation earned income of $1,800,000 and paid dividends of $700,000 during 20X7.

   A. What method should be used to account for the investment in Prince Corporation?

   B. How much revenue will be recorded by King Co. in 20X7 from the investment in Prince Corporation?

   C. What is the balance in the Investment account at the end of 20X7?

3. Hunter Company purchased 100% of the common stock of Prey Corporation for $1,315,000. Prey Corporation showed Common Stock of $280,000 and Retained Earnings of $510,000. Compute the amount of goodwill resulting from the purchase. Assume no other stockholders' equity accounts.

4. Prepare journal entries for the following available-for-sale stock investment:

Jun 10 Purchased 1,000 shares of Sure-Tech Corporation common stock at 35 1/4, plus a broker's commission of $205.

Oct 2 Received a $1.50 per share cash dividend.

Nov 15 Sold 400 shares at 40 1/4 per share, less a commission of $80.

Dec 31 Sure-Tech Corporation stock closed at $39 1/8.

Date	Account and Explanation	Debit	Credit

5. Prepare journal entries for the following foreign currency transactions. Assume a perpetual inventory system.

Jan 5   Purchased 5,000 cases of dry cider from a British wholesaler for 4.55 pounds sterling per case. Today's exchange rate is $1.62 = 1 pound sterling.

Jan 20   Purchased 2,000 cases of red wine from a cooperative in Coustouge, France. The price was 64 francs per case. Today's exchange rate is $1.00 = 6.10 French francs.

Feb 10   Paid the British wholesaler. Today's exchange rate is $1.59 = 1 pound sterling.

Mar 20 Paid for the French wine. Today's exchange rate is $1.00 = 5.90 French francs.

Date	Account and Explanation	Debit	Credit

VI. Beyond the Numbers

Review the information in Exercise 4 and change the October 2 entry to the following:

Oct 2   Received a 15% stock dividend. The stock was trading at $38 per share.

Prepare journal entries for Oct 2, Nov 15 and Dec 31

Date	Account and Explanation	Debit	Credit

VII. Demonstration Problems

Demonstration Problem #1

At December 31, 2009, Knox Corporation had the following Long-Term Investments in its portfolio:

	Cost	Market Value
Available-for-sale securities		
2,500 shares Bibtech, Inc.	$25 1/4	$28
6,000 shares FFA Industries	10 3/8	18 ½
3,800 shares Globex	48	37 3/4
1,400 shares Textronics	63 ½	66 7/8
Held-to-maturity bonds		
$100,000, 9% NatSci, Inc., due 10/1/2019	$100,000	$100,000

Requirement 1

In the space below, present the Long-Term Investments as they would appear on Knox Corporation's December 31, 2009 balance sheet. None of the stock investments are influential. The bonds pay interest semiannually on April 1 and October 1.

Requirement 2

Record the following 2010 events related to Knox Corporation's Long-Term Investments:

Bibtech, Inc.—these shares paid quarterly dividends of $.15/share on February 10 and May 10. The shares were sold on July 2 for $32/share less a broker's commission of $185.

FFA Industries—these shares pay no cash dividends; however, a 10% stock dividend was received on August 10. The investment remained in the portfolio at the end of the year, at which time its market value was $24 1/4 per share.

Globex—these shares continued to decline in value throughout January and management decided to sell them on Feb 8 for $31/share, less a commission of $205.

Textronics—these shares remained in the portfolio throughout the year. On September 15 the stock split 3 for 2. At year-end, the shares were trading for $55/share.

NatSci, Inc.—Checks for interest were received April 1 and October 1. The bonds remained in the portfolio at year-end.

On November 1, 2010 Knox Corporation purchased $250,000, 10-year, 6% bonds from Wood, Inc., for 97. The bonds pay semiannual interest on May 1 and November 1. The bonds mature on November 1, 2020. Knox plans to hold the bonds until maturity.

Date	Account and Explanation	Debit	Credit

Requirement 3

Record the necessary adjusting entries at December 31, 2010 (fiscal year end.)

Date	Account and Explanation	Debit	Credit

Requirement 4

Present the Long-Term Investments as they would appear on Knox Corporation's 12/31/2010 balance sheet, taking into consideration the events described in Requirement 2 above.

SOLUTIONS

I. Matching

1. D	5. I	9. M	13. H	17. Q
2. A	6. P	10. C	14. E	18. R
3. K	7. L	11. O	15. F	
4. J	8. N	12. G	16. B	

II. Multiple Choice

1. D The Close is the last price at which the stock traded yesterday. Net Change is the increase (+) or decrease (-) in the Close compared to the previous day. The previous day's close is 43 1/2 - 1 1/4 or $43.50 - $1.25 = $42.25.

2. D Note that besides the determinable liquidity of the investment, the intent of management determines an investment's classification as a Short-Term Investment.

3. D GAAP requires available-for-sale securities to be reported on the balance sheet at market value.

4. D GAAP requires trading securities to be reported on the balance sheet at market value.

5. B When an investor owns 20-50% of the voting stock of an investee, the investor can significantly influence the decisions of the investee. The equity method of accounting for these investments requires that the investor participate proportionately in any income and dividends. The Long-Term Equity-Method Investment account is increased for net income and decreased for dividends.

6. C The Minority Interest account represents the ownership interest of parties outside of the Parent-Subsidiary relationship. In actual practice it is most often reported as part of the liability section on the balance sheet.

7. C The exchange rate is used to convert one currency into another.

8. C Strong currencies are those that increase relative to other currencies.

9. D Available-for-sale securities are stock investments other than trading securities and bond investments other than trading securities and held-to-maturity securities.

10. A Unrealized gains (or losses) are a result of the market value method applied to available-for-sale securities.

III. Completion

1. market (The market allows buyers and sellers with opposing interests to arrive at a price acceptable to both.)
2. income statement, other gains and losses
3. cost
4. equity

5. controlling interest
6. intangible
7. foreign-currency transaction gain or loss
8. Consolidated financial statements
9. minority interest
10. balance sheet; stockholders' equity

IV. Daily Exercises

1. $18,430 (1,000 × $18 3/8 = $18,375 + $55). The dividends would be credited to a Dividend Revenue Account.

2.

Short-term Investment	2,320	
Gain on Trading Investment		2,320

The market value method requires trading securities to be listed on the balance sheet at their current market value. The shares are currently worth $20,750 (1,000 × $20 ¾) but listed in the account at $18,430. The difference, $2,320, is a gain on trading investment.

> **Study Tip:** Gains and losses on trading securities are reported on the income statement under "other gains and losses."

3.

Allowance to Adjust Investment to Market	2,320	
Unrealized Gain on Investment		2,320

4. Available-for-sale securities are defined by exception. In other words, if the investment is not a trading investment, then it is classified as an available-for-sale investment.

5.

Long-Term Investment in Bonds	98,000	
Cash		98,000

The discount is not recorded on the books of the purchaser, only on the books of the selling corporation.

6.

Interest Receivable	2,000	
Interest Revenue		2,000
($100,000 × 8% × 3/12)		
Long-Term Investment in Bonds	50	
Interest Revenue		50
($2,000 ÷ 10 years × 3/12)		

V. Exercises

1. A. market value
   B. 10% of $80,000 = $8,000 dividend revenue
   C. $520,625 ($425,000 balance in the Investment account plus $95,625 (1 1/8 per share gain × 85,000 shares) in the Allowance to Adjust Investment account)

2. A. equity method
   B. .40 × $1,800,000 = $720,000
   C. $6,750,000 + $720,000 - (.40 × $700,000) = $7,190,000

3. $1,315,000 - ($280,000 + $510,000) = $525,000

4.

Jun 10	Investment—Sure-Tech	35,455	
	Cash		35,455

(1,000 shares × $35.25 plus $205)
Actual cost/share is 35,455 / 1000 = $35.455

Oct 2	Cash	1,500	
	Dividend Revenue		1,500

Nov 15	Cash	16,020	
	Investment—Sure-Tech		14,182
	Gain on Sale of Investment		1,838

The gain is the difference between the proceeds and our cost. Our cost is 400 shares × $35.455/share (see 6/10)

Dec 31	Allowance to Adjust Investment to Market	2,202	
	Unrealized Gain on Investment		2,202

Our cost basis was $35.455/share and we have 600 shares for a total of $21,273. The current market value is 600 × $39 1/8 = $23,475. Therefore, $2,202 is needed to adjust the Investment to market. Since the $2,202 represents an increase in value, it represents an unrealized gain on the investment.

5.

Jan 5	Inventory	36,855.00	
	Accounts Payable		36,855.00

(5,000 cases × 4.55 pounds sterling × $1.62)

Jan 20	Inventory	20,983.61	
	Accounts Payable		20,983.61

(2,000 cases × 64 francs / 6.10)

Feb 10	Accounts Payable	36,855.00	
	Foreign Currency Transaction Gain		682.50
	Cash		36,172.50

(5,000 cases × 4.55 pounds sterling × $1.59)

Mar 20   Accounts Payable   20,983.61

             Foreign Currency Transaction Loss   711.31

                 Cash   21,694.92

             (2,000 cases × 64 francs / 5.90)

On the first purchase, because the dollar strengthened relative to the British pound (on 1/5 it took $1.62 to purchase 1 pound sterling - a month later the same pound would only cost $1.59), a foreign currency transaction gain was realized when we paid the bill. Conversely, on the second purchase the dollar weakened relative to the French franc, so we realized a foreign currency transaction loss. Foreign currency transaction gains and losses are reported on the income statement as "other gains and losses."

VI. Beyond the Numbers

Oct 2   No entry - however we need to note the receipt of the additional 150 shares. We now own 1,150 shares that cost us $35,455, or $30.83 (rounded) per share.

Study Tip: The current trading value of the shares is irrelevant from our perspective. It is only relevant to Sure-Tech. They used it to record the charge against Retained Earnings when the dividend was declared.

Nov 15   Cash   16,020

             Investment— Sure-Tech   12,332

             Gain on Sale of Investment   3,688

Our cost per share was $30.83 (rounded)—see 10/2 details. We sold 400 shares at $40.25/share, less the $80 commission. The gain is the difference between our proceeds (400 shares × $40.25 less $80) and the cost basis of those shares, $30.83 × 400.

Dec 31   Allowance to Adjust Investment to Market   6,221

             Unrealized Gain on Investment   6,221

Make sure you give some thought to this adjustment. Remember our adjusted cost per share is $30.83 and we have 750 shares (the original 1,000 plus the 150 share dividend less the 400 shares sold on Nov 15). Therefore, our cost basis for those remaining shares is $23,123 (rounded) (750 shares × $30.83/share). On Dec 31, the shares were trading at $39 1/8 ($39.125), so their market value is $29,344 (rounded); the Unrealized Gain is the difference between $29,344 and $23,123, or $6,221. Available-for-sale stock securities are reported on the balance sheet at their market value. The amount in the Allowance to Adjust account will be added to the balance in the Investment account, thereby reporting the investment in stock at the market value.

VII. Demonstration Problems

Demonstration Problem #1 Solved and Explained

Requirement 1

Long-Term Investments (at market value) $518,075

The cost of the combined Long-Term Investments (both equity and debt) is $496,675, while the 12/31/09 market value of the portfolio is $518,075. Recall that Long-Term Investments are reported on the balance sheet at market value. Prior to the preparation of the balance sheet, an adjusting entry would have been recorded, as follows:

Allowance to Adjust Investment to Market	21,400	
Unrealized Gain on Long-Term Investments		21,400

The effect of this adjustment is to increase the Investments to their market value. Most companies would report the Investments at market value, and then report the cost in a footnote. The Unrealized Gain would be added into the stockholders' equity section. Knox would also have adjusted for the accrued interest on the NatSci bond; however, the amount ($2,250) is NOT included with the Long-Term Investments, but reported separately as Interest Receivable in the current asset section.

Requirement 2

Bibtech, Inc.

Feb 10	Cash	375	
	Dividend Revenue		375
May 10	Cash	375	
	Dividend Revenue		375
Jul 2	Cash	79,815	
	Long-Term Available-for-Sale Investment		63,125
	Gain on Sale of Investment		16,690

The gain is the difference between the proceeds (2,500 shares × $32/share less the $185 commission) and the cost (2,500 shares × $25 1/4).

FFA Industries

Aug 10 no entry—memo only reflecting 6,600 shares now in the portfolio

Globex

Feb 8	Cash	117,595	
	Loss on Sale of Investment	64,805	
	Long-Term Available-for-Sale Investment		182,400

The loss is the difference between the cost (3,800 × $48) and the proceeds (3,800 × $31 less the $205 commission).

Textronics

Sep 15 no entry—memo only reflecting 2,100 shares now in the portfolio

NatSci

Apr 1	Cash	4,500	
	Interest Receivable		2,250
	Interest Revenue		2,250
Oct 1	Cash	4, 500	
	Interest Revenue		4,500

Wood, Inc.

Nov 1	Long-Term Investment in Bonds	242,500	
	Cash		242,500

As the purchaser of the bonds, we do not record the $7,500 discount in a contra account.

Requirement 3 (adjusting entries)

Dec 31	Allowance to Adjust Investments to Market	103,000	
	Unrealized Gain on Long-Term Investments		103,000

As of the end of 2009, the Allowance to Adjust account has a debit balance of $21,400 (see Requirement 1 Solution). At the end of 2010, the cost and market values of the remaining available-for-sale equity securities are as follows:

	Cost	Market
FFA Industries	$62,250	$160,050
Textronics	88,900	115,500
Totals	$151,150	$275,550

These totals reflect a difference of $124,400. Given the existing debit balance of $21,400, we need to adjust for $103,000 to increase the Allowance account to the desired $124,400 figure.

Dec 31	Interest Receivable	2,250	
	Interest Revenue		2,250
	To adjust accrued interest ($100,000 × .09 × 3/12) on NatSci bonds		

Dec 31	Interest Receivable	2,500	
	Long-Term Investment in Bonds	125	
	Interest Revenue		2,625
	To adjust for accrued interest ($250,000 × .06 × 2/12) and amortize the discount ($7,500/10 years × 2/12).		

Recall that Long-Term Investments in Bonds must be reported on the balance sheet at their fully amortized cost. When bonds are purchased at a discount, the amortized cost will increase over the life of the bonds. At the maturity date, the amortized cost will equal the bond's maturity value.

Requirement 4

Long-Term Investments (at market) $618, 175

The balance in the Long-Term Investments account consists of the following:

Stocks	($151,150 cost + $124,400 Allowance)	$275,550
Bonds	NatSci	100,000
	Wood, Inc. ($242,500 + $125)	242,625
	Total	$618,175

Interest Receivable will be listed among the current assets, Interest Revenue under "Other Revenues" on the Income Statement, and the Unrealized Gain with stockholders' equity on the balance sheet.

Chapter 17 - The Statement of Cash Flows

CHAPTER OVERVIEW

In Chapter 1, you were introduced to the four principal financial statements—the income statement, statement of owner's equity, the balance sheet, and the statement of cash flows. However, since the beginning of this course, the focus has been on the first three financial statements. We are now going to turn our attention to the statement of cash flows. Many people think the statement of cash flows is the most important of the four statements, even more so than the income statement and the balance sheet. This is because it shows the actual "flow" of cash, whereas the other financial statements do not. The learning objectives for this chapter are to

1. Identify the purposes of the statement of cash flows.
2. Distinguish among operating, investing, and financing cash flows.
3. Prepare a statement of cash flows by the indirect method.
4. Prepare a statement of cash flows by the direct method.

CHAPTER REVIEW

Objective 1 - Identify the purposes of the statement of cash flows.

Cash flows are cash receipts and cash payments (disbursements). The **statement of cash flows** focuses only on the cash account and reports all of the cash receipts (inflows) and disbursements (outflows). By reporting all of the cash receipts and disbursements for the period, the statement of cash flows successfully explains the causes for the change in the cash balance from one period to the next. Every cash receipt or payment must be classified under one of the three major business activities--operating, investing, and financing. The statement is used to:

1. Predict future cash flows
2. Evaluate management's decisions
3. Predict the company's ability to make debt payments to lenders and to pay dividends to stockholders

The term cash is used to include **cash equivalents** that are highly liquid short-term investments (such as T-bills and money market accounts).

Objective 2 - Distinguish among operating, investing, and financing cash flows.

Operating activities create revenues and expenses from the entity's major line of business. Therefore, operating activities are related to the transactions that make up net income (or loss) on the income statement. Cash flows from operating activities include:

1. Collections from customers (inflow)
2. Payments to suppliers and employees (outflow)
3. Interest revenue (inflow) and interest expense (outflow)
4. Taxes (outflow)
5. Dividends received on investments (inflow)

Operating activities are always listed first because they are the largest and most important source of cash for a business. Determining cash flows from operating activities requires analysis of the accounts that appear on the income statement as well as the current asset and current liability accounts.

Investing activities increase and decrease long-term assets. Investing activities require analysis of the long-term asset accounts and include:

1. Buying (outflow) plant assets
2. Selling (inflow) plant assets

Investing activities are listed after the cash flows from operating activities.

Financing activities obtain the funds from investors and creditors needed to launch and sustain the business. Financing activities require analysis of the long-term liability accounts and the owners' equity accounts and include:

1. Issuing stock (inflow)
2. Purchase (outflow) and sale (inflow) of treasury stock
3. Paying dividends (outflow)
4. Borrowing money (inflow) and repaying (outflow) the principal

Financing activities are listed after the cash flows from investing activities.

> **Study Tip:** While *principal* payments on notes and bonds payable are classified as a financing activity, the interest payments (interest expense) are classified as an operating activity.

> **Study Tip:** The following relationships are important to remember:
> 1. Operating activities relate to net income
> 2. Investing activities relate to long-term assets
> 3. Financing activities relate to long-term liabilities and owners' equity

Review Exhibit 17-2 in your text and become familiar with both the format and content of a cash flow statement.

Objective 3 - Prepare a statement of cash flows by the indirect method.

The statement of cash flows reports cash flows from operating activities, investing activities, and financing activities, calculates the net increase or decrease in cash over the year, and adds that to the previous year's cash balance in order to arrive at the current year's cash balance. It shows where cash came from and how it was spent. There are two methods to present the operating activities section of the statement of cash flows: direct and indirect. We will first look at the indirect method since it is the most widely used.

The **indirect method** reconciles net income, derived by using accrual-basis accounting, to net cash flows from operations and affects only the operating activities section of the statement. In essence, the indirect method converts net income determined under the accrual-basis of accounting (GAAP), to what it would be if it had been determined using the cash-basis of accounting (not GAAP). To prepare the statement of cash flows, you need the income statement and the balance sheet.

Preparing the statement of cash flows requires these steps:

1. Identify items that affect cash
2. Classify the items as operating activities, investing, or financing activities
3. Determine the increase or decrease in cash for each item

To prepare the operating activities section using the indirect method, you begin with net income off the income statement, and then make the following adjustments:

1. Depreciation, amortization, and depletion are noncash expenses that are subtracted in determining net income on the income statement. Because these are noncash expenses, we need to add them back to net income as part of our effort to arrive at cash flow from operations.
2. Gains and losses from the sale of plant assets are reported on the income statement as part of net income. However, the cash proceeds from the sale are reported in the investing activities section because the cash flows relate to long-term asset accounts. To avoid counting gains and losses twice, we must remove their effect from net income. Therefore, gains are subtracted from net income and losses are added to net income.
3. Changes in current assets and current liabilities:
   a. Increases in current assets, other than cash, are subtracted from net income.
   b. Decreases in current assets, other than cash, are added to net income.
   c. Decreases in current liabilities, other than dividends payable, are subtracted from net income. (Payments for dividends appear under financing activities.)
   d. Increases in current liabilities, other than dividends payable, are added to net income.

Study Tip: Under the indirect method, only the net change in current asset and current liability accounts are used.

Cash flows from investing activities include:

1. payments (outflow) for acquisition of plant assets.
2. proceeds (inflow) from the sale of plant assets.

Cash flows from financing activities include:

1. proceeds (inflow) from issuance of stock and notes payable.
2. payments (outflow) of notes payable and purchases of treasury stock.
3. payment (outflow) of cash dividends.

Review Exhibits 17-3; 17-4; 17-5; 17-6 and 17-7 in your text.

Noncash investing and financing activities

Some investing and financing activities are noncash. Some typical noncash investing and financing activities include:

1. Acquisition of assets by issuing stock
2. Acquisition of assets by issuing debt
3. Payment of long-term debt by transferring investment assets to the creditor

Noncash activities are included in a schedule or a note to the statement of cash flows.

Objective 4 - Prepare a statement of cash flows by the direct method.

Cash flows from operating activities using the direct method include:

1. cash collections from customers.
2. cash receipts of interest.
3. cash receipts of dividends.
4. payments to suppliers.
5. payments to employees.
6. payments for interest and income tax.

The investing activities and financing activities sections are identical to the sections prepared using the indirect method.

When the direct method of computing operating cash flows is used, FASB requires companies to include a reconciliation from net income to net cash flows from operating activities. This reconciliation is identical to operating activity section of the cash flow statement under the indirect method.

Cash flows are only one source of information creditors and investors use to evaluate a company. The Decision Guidelines in your text provide an excellent summary of using cash flow and related information to evaluate investments.

Free cash flow is defined as the amount of cash available from operations after paying for planned investments in plant, equipment, and other long-term assets. Free cash flow refers to the amount of cash flow that a company could access quickly should a need/opportunity arise. When net cash flows from operations exceed the amount of cash required for investments in long-term assets, the excess is available for additional investments. Obviously, a positive free cash flow is preferable to a negative amount. Free cash flow is yet another tool to be used in evaluating a company's performance.

TEST YOURSELF

All the self-testing materials in this chapter focus on information and procedures that your instructor is likely to test in quizzes and examinations.

I. Matching *Match each numbered term with its lettered definition.*

_____ 1. Cash Equivalents
_____ 2. Direct method
_____ 3. Indirect method
_____ 4. Operating activity

_____ 5. Cash flows
_____ 6. Financing activity
_____ 7. Investing activity
_____ 8. Statement of cash flows

A. A report of cash receipts and cash disbursements classified according to the entity's major activities: operating, investing, and financing
B. Activity that creates revenue or expense in the entity's major line of business
C. Activity that increases or decreases the long-term assets with which the business has to work
D. Activity that obtains from creditors the funds needed to launch and sustain the business or repays such funds
E. Cash receipts and cash disbursements
F. Format of the operating activities section of the statement of cash flows that lists the major categories of operating cash receipts and cash disbursements
G. Format of the operating activities section of the statement of cash flows that starts with net income and shows the reconciliation from net income to operating cash flows
H. Highly liquid short-term investments that can be readily converted into cash

II. Multiple Choice *Circle the best answer.*

1. All of the following are uses of the statement of cash flows except

   A. evaluate employee's performance.
   B. evaluate management's decisions.
   C. predict future cash flows.
   D. relate net income to changes in cash.

2. Activities that increase or decrease business assets such as machinery are called

   A. financing activities.
   B. investing activities.
   C. operating activities.
   D. reporting activities.

3. Transactions involving capital or debt activities are called

   A. financing activities.
   B. investing activities.
   C. operating activities.
   D. reporting activities.

4. Which of the following is considered a cash equivalent?

   A. Accounts receivable
   B. Inventory
   C. Supplies
   D. Treasury bills

5. The receipt of dividend revenues would be reported on the

A. balance sheet.
B. income statement.
C. statement of cash flows only.
D. both the income statement and the statement of cash flows.

6. All of the following are examples of operating activities except

A. purchases from suppliers.
B. sales to customers.
C. sales of equipment.
D. recording rent expense.

7. All of the following are examples of investing activities except

A. sale of building.
B. payment of dividends.
C. purchase of equipment.
D. receipt of cash from sale of California State bonds.

8. All of the following are financing activities except

A. issuing stock.
B. paying dividends.
C. selling equipment.
D. long-term borrowing.

9. Cash collections from customers are computed by

A. Sales Revenue + Increase in Accounts Receivable
B. Sales Revenue - Increase in Accounts Receivable
C. Sales Revenues - Decrease in Accounts Receivable
D. Sales Revenue + Decrease in Accounts Receivable
E. Either B or D.

10. Which of the following accounts must be analyzed to determine the cash paid for dividends?

A. Dividends Payable
B. Retained Earnings
C. Common Stock
D. Both A. and B.

III. Completion *Complete each of the following statements.*

1. The _____ is the only financial statement that is dated as of the end of the period.
2. The largest cash inflow from operations is _____.
3. Both the _____ method and the _____ method of preparing the statements of cash flows are permitted by the FASB.
4. Payments of dividends is a(n) _____ activity on the statement of cash flows.
5. Purchasing equipment is a(n) _____ activity on the statement of cash flows.
6. Depreciation is included in the _____ activity section on the statement of cash flows when using the indirect method.
7. The sale of equipment is a(n) _____ activity on the statement of cash flows.
8. While permitting both methods, FASB recommends the _____ method.
9. The _____ method begins with net income.
10. The difference between the direct and indirect method is found in the _____ section of the statement of cash flows.

IV. Daily Exercises

1. Classify each of the following as an operating, investing, or financing activity.

Item	Classification
a) Payment to employees	_____
b) Receiving dividends on investments	_____
c) Selling treasury stock	_____
d) Raising funds by selling bonds	_____
e) Receiving cash from customers	_____
f) Paying taxes	_____
g) Purchasing equipment by paying cash	_____
h) Purchasing equipment and signing a long-term note payable	_____
i) Purchasing inventory on account	_____
j) Receiving interest revenue	_____
k) Paying dividends to stockholders	_____
l) Selling shares of common stock	_____

2. When using the indirect method and analyzing changes in balance sheet accounts, how do you treat (add or deduct) each of the following specific changes?

   a. _____ Increase in interest payable
   b. _____ Decrease in salary payable
   c. _____ Increase in accounts receivable
   d. _____ Decrease in prepaid expenses
   e. _____ Decrease in inventory
   f. _____ Decrease in accrued liabilities
   g. _____ Increase in income tax payable
   h. _____ Decrease in interest receivable
   i. _____ Decrease in accounts payable

3. When preparing the operating activities section of a cash flows statement using the indirect method, indicate (using a + or -) the effect on net income of each of the following items:

   a. _____ Amortization expense
   b. _____ Gain on sale of equipment
   c. _____ Increase in inventory
   d. _____ Depreciation expense
   e. _____ Loss on sale of building
   f. _____ Increase in accrued liabilities
   g. _____ Depletion expense
   h. _____ Decrease in inventory
   i. _____ Decrease in accounts payable
   j. _____ Decrease in accounts receivable

4. Depreciation expense is ignored when preparing the operating activities section using the direct method, but needs to be considered when using the indirect method. Why?

V. Exercises

1. Shimer Company had cost of goods sold of $400,000, an increase in inventory of $10,000, and an increase in Accounts Payable of $18,000 in 20X6. How much cash was paid to suppliers?

2. Mancuzo Company had sales of $1,250,000 in 20X6. Eighty percent of sales are on credit. During the year, Accounts Receivable increased from $35,000 to $81,000. How much cash was received from customers during 20X6?

3. Seraphim Company purchased machinery for $91,000, and sold a building with a book value of $100,000 for a $12,000 gain. What was the net cash flow from investing activities?

4. From the following list of cash receipts and payments, present the cash flows from the operating activities section of the cash flows statement, using the direct method.

Cash receipts from interest revenues	$ 2,440
Cash paid for taxes	32,855
Cash payments to suppliers	287,990
Cash receipts from customers	451,385
Cash paid for dividends	4,660
Cash payments to employees	61,075
Cash receipts from dividend revenues	1,565
Cash payments for interest	1,010

VI. Beyond the Numbers

Brendell Company has net cash flows from operating activities ($13,000), net cash flows from investing activities $20,000, and net cash flows from financing activities of $50,000. What is your analysis of the Brendell's overall business performance based on the information provided?

_____
_____
_____
_____
_____
_____

VII. Demonstration Problems

Demonstration Problem #1

The income statement, schedule of current account changes, and additional data for Johnson Jones Corporation follows:

Johnson Jones Corporation
Income Statement
For the Year Ended December 31, 20X7

Revenues:		
Net sales revenue	$1,405,000	
Dividend revenue	27,000	$1,432,000
Expenses:		
Cost of goods sold	1,081,000	
Salary expense	129,000	
Other operating expense	31,000	
Depreciation expense	55,000	
Interest expense	65,000	
Amortization expense-patents	5,000	1,366,000
Net income		$ 66,000

Additional data:

a. Collections exceeded sales by $7,000.
b. Dividend revenue equaled cash amounts received, $27,000.
c. Payments to suppliers were $18,000 less than cost of goods sold. Payments for other operating expense and interest expense were the same as Other Operating Expenses and Interest Expense.
d. Payments to employees were equal to salary expense.
e. Acquisition of plant assets totaled $130,000. Of this amount, $20,000 was paid in cash and the balance was financed by signing a note payable.
f. Proceeds from the sale of land were $85,000.
g. Proceeds from the issuance of common stock were $50,000.
h. Full payment was made on a long-term note payable, $40,000.
i. Dividends were paid in the amount of $16,000.
j. A small parcel of land located in an industrial park was purchased for $74,000.
k. Current asset and liability activity changes were as follows:

	December 31	
	20X7	20X6
Cash and cash equivalents	228,000	92,000
Accounts receivable	236,000	243,000
Inventory	378,000	384,000
Accounts payable	214,000	202,000
Income tax payable	3,200	3,200

Required

1. Using the direct method, prepare the December 31, 20X7, statement of cash flows and accompanying schedule of noncash investing and financing activities for Johnson Jones Corporation.

Requirement 1 (statement of cash flows—direct method)

Johnson Jones		
Statement of Cash Flows		
For the Year Ended December 31, 20X7		

Demonstration Problem #2

Using the information in Problem 1, prepare a statement of cash flows and accompanying schedule of noncash investing and financing activities using the indirect method.

Indirect Method

Johnson Jones
Statement of Cash Flows
For the Year Ended December 31, 20X7

SOLUTIONS

I. Matching

1. H	3. G	5. E	7. C
2. F	4. B	6. D	8. A

II. Multiple Choice

1   A   Replace A with "to determine ability to pay dividends and interest" and you have a list of all the purposes for the statement of cash flows.

2.   B   Changes in property, plant, and equipment are investing activities.

3.   A   Changes in capital and debt are financing activities.

4.   D   Cash and cash equivalents are highly liquid, short-term investments that can be converted into cash with little delay and include money market investments and investments in T-bills.

5.   D   Recall that the receipt of a dividend from an investment accounted for under the cost method is treated as income and accordingly will be included in the income statement. For cash flow statement purposes, the receipt of dividends is considered an operating activity and will be reflected in that portion of the statement.

6.   C   Operating activities create revenues and expenses in the entity's major line of business. Equipment sales are assumed not to be this entity's major line of business.

7.   B   Investing activities increase and decrease the long-term assets the business has to work with. Payment of a dividend is a financing activity. Note that while the receipt of interest on a bond is an operating activity, buying and selling bonds is an investing activity.

8.   C   Financing activities include transactions with investors and creditors needed to obtain funds to launch and sustain the business. Of the items listed, only C, an investing activity, does not fit that definition.

9.   E   Sales revenue is recorded on the accrual basis. To convert this to a cash flow, the net change in accounts receivable must be considered. A decrease in accounts receivable indicates that customers have paid more than they purchased and should be added to sales. An increase in accounts receivable indicates that customers have purchased more than they paid and should be subtracted from sales.

10.   D   To calculate the cash paid for dividends, you must analyze both the retained earnings account and dividends payable account, if any.

III. Completion

1. balance sheet (The income statement, statement of retained earnings, and statement of cash flows all cover a period of time. Only the balance sheet is as of a particular date.)
2. collections of cash from customers
3. direct, indirect (order not important)
4. financing
5. investing
6. operating (Recall from our previous discussion that depreciation is a noncash expense.)
7. investing
8. direct
9. indirect
10. operating activities

IV. Daily Exercises

1.
   a) operating activity
   b) operating activity
   c) financing activity
   d) financing activity
   e) operating activity
   f) operating activity
   g) investing activity
   h) none (this is a noncash investing activity)
   i) operating activity
   j) operating activity
   k) financing activity
   l) financing activity

> **Study Tip:** Remember, operating activities relate to the income statement, investing activities to long-term assets, and financing activities to long-term liabilities and owners' equity.

2.
   a. add (current liability)
   b. deduct (current liability)
   c. deduct (current asset)
   d. add (current asset)
   e. add (current asset)
   f. deduct (current liability)
   g. add (current liability)
   h. add (current asset)
   i. deduct (current liability)

3.

a.	+	
b.	-	
c.	-	
d.	+	
e.	+	
f.	+	
g.	+	
h.	+	
i.	.	-
j.	+	

4. The direct method ignores net income; therefore, the operating activities lists cash receipts and payments. Since depreciation expense is a non-cash item, it can be ignored. The indirect method begins with net income, which includes a deduction for depreciation expense. Since the latter is a non-cash item, it needs to be added back to net income.

V. Exercises

1.

	Cost of Goods Sold	$400,000
+	Increase in Inventory	10,000
=	Subtotal	410,000
-	Increase in Accounts Payable	18,000
=	Cash paid to suppliers	$392,000

2. Cash received from credit sales:

	Accounts Receivable (beginning)	$35,000
+	Credit sales (80% × 1,250,000)	1,000,000
=	Subtotal	1,035,000
-	Cash collected from customers	?
=	Accounts Receivable (ending)	$81,000

Cash received from credit sales ($1,035,000 - $81,000) $ 954,000
Cash collected from cash sales (20% × 1,250,000)   250,000
= Total cash collected from customers $1,204,000

3. Purchase of machinery $(91,000)
   Sale of building ($100,000 + $12,000)   112,000
   Net cash flow from investing activities $ 21,000

4.

Cash flows from operating activities:		
Cash receipts from customers	451,385	
Cash receipts from dividends	1,565	
Cash receipts from interest	2,440	
Cash payments to suppliers	(287,990)	
Cash payments to employees	(61,075)	
Cash paid for taxes	(32,855)	
Cash payments for interest	(1,010)	
Net cash inflow from operating		$72,460

The cash paid for dividends is not an operating activity. Dividends paid to shareholders relate to stockholders' equity on the balance sheet and are, therefore, a financing activity.

VI. Beyond the Numbers

When evaluating the statement of cash flows, the most important sign of financial strength is whether the company is generating a positive net cash flow from operating activities. Brendell has a negative cash flow from operating activities, which might not be cause for concern if this occurs in the early years of operations when it may take time initially to generate a positive cash flow. However, if the company has been in business for several years, a negative cash flow from operating activities could indicate financial trouble. You must also evaluate the cash flows from investing and financing activities. A positive net cash flow from investing activities will result when a business has sold more long-term assets than it has acquired. If the company is selling off its assets to compensate for the negative cash flow from operating activities, this could also be a sign of financial trouble. A positive net cash flow from investing activities could also indicate that the business is selling its older, less productive assets. If the company were selling off old assets, then you would expect to see the acquisition of additional operational assets in the future. A positive cash flow from financing activities indicates that the company is either borrowing money and/or issuing stock in an effort to generate additional funds. These activities could be positive or negative depending on the business context in which they occur. If the company wants to expand their operations, then raising additional funds via financing activities is appropriate. However, if the company is having difficulty generating cash flows from operating activities, and is borrowing money or issuing stock to pay for day-to-day operations, then the company may be in trouble.

VII. Demonstration Problems

Demonstration Problem #1 Solved and Explained

Requirement 1 (direct method)

Johnson Jones
Statement of Cash Flows
For the Year Ended December 31, 20X7

Cash flows from operating activities:		
Receipts:		
Collections from customers	$1,412,000 (A)	
Dividends received on investments in stock	27,000 (B)	
Total cash receipts		$1,439,000
Payments:		
To suppliers	1,094,000 (C)	
To employees	129,000 (D)	
For interest	65,000 (C)	
Total cash payments		1,288,000
Net cash inflow from operating activities		151,000
Cash flows from investing activities:		
Acquisition of plant assets	(20,000) (E)	
Proceeds from sale of land	85,000 (F)	
Acquisition of industrial park land	(74,000) (E)	
Net cash outflow from investing activities		(9,000)
Cash flows from financing activities:		
Proceeds from common stock issuance	50,000 (G)	
Payment of long-term note payable	(40,000) (G)	
Dividends	(16,000) (G)	
Net cash outflow from financing activities		(6,000)
Net increase in cash		136,000
Cash balance beginning of year		92,000
Cash balance end of year		228,000
Noncash investing and financing activities:		
Acquisition of plant assets by issuing note payable		$ 110,000 (E)

Computations and Explanations

(A) The largest cash inflow from operations will almost always be the collection of cash from customers. Cash sales obviously will bring in cash immediately. Since sales on account increase Accounts Receivable (not Cash), companies need to know the actual collections from customers. Item (a) of the additional data indicates that collections from customers were more than sales by $7,000. Thus, collections must have been $1,412,000 ($1,405,000 sales plus $7,000).

(B) Dividends do not accrue with the passage of time, but rather are recorded when received. Item (b) of the additional data states that $27,000 was received, the identical amount shown in the income statement. Thus, no adjustment is necessary. Note that dividends received result in a cash inflow

158

reported as an operating activity. Although the origin of the dividend was from an investment activity, in accordance with the FASB, dividends received were accounted for as part of operating activities because they have a direct impact on net income.

(C) Payments to suppliers is a broad category which includes all cash payments for inventory and all operating expenses except disbursements for:

1. employee compensation expense
2. interest expense
3. income tax expense

A review of Item (c) indicates that payments to suppliers were $1,094,000 ($1,063,000 + $31,000) as follows:

Cost of goods sold	$1,081,000
Less: Additional amounts owed to suppliers	18,000
Payments for inventory	$1,063,000
Payments for Operating expense	$31,000

Payments to suppliers include all payments (except those listed above as exceptions) to those who supply the business with its inventory and essential services. Note that interest payment equals interest expense, an item that is separately disclosed in the statement of cash flows.

(D) Payments to employees include all forms of employee compensation. The income statement reports the expense (including accrued amounts), whereas the statement of cash flows reports only the payments. Item (d) indicates that actual payments were $129,000, which is same as the $129,000 reported in the income statement as salary expense.

(E) The purchase of $130,000 in plant assets used $20,000 in cash. The balance was financed with a $110,000 promissory note. Because the note is not an outflow of cash, it is separately disclosed as a noncash investing activity at the bottom of the statement of cash flows.

The $74,000 industrial park land (Item j) used $74,000 cash and is shown as a cash outflow or "use." A firm's investment in income-producing assets often signals to investors the direction that the firm is taking.

(F) The receipt of $85,000 from the land sale (Item f) is essentially the opposite of the acquisition of a plant asset, and should be reported as a cash inflow from an investment transaction.

(G) Investors and other financial statement users want to know how an entity obtains it's financing. The financing activities section of the cash flow statement for Johnson Jones Corporation discloses the effect of the sale of common stock (inflow of $50,000, Item g), payment of a long-term note (outflow of $40,000, Item h), and payment of cash dividends (outflow of $16,000, Item i).

Demonstration Problem #2 Solved and Explained

Indirect Method

Johnson Jones Corporation
Statement of Cash Flows
For the Year Ended December 31, 20X7

Cash flows from operating activities:		
Net income (from income statement):		$ 66,000
Add (subtract) items that affect net income and cash flow differently:		
Depreciation expense	55,000	
Amortization expense	5,000	
Decrease in accounts receivable	7,000	
Decrease in inventory	6,000	
Increase in accounts payable	12,000	85,000
Net cash inflow from operating activities		151,000
Cash flows from investing activities:		
Acquisition of plant assets	(20,000)	
Proceeds from sale of land	85,000	
Acquisition of industrial park land	(74,000)	
Net cash outflow from investing activities		(9,000)
Cash flows from financing activities:		
Proceeds from common stock issuance	50,000	
Payment of long-term note payable	(40,000)	
Dividends	(16,000)	
Net cash outflow from financing activities		(6,000)
Net increase in cash		$136,000
Cash balance beginning of year		92,000
Cash balance end of year		$228,000
Noncash investing and financing activities:		
Acquisition of plant assets by issuing note payable		$110,000

160

As emphasized many times in this chapter, the difference between the direct method and the indirect method appears only in the presentation of the cash flows from operating activities section of the statement. The indirect method begins with net income, and then "adjusts" the net income figure in order to convert it to a cash based value. Regardless of method, the presentation of cash flows from investing activities and financing activities are the same. FASB Statement No. 95 permits either method, but recommends the direct method because it is thought to be more "user friendly."

Chapter 18 - Financial Statement Analysis

CHAPTER OVERVIEW

Financial statements are the primary resource a prospective investor or creditor uses to evaluate a company and/or compare it with other companies. There are a variety of methods used to evaluate performance. In this chapter you are introduced to some of these techniques. The learning objectives for the chapter are to

1. Perform a horizontal analysis of comparative financial statements.
2. Perform a vertical analysis of financial statements.
3. Prepare and use common-size financial statements.
4. Compute the standard financial ratios.
5. Measure economic value added.

CHAPTER REVIEW

Financial statement analysis is based on information taken from the annual report, SEC reports, articles in the business press, and so on. The objective of financial statement analysis is to provide information to creditors and investors to help them 1) predict future returns and 2) assess the risk of those returns. Many times past performance can be a good indicator of future performance. Three categories of financial statement analysis are: horizontal, vertical, and ratio analysis.

Objective 1 - Perform a horizontal analysis of comparative financial statements.

The study of percentage changes of a financial statement item in comparative statements is called **horizontal analysis**. Horizontal analysis highlights changes in an item over time. Computing a percentage change in an item in comparative statements requires two steps: 1) compute the dollar amount of the change in the item from the base period to the later period, and 2) divide the dollar amount of the change by the base period amount.

The **base period** for horizontal analysis is the year prior to the year being considered. Suppose there are three years of data. The percentage change from Year 1 to Year 2 is:

$$\frac{\text{\$ YEAR 2 - \$ YEAR 1}}{\text{\$ YEAR 1}}$$

And, the percentage change from Year 2 to Year 3 is:

$$\frac{\text{\$ YEAR 3 - \$ YEAR 2}}{\text{\$ YEAR 2}}$$

No percentage changes are computed if the base year amount is zero or negative. Exhibits 18-2 and 18-3 illustrate horizontal analysis on an income statement and balance sheet.

Trend percentages are a form of horizontal analysis.. Trends indicate the direction a business is taking by comparing numbers over a span of several years. Trend percentages are computed by selecting a base year and expressing the amount of each item for each of the following years as a percentage of the base year's amount for that item.

Objective 2 - Perform a vertical analysis of financial statements.

Vertical analysis of a financial statement shows the relationship of each item to the base amount of another item. Vertical analysis reveals the percentage of the total base amount that each statement item represents. For example, percentages on a comparative income statement are computed by dividing all items by net sales. Percentages on the comparative balance sheet are shown as a percentage of total assets.

Vertical analysis of the income statement highlights changes in such items as the gross profit percentage and net income.

Vertical analysis of the balance sheet shows the composition of the balance sheet items. Trend analysis can be used to highlight year-to-year percentage changes.

Exhibits 18-4 and 18-5 in your text illustrate vertical analysis of the comparative income statement and balance sheet, respectively.

Objective 3 - Prepare and use common-size financial statements.

Common-size statements report financial statement items in percentages only (no dollar amounts). The common-size statement is a form of vertical analysis. On a common-size income statement, each item is expressed as a percentage of the net sales amount. On the balance sheet, the common-size is total assets. Note that common-size percentages are the same percentages shown on financial statements using vertical analysis. Review Exhibit 18-6 in your text for an example of the common-size analysis of current assets.

Benchmarking is the practice of comparing a company's financial statement results to a standard set by other companies. Benchmarking is used to compare a company's results with the average for their industry. In addition, common-size statements can be compared with those of specific competitors within the industry. Exhibits 18-7 and 18-8 in your text illustrate these two uses of benchmarking.

Common-size percentages can be used to compare financial statements of different companies or to compare one company's financial statements to industry averages.

Objective 4 - Compute the standard financial ratios.

There are many different ratios used in financial analysis. Sometimes a ratio is used alone but more frequently a group of ratios are calculated and used to analyze a particular aspect of the company. The ratios discussed in this chapter may be classified as those:

1. Measuring the company's ability to pay current liabilities
2. Measuring the company's ability to sell inventory and collect receivables
3. Measuring the company's ability to pay long-term debt
4. Measuring the company's profitability
5. Analyzing the company's stock as an investment

1. **Ratios that measure the company's ability to pay current liabilities**

Working capital is used to measure a business's ability to meet its short-term obligations with its current assets.

$$\text{WORKING CAPITAL} = \text{CURRENT ASSETS} - \text{CURRENT LIABILITIES}$$

The **current ratio** measures a company's ability to pay current liabilities with current assets.

$$\text{CURRENT RATIO} = \frac{\text{CURRENT ASSETS}}{\text{CURRENT LIABILITIES}}$$

For example, a current ratio of 1.50 means that for every $1 of current liabilities, the company has $1.50 in current assets. This ratio must be compared to the industry average to evaluate whether this is a positive or negative indicator for the company.

The **acid-test** (or **quick**) **ratio** measures the ability of a business to pay all of its current liabilities if they came due immediately. Therefore, the numerator identifies the company's most liquid current assets and divides by total current liabilities.

$$\text{ACID-TEST RATIO} = \frac{\text{CASH} + \substack{\text{SHORT-TERM} \\ \text{INVESTMENTS}} + \substack{\text{NET CURRENT} \\ \text{RECEIVABLES}}}{\text{CURRENT LIABILITIES}}$$

> **Study Tip:** Inventory and prepaid expenses are not used to compute the acid-test ratio because they are the least liquid of the current assets.

2. **Ratios that measure the company's ability to sell inventory and collect receivables**

Inventory turnover measures the number of times a company sells its average level of inventory during a year.

$$\text{INVENTORY TURNOVER} = \frac{\text{COST OF GOODS SOLD}}{\text{AVERAGE INVENTORY}}$$

$$\text{AVERAGE INVENTORY} = \frac{\text{BEGINNING INVENTORY} + \text{ENDING INVENTORY}}{2}$$

An inventory turnover of 5.0 indicates that, on average, a company sells its inventory 5 times per year.

Accounts receivable turnover measures the company's ability to collect cash from its credit customers.

$$\substack{\text{ACCOUNTS} \\ \text{RECEIVABLE} \\ \text{TURNOVER}} = \frac{\text{NET CREDIT SALES}}{\text{AVERAGE NET ACCOUNTS RECEIVABLE}}$$

$$\substack{\text{AVERAGE NET} \\ \text{ACCOUNTS} \\ \text{RECEIVABLE}} = \frac{\substack{\text{BEGINNING} \\ \text{ACCOUNTS RECEIVABLE}} + \substack{\text{ENDING} \\ \text{ACCOUNTS RECEIVABLE}}}{2}$$

An accounts receivable turnover ratio of 7.5 means that, on average, a company collects its receivables, 7.5 times per year.

Days' sales in receivables also referred to as the *collection period,* measures how many days it takes to collect the average level of accounts receivable. To compute the ratio, follow a two-step process:

$$\text{ONE DAY'S SALES} \quad = \quad \frac{\text{NET CREDIT SALES}}{365}$$

$$\begin{matrix} \text{DAYS' SALES IN} \\ \text{ACCOUNTS} \\ \text{RECEIVABLE} \end{matrix} \quad = \quad \frac{\text{AVERAGE NET ACCOUNTS RECEIVABLE}}{\text{ONE DAY'S SALES}}$$

To compute the ratio for the beginning of the year, substitute beginning net Accounts Receivable for average net Accounts Receivable. To compute the ratio for the end of the year, substitute ending net Accounts Receivable for average net Accounts Receivable.

3. **Ratios that measure the company's ability to pay long-term debt**

The **debt ratio** shows the relationship between total liabilities and total assets by measuring the proportion of a company's assets that is financed with debt.

$$\text{DEBT RATIO} \quad = \quad \frac{\text{TOTAL LIABILITIES}}{\text{TOTAL ASSETS}}$$

A debt ratio of .40 means that 40% of the company's assets are financed with debt.

The **times-interest-earned ratio** measures the ability of a business to pay interest expense.

$$\begin{matrix} \text{TIMES-} \\ \text{INTEREST-EARNED} \\ \text{RATIO} \end{matrix} \quad = \quad \frac{\text{INCOME FROM OPERATIONS}}{\text{INTEREST EXPENSE}}$$

A high times-interest-earned ratio indicates ease in paying interest expense while a low value suggests difficulty. Remember that income from operations does not include interest revenue, interest expense, or income tax expense.

4. **Ratios that measure the company's profitability**

Rate of return on net sales (or return on sales) shows the relationship between net income and sales by measuring the percentage of each sales dollar earned as net income.

$$\begin{matrix} \text{RATE OF} \\ \text{RETURN ON} \\ \text{NET SALES} \end{matrix} \quad = \quad \frac{\text{NET INCOME}}{\text{NET SALES}}$$

A return on sales of .045 means that for every $1 in net sales, the company generates $.045 in net income.

165

Rate of return on total assets measures how successful a company is in using its assets to earn A profit for the persons who finance the business. In the numerator, net income represents the return to the stockholders and interest expense represents the return to the creditors. The sum of interest expense and net income is the return to the two groups that have financed the company.

$$\text{RATE OF RETURN ON TOTAL ASSETS} = \frac{\text{NET INCOME} + \text{INTEREST EXPENSE}}{\text{AVERAGE TOTAL ASSETS}}$$

$$\text{AVERAGE TOTAL ASSETS} = \frac{\text{BEGINNING TOTAL ASSETS} + \text{ENDING TOTAL ASSETS}}{2}$$

The **rate of return on common stockholders' equity** shows the relationship between net income and the common stockholders' investment in the company and measures how much income is earned for every $1 invested by the common shareholders.

$$\text{RATE OF RETURN ON COMMON STOCKHOLDERS' EQUITY} = \frac{\text{NET INCOME} - \text{PREFERRED DIVIDENDS}}{\text{AVERAGE COMMON STOCKHOLDERS' EQUITY}}$$

$$\text{AVERAGE COMMON STOCKHOLDERS' EQUITY} = \frac{\text{BEGINNING} + \text{ENDING COMMON STOCKHOLDERS' EQUITY}}{2}$$

Earnings per share (EPS) is the amount of net income earned for each share of the company's common stock.

$$\text{EPS} = \frac{\text{NET INCOME} - \text{PREFERRED DIVIDENDS}}{\text{NUMBER OF SHARES OF COMMON STOCK OUTSTANDING}}$$

> **Study Tip:** Remember, earnings per share (EPS) is the only ratio that is required to appear on the face of the income statement.

5. **Ratios used to analyze the company's stock as an investment**

The **price/earnings (P/E) ratio** is the ratio of the market price of a share of common stock to the company's EPS, which measures the value that the stock market places on $1 of a company's earnings.

$$\text{PRICE/EARNINGS RATIO} = \frac{\text{MARKET PRICE PER SHARE OF COMMON STOCK}}{\text{EARNINGS PER SHARE}}$$

Dividend yield is the ratio of dividends per share of stock to the stock's market price per share, which measures the percentage of a stock's market value that the company returns to stockholders as dividends.

$$\text{DIVIDEND YIELD ON COMMON STOCK} = \frac{\text{DIVIDENDS PER SHARE OF COMMON STOCK}}{\text{MARKET PRICE PER SHARE OF COMMON STOCK}}$$

The formula for calculating **book value per share of common stock** is:

$$\text{BOOK VALUE PER SHARE OF COMMON STOCK} = \frac{\text{TOTAL STOCKHOLDERS' EQUITY - PREFERRED EQUITY}}{\text{NUMBER OF SHARES OF COMMON STOCK OUTSTANDING}}$$

Objective 5 - Measure economic value added.

Economic value added (EVA) is one measure many companies use to evaluate whether the company has increased stockholder wealth from operations. The formula for EVA is

Net income + interest expense - capital charge

Capital charge = (Notes payable + Bonds payable + Stockholders' equity) × cost of capital

The **cost of capital** is a weighted average of the returns demanded by the company's stockholders and lenders. Newer companies, because of the added risk, have a higher cost of capital compared with older, more established companies. The underlying assumption behind EVA is that returns to both stockholders and lenders should be greater than the company's capital charge. If the calculation results in a positive value, the result indicates an increase in stockholder wealth. If negative, stockholders may consider selling the stock, which, if done in large enough amounts, could lower the price of the stock. Obviously, companies who use this measure strive to achieve a positive result.

TEST YOURSELF

All the self-testing materials in this chapter focus on information and procedures that your instructor is likely to test in quizzes and examinations.

I. Matching   *Match each numbered term with its lettered definition.*

_____ 1. Accounts receivable turnover
_____ 2. Working capital
_____ 3. Common-size statements
_____ 4. Days' sales in receivables
_____ 5. Dividend yield
_____ 6. Inventory turnover
_____ 7. Return on total assets
_____ 8. Times-interest-earned ratio
_____ 9. Vertical analysis
_____ 10. Acid-test ratio

_____ 11. Current ratio
_____ 12. Debt ratio
_____ 13. Horizontal analysis
_____ 14. Price/earnings ratio
_____ 15. Return on net sales
_____ 16. Book value per share of common stock
_____ 17. Return on common stockholders' equity
_____ 18. Benchmarking
_____ 19. Cost of capital
_____ 20. Economic value added

A. Analysis of a financial statement that reveals the relationship of each statement item to total assets or net sales
B. Common stockholders' equity divided by the number of shares of common stock outstanding
C. Current assets divided by current liabilities
D. Current assets minus current liabilities
E. Financial statements that report only percentages (no dollar amounts) for financial statement items
F. Measures the number of times that operating income can cover interest expense
G. Measures the number of times a company sells its average level of inventory during a year
H. Ratio of the market price of a share of common stock to the company's earnings per share
I. Measures the success a company has in using its assets to earn a profit
J. Net income minus preferred dividends, divided by average common stockholders' equity; a measure of profitability
K. Ratio of average net accounts receivable to one day's sales
L. Ratio of dividends per share to the stock's market price per share
M. Ratio of net income to net sales; a measure of profitability
N. Study of percentage changes in financial statement items from comparative financial statements
O. Tells the proportion of a company's assets that it has financed with debt
P. Tells whether an entity could pay all its current liabilities if they came due immediately
Q. The ratio of net credit sales to average net accounts receivable; it measures ability to collect cash from credit customers
R. Used to measure if a company has increased shareholder wealth from operations
S. The practice of comparing a company with other companies with a view toward improvement
T. A weighted average of the returns demanded by the company's stockholders and lenders

II. Multiple Choice   *Circle the best answer.*

1. In vertical analysis, the relationship between net income and net sales is also shown by the

   A. income from operations percentage.
   B. net income percentage.
   C. rate of return on sales.
   D. gross profit percentage.

2. Which of the following measures profitability?

   A. Return on assets
   B. Current ratio
   C. Earnings per share
   D. Both A. and C.

3. Which of the following current assets is not used to compute the acid-test ratio?

   A. Accounts receivable
   B. Cash
   C. Prepaid expenses
   D. Short-term investments

4. Which of the following is a common measure of a firm's ability to meet short-term obligations?

   A. Acid-test ratio
   B. Rate of return on assets
   C. Book value
   D. Earnings per share

5. The times-interest-earned ratio measures

   A. profitability.
   B. ability to pay interest expense on debt.
   C. ability to pay current liabilities.
   D. ability to collect receivables.

6. The proportion of a firm's assets financed by debt is measured by the

   A. current ratio.
   B. debt ratio.
   C. dividend yield ratio.
   D. times-interest-earned ratio.

7. Assume that a company's current ratio is greater than one. If the company pays some or all current liabilities with cash, the new current ratio will

   A. increase.
   B. decrease.
   C. remain unchanged.
   D. cannot be determined.

8. The price/earnings ratio measures

   A. the ability to pay current debt.
   B. profitability.
   C. stock as an investment.
   D. ability to pay long-term debt.

9. The excess of current assets less current liabilities is

   A. a measure of profitability.
   B. economic value added.
   C. a measure of short-term liquidity.
   D. a measure of long-term debt paying ability.

10. Economic value added measures

    A. profitability.
    B. short-term liquidity.

    C. long-term debt paying ability.
    D. whether the company's operations have increased stockholder wealth.

III. Completion *Complete each of the following statements.*

1. The study of percentage changes in comparative financial statements is called _____ analysis.

2. Vertical analysis percentages on the income statement are computed by dividing all amounts by _____.

3. Vertical analysis percentages on the balance sheet are computed by dividing all amounts by _____.

4. Working capital is _____.

5. _____ and _____ are the two most common measures of firm working capital.

6. Leverage _____ the risk to common stockholders.

7. The _____ ratio measures the value that the stock market places on $1 of a company's earnings.

8. The rate of return on total assets equals _____.

9. The most widely quoted of all financial statistics is _____.

10. The _____ is the recorded accounting value of each share of common stock outstanding.

IV. Daily Exercises

1. Net income was $300,000 in Year 1, $400,000 in Year 2, and $320,000 in Year 3. What were the percentage changes in net income?

2. For the year 20X5, a company had 525,000 shares of common stock outstanding, 5,000 shares of 6%, $50 par preferred stock, net income of $1,570,000, and average total assets of $1,200,750 . Calculate earnings per share.

3. Refer to The Complex Corporation income statement in Demonstration Problem #1 and complete a vertical analysis.

	Amount	%
Net sales		
Cost of products sold		
Selling, delivery, and administration		
Advertising		
Research and development		
Interest expense		
Other (income) expense, net		
Total costs and expenses		
Earnings before income taxes		
Income Taxes		
Net earnings		

4. Examine your results in Daily Exercise #3, and calculate Complex's gross profit rate for 20X7.

5. Presented below are The Complex Corporation's net sales (in thousands) and net earnings (in thousands) for the past five years. Calculate trend percentages. Assume the base year is 20X3.

	20X7	20X6	20X5	20X4	20X3
Net Sales	$2,532,651	$2,217,843	$1,984,170	$1,836,949	$1,634,171
Net Earnings	249,442	222,092	200,832	212,057	167,051

V. Exercises

1. Hoffman Industries had the following information for 20X9:

Cost of goods sold	$400,000
Beginning inventory	30,000
Ending inventory	60,000
Net credit sales	725,000
Beginning accounts receivable	75,000
Ending accounts receivable	85,000

A. What is inventory turnover?

B. What is the accounts receivable turnover?

C. What is the days' sales in accounts receivables?

2. The following information is given for Ramirez Corporation for 20X9:

Net sales	$825,000
Net income	60,000
Average common stockholders' equity	3,150,000
Average total assets	4,225,000
Interest expense	75,000
Preferred dividends	20,000
Common dividends	55,000
Common stock outstanding	240,000 shares

A. What is the rate of return on net sales?

B. What is the rate of return on total assets?

C. What is the rate of return on common stockholders' equity?

3. The following information is given for Williams Corporation:

Assets:

Cash	$ 60,000
Marketable securities	118,000
Accounts receivable	214,000
Inventory	141,000
Equipment	420,000
Total Assets	$953,000

Liabilities and Stockholders' Equity:

Accounts payable	$105,000
Salary payable	17,000
Long-term bonds payable	165,000
Common stock	200,000
Retained earnings	466,000
Total Liabilities and Stockholders' Equity	$953,000

A. What is the current ratio?

B. What is the acid-test (quick) ratio?

C. What is the debt ratio?

4. Calvin, Inc., has a price/earnings ratio of 19, dividends of $1.50 per share, and earnings per share of $1.28.

A. What is the market price per share?

B. What is the dividend yield?

VI. Beyond the Numbers

The operating cycle is the length of time between the purchase of merchandise and its conversion to cash following the sale and receipt of payment (you were introduced to the operating cycle in Chapter 5). Using the information in Exercise 1 above, calculate the operating cycle for Hoffman Industries.

VII. Demonstration Problems

Demonstration Problem #1

The Complex Company, headquartered in San Jose, California, manufactures household products. Figures from their 20X7 annual report (slightly modified for ease of presentation) follow:

The Complex Company
Statement of Consolidated Earnings
For Year Ended June 30, 20X7

	(In thousands)
Net sales	$2,532,651
Cost and expenses	
Cost of products sold	1,123,459
Selling, delivery, and administration	543,804
Advertising	348,521
Research and development	50,489
Interest expense	55,623
Other (income) expense, net	(5,260)
Total costs and expenses	2,116,636
Earnings before income taxes	416,015
Income Taxes	166,573
Net earnings	$ 249,442
Average shares outstanding	103,165

The Complex Company
Consolidated Balance Sheet
June 30, 20X7

| | (In thousands) | |
	20X7	20X6
Assets		
Current assets:		
Cash and short-term investments	$ 101,046	$ 90,828
Accounts receivable, less allowance	356,996	315,106
Inventories	170,340	138,848
Prepaid expenses	22,534	18,076
Deferred income taxes	22,581	10,987
Total current assets	673,497	573,845
Property, plant, and equipment—net	570,645	551,437
Brands, trademarks, patents and other intangibles—net	1,186,951	704,669
Investment in affiliates	93,004	99,033
Other assets	253,855	249,910
Total Assets	$2,777,952	$2,178,894
Liabilities and Stockholders' Equity		
Current liabilities:		
Accounts payable	$ 143,360	$ 155,366
Accrued liabilities	358,785	266,192
Short-term debt	369,973	192,683
Income tax payable	17,049	9,354
Current maturity of long-term debt	3,551	291
Total current liabilities	892,718	623,886
Long-term debt	565,926	356,267
Other obligations	112,539	100,246
Deferred income taxes	170,723	148,408
Stockholders' equity		
Common stock - authorized, 375,000,000 shares,		
$1 par value; issued: 110,844,594 shares	110,844	110,844
Additional paid-in capital	66,803	56,360
Retained earnings	1,207,524	1,078,789
Treasury shares, at cost: 20X7, 7,680,056 shares;		
20X6, 7,848,942 shares	(289,075)	(251,393)
Cumulative translation adjustments	(60,050)	(44,513)
Total Stockholders' equity	1,036,046	950,087
Total liabilities and stockholders' equity	$2,777,952	$2,178,894

Required:

Assume annual dividends of $1.16 and a market price of 79 5/16 per share. Assume all sales are on credit. Compute the following for 20X7:

A) Working capital

B) Current ratio

C) Acid-test (quick) ratio

D) Inventory turnover

E) Accounts receivable turnover

F) Days' sales in receivables

G) Debt ratio

H) Times-interest-earned ratio

I) Rate of return on sales

J) Rate of return on total assets

K) Rate of return on common stockholders' equity

L) Earnings per share

M) Price/earnings ratio

N) Dividend yield

O) Book value per share of common stock

Demonstration Problem #2

Chris Daniel Corporation's balance sheets and income statements are presented below:

Chris Daniel Corporation
Balance Sheet
At December 31, 20X9 and 20X8

	20X9	20X8
Assets		
Current assets:		
Cash	$ 13,300	$ 20,350
Short-term investments	8,200	8,000
Receivables, net	26,000	24,000
Inventories	45,000	40,000
Prepaid expenses	2,500	4,650
Total current assets	95,000	97,000
Property, plant, and equipment—net	185,680	196,500
Land	40,000	35,000
Intangibles and other assets	2,400	2,400
Total assets	$323,080	$330,900
Liabilities and Stockholders' Equity		
Current liabilities:		
Notes payable	$ 10,000	$ 10,500
Current installments of long-term debt	3,550	3,445
Accounts payable-trade	14,447	18,500
Accrued liabilities	3,670	1,605
Total current liabilities	31,667	34,050
Long-term debt, less current installments	95,500	93,330
Capital lease obligations, less current portion	1,100	2,150
Deferred income and deferred income taxes	4,813	4,370
Total common stockholders' equity	190,000	197,000
Total liabilities and stockholders' equity	$323,080	$330,900

177

Chris Daniel Corporation
Income Statements
For the Years Ended December 31, 20X9 and 20X8

	20X9	20X8
Net sales	$416,500	$406,316
Cost and expenses:		
Cost of goods sold	322,593	315,812
Operating expenses	41,219	43,200
Total Costs and Expenses	363,812	359,012
Income from operations	52,688	47,304
Interest expense	3,251	3,150
Earnings before income taxes	49,437	44,154
Income taxes	7,437	6,554
Net income	$ 42,000	$ 37,600

Required:

1. Prepare a horizontal analysis for 20X9 of the balance sheet, using the 20X8 amounts as the base.

Chris Daniel Corporation				
Balance Sheet				
At December 31, 20X9 and 20X8				
	20X9	20X8	Amount Increase (Decrease)	% Change
Assets:				
Current assets:				
Cash	$ 13,300	$ 20,350		
Short-term investments	8,200	8,000		
Receivables, net	26,000	24,000		
Inventories	45,000	40,000		
Prepaid expenses	2,500	4,650		
Total current assets	95,000	97,000		
Property, plant, and equipment—net	185,680	196,500		
Land	40,000	35,000		
Intangibles and other assets	2,400	2,400		
Total assets	$323,080	$330,900		
Liabilities and stockholders' equity:				
Current liabilities:				
Notes payable	$ 10,000	$ 10,500		
Current installments of long-term debt	3,550	3,445		
Accounts payable-trade	14,447	18,500		
Accrued liabilities	3,670	1,605		
Total current liabilities	31,667	34,050		
Long-term debt, less current installments	95,500	93,330		
Capital lease obligations, less current portion	1,100	2,150		
Deferred income and deferred income taxes	4,813	4,370		
Total common stockholders' equity	190,000	197,000		
Total liabilities and stockholders' equity	$323,080	$330,900		

179

2. Convert the 20X9 and 20X8 Income Statements to common-size statements, using net sales as the base figures.

Chris Daniel Corporation				
Income Statements				
For the Years Ended December 31, 20X9 and 20X8				
	20X9		20X8	
	Amount	%	Amount	%
Net sales	$416,500		$406,316	
Cost and expenses:				
Cost of goods sold	322,593		315,812	
Operating expenses	41,219		43,200	
Total costs and expenses	363,812		359,012	
Income from operations	52,688		47,304	
Interest expense	3,251		3,150	
Earnings before income taxes	49,437		44,154	
Income taxes	7,437		6,554	
Net income	$ 42,000		$ 37,600	

SOLUTIONS

I. Matching

1. Q	5. L	9. A	13. N	17. J
2. D	6. G	10. P	14. H	18. S
3. E	7. I	11. C	15. M	19. T
4. K	8. F	12. O	16. B	20. R

II. Multiple Choice

1. B The rate of return on sales is net income / net sales. But, in vertical analysis, net income is expressed as a percentage of net sales.

2. D The current ratio measures the ability to pay current liabilities.

3. C Only the most liquid current assets are used to calculate the acid-test ratio.

4. A Acid-test ratio is (cash + short-term investments + net current receivables)/current liabilities. It measures a firm's ability to meet short-term obligations.

5. B Times-interest-earned ratio measures how many times operating income is greater than interest expense.

6. B Current ratio measures the ability to pay current liabilities. Debt yield ratio has no meaning. Times-interest-earned ratio measures ability to pay interest on debt. The debt ratio is total liabilities / total assets.

7. A Suppose a company has current assets of $100 and current liabilities of $50. The current ratio is 2.0 or ($100/$50). If the company pays $25 of the current liabilities with cash, then current assets decrease to $75 and current liabilities decrease to $25. The new current ratio is 3.0 or ($75/$25).

> **Study Tip:** In a firm with current assets greater than current liabilities, the current ratio can be improved by using cash to pay current liabilities.

8. C Price/earnings ratio measures the value that the stock market places on $1 of a company's earnings and therefore is one way to evaluate a stock as a potential investment.

9. C Working capital (the excess of current assets over current liabilities) measures short-term liquidity.

10. D Economic value added (EVA) is used to evaluate a company's operating performance. EVA combines the concepts of accounting income and corporate finance to measure whether the company's operations have increased stockholder wealth.

III. Completion

1. horizontal
2. net sales
3. total assets
4. current assets minus current liabilities
5. Current ratio, acid-test ratio
6. increases (Financial leverage is the practice of increasing the debt financing of an entity with respect to owner financing. Financial leverage is a two-edged sword, increasing profits (and returns to stockholders') during good times but compounding losses during bad times.)
7. price/earnings
8. (net income + interest expense) / average total assets
9. earnings per share
10. book value

IV. Daily Exercises

1. Year 2 = $100,000 / $300,000 = 33.33%
   Year 3 = ($80,000) / $400,000 = (20%)

2.
   ($1,570,000 - $15,000) ÷ 525,000 = $2.96 (rounded)
   Preferred dividend = $15,000 (5,000 shares × $50 par × .06)

Study Tip: When a company has issued preferred stock, the preferred dividend must be subtracted from net income when calculating earnings per share.

3.

	Amount	%
Net sales	$2,532,651	100%
Cost of products sold	1,123,459	44.4%
Selling, delivery, and administration	543,804	21.5%
Advertising	348,521	13.8%
Research and development	50,489	2.0%
Interest expense	55,623	2.2%
Other (income) expense, net	(5,260)	(.2%)
Total costs and expenses	2,116,636	83.6%
Earnings before income taxes	416,015	16.4%
Income Taxes	166,573	6.6%
Net earnings	$ 249,442	9.8%

4. If Cost of products sold is 44.4% of net sales, the gross profit (gross profit = net sales - cost of products sold) must be 55.6% (100% - 44.4%).

5.

	20X7	20X6	20X5	20X4	20X3
Net Sales	155%	136%	121%	112%	100%
Net Earnings	149%	133%	120%	127%	100%

V. Exercises

1. A. Cost of goods / Average inventory = [$400,000 / ($30,000 + $60,000) / 2] = 8.89
    B. Net credit sales / Average accounts receivable = [$725,000 / ($75,000 + $85,000) / 2] = 9.06
    C. Average accounts receivable / One day's sales = [($75,000 + $85,000) / 2] / ($725,000 / 365) = 40.3 days

2. A. Net income / Net sales = $60,000 / $825,000 = .073 = 7.3%
    B. (Net income + Interest expense) / Average total assets = ($60,000 + $75,000) / $4,225,000 = .032 = 3.2%
    C. (Net income - Preferred dividends) / Average common stockholders' equity = ($60,000 - $20,000) / $3,150,000 = .013 = 1.3%

3. A. Current assets / Current liabilities = ($60,000 + $118,000 + $214,000 + $141,000) / ($105,000 + $17,000) = 4.4 (rounded)
    B. (Cash + Short-term investments + Net current receivables) / Current liabilities = ($60,000 + $118,000 + $214,000) / ($105,000 + $17,000) = 3.2

> **Study Tip:** Remember only the assets that will convert to cash "quickly" are called quick assets. Inventory is not considered a "quick" asset.

    C. Total liabilities / Total assets = ($105,000 + $17,000 + $165,000) / $953,000 = .301 = 30.1%

4. A. Market price per share of common stock / Earnings per share = P / $1.28 = 19; P = $24.32 or $24 1/3.

    B. Dividends per share of common stock / Market price per share of common stock = $1.50 / $24.32 = .06 = 6%

VI. Beyond the Numbers

The operating cycle for Hoffman Industries is 81 days (rounded). Instruction (C) in the exercise asked you to calculate the days' sales in average receivables. The correct figure was 40.3 days. Another way of characterizing this result is to say that it takes approximately 40 days to collect an average account receivable. Instruction (A) asked you to calculate inventory turnover. The correct amount was 8.89—in other words, inventory "turns" slightly less than 9 times each year. Divide this result into 365 to convert it to days, or 41 days. In other words, on average it takes 41 days for an item to sell and 40 days on average to collect a receivable. Therefore, the operating cycle is 81 days.

VII. Demonstration Problems

Demonstration Problem #1 Solved and Explained

A) Working capital = current assets - current liabilities = $673,497 - 892,718 = ($219,221)

Study Tip: When current liabilities exceed current assets, the result is negative working capital. Negative working capital always exists when the current ratio is less than 1.

B) Current ratio = current assets ÷ current liabilities = $673,497 ÷ $892,718 = .75 (rounded)

C) Acid-test (quick) = quick assets ÷ current liabilities
   = ($101,046 + $356,996) ÷ $892,718 = 0.51 (rounded)

This means Complex has 51 cents of quick assets (cash and short-term investment plus net accounts receivable) for every dollar of current liability.

D) Inventory turnover = cost of goods sold / average inventory
   = $1,123,459 ÷ [($138,848 + $170,340) ÷ 2] = 7.27 times

Complex "turns" its inventory 7.27 times each year. Another way of stating this ratio is to convert it to days by dividing the "turn" into 365. For Complex, the turnover averages 50 days (365 ÷ 7.27).

E) Accounts receivable turnover = net credit sales ÷ average accounts receivable
   = $2,532,651 ÷ [($315,106 + $356,996) ÷ 2] = 7.54 times

F) Days' sales in receivables = average net accounts receivable ÷ one day's sales
   = $336,051 ÷ ($2,532,651 ÷ 365) = 48.4 days

The numerator for this ratio was the denominator for the previous ratio.

G) Debt ratio = total liabilities ÷ total assets
   = $1,741,906 ÷ $2,777,952
   = 0.627 or 62.7%

This means that 62.7% of the Complex assets were financed with debt. Notice the numerator (total liabilities) was not presented on the balance sheet but had to be calculated by subtracting total stockholders' equity from total liabilities and stockholders' equity.

H) Times-interest-earned = income from operations / interest expense
   = $471,638 ÷ $55,623
   = 8.48 times

Note we used earnings before income taxes plus interest expense as the numerator because interest expense had already been deducted from the earnings before income taxes amount.

I) Rate of return on sales = net income ÷ net sales
   = $249,442 ÷ $2,532,651
   = 0.098 0r 9.8%

J) Rate of return on total assets = (net income + interest expense) / average total assets
= ($249,442 + $55,623) ÷ [($2,178,894 + $2,777,952) ÷ 2]
= 0.123 or 12.3%

This ratio measures the return on assets generated by this year's operations.

K) Rate of return on common stockholders' equity = (net income - preferred dividends) ÷ average common stockholders' equity
= ($249,442 - 0) ÷ [($950,087 + $1,036,046) ÷ 2]
= 0.251 or 25.1%

Complex does not have preferred stock outstanding, so the numerator is the same as net earnings.

L) Earnings per share = (net income - preferred dividends) ÷ number of shares of common stock outstanding
= $249,442 ÷ 103,165 (110,844,594 –7,680,056)
= $2.42 (rounded)

This should be calculated for each "net earnings" amount. Companies are required to include these per share amounts on the income statement, not in the footnotes.

M) Price/earnings ratio = market price per share of common stock ÷ earnings per share
= $79.3125 ÷ $2.42 = 33 (rounded)

N) Dividend yield = dividend per share of common stock ÷ market price of common stock
= $1.16 ÷ $79.3125
= 0.0146 or 1.46%

O) Book value per share of common stock = (total stockholders' equity - preferred equity) ÷ number of shares of common stock outstanding
= 1,036,046,000 ÷ 103,164,538
= $10.04 per share

The dollars are presented "in thousands," so you must add three zeroes to the total stockholders' equity amount. To determine the number of shares outstanding, deduct the treasury shares (7,680,056) from the issued shares (110,844,594). As emphasized in your text, these ratios would have more meaning if you did them over consecutive years. In addition, to properly evaluate a company you would also want to compare the ratios with those of competitors and with the industry as a whole.

Demonstration Problem #2 Solved and Explained

1.

Chris Daniel Corporation				
Balance Sheet				
At December 31, 20X9 and 20X8				
	20X9	20X8	Amount Increase (Decrease)	% Change
Assets				
Current assets:				
Cash	$ 13,300	$ 20,350	$(7,050)	(34.6)
Short-term investments	8,200	8,000	200	2.5
Receivables, net	26,000	24,000	2,000	8.3
Inventories	45,000	40,000	5,000	12.5
Prepaid expenses	2,500	4,650	(2,150)	(46.2)
Total current assets	95,000	97,000	(2,000)	(2.1)
Property, plant, and equipment—net	185,680	196,500	(10,820)	(5.5)
Land	40,000	35,000	5,000	14.3
Intangibles and other assets	2,400	2,400	0	0
Total Assets	$323,080	$330,900	$(7,820)	(2.4)
Liabilities and Stockholders' Equity				
Current liabilities:				
Notes payable	$ 10,000	$ 10,500	$ (500)	(4.8)
Current installments of long-term debt	3,550	3,445	105	3.0
Accounts payable-trade	14,447	18,500	(4,053)	(21.9)
Accrued liabilities	3,670	1,605	2,065	128.7
Total current liabilities	31,667	34,050	(2,383)	(7.0)
Long-term debt, less current installments	95,500	93,330	2,170	2.3
Capital lease obligations, less current portion	1,100	2,150	(1,050)	(48.8)
Deferred income and deferred income taxes	4,813	4,370	443	10.1
Total common stockholders' equity	190,000	197,000	(7,000)	(3.6)
Total Liabilities and Stockholders' Equity	$323,080	$330,900	$(7,820)	(2.4)

2.

Chris Daniel Corporation				
Income Statements				
For the Years Ended December 31, 20X9 and 20X8				
	20X9		20X8	
	Amount	%	Amount	%
Net sales	$416,500	100.0	$406,316	100.0
Cost and expenses:				
Cost of goods sold	322,593	77.5	315,812	77.7
Operating expenses	41,219	9.9	43,200	10.6
Total costs and expenses	363,812	87.3	359,012	88.4
Income from operations	52,688	12.7	47,304	11.6
Interest expense	3,251	0.8	3,150	0.8
Earnings before income taxes	49,437	11.9	44,154	10.9
Income taxes	7,437	1.8	6,554	1.6
Net income	$42,000	10.1	$37,600	9.3

Points to remember:

1. When presenting horizontal analysis, each year's change in a financial statement item is divided by the base-year amount (in this case 20X8) and converted to a percentage. While the change in any single item in any single year may not be significant, applying horizontal analysis over a number of years may highlight significant changes.

2. Common-size statements for a single year are only meaningful when the results are compared to other companies or industry data. However, common-size statements covering two or more years permit analysis of the particular company being examined. In this case, we see that 20X9 results improved over 20X8 due to lower cost of goods sold and lower operating expenses.

3. Financial ratios are mathematical formulas that quantify the relationship between two or more items reported in the financial statements. Ratios are used to assess a firm's liquidity, profitability, rate of return, and ability to meet debt obligations.

Study Tip: One of the most common mistakes students make is forgetting to use the average amount of inventory, accounts receivable, or stockholders' equity in some of the formulas. It is important that an average be used to reduce distortions that might occur if only year-end balances were used.

Chapter 19 - Introduction to Management Accounting

CHAPTER OVERVIEW

This chapter is the first of eight introducing you to management accounting. You will learn about techniques businesses use to assist management in planning and controlling activities. In this chapter you are introduced to management accounting. The learning objectives for the chapter are to

1. Distinguish financial accounting from management accounting.
2. Describe service, merchandising, and manufacturing companies and classify their costs by value-chain element.
3. Distinguish among (a) direct costs and indirect costs; and (b) full product costs, inventoriable product costs, and period costs.
4. Prepare the financial statements of a manufacturing company.
5. Identify trends in the business environment, and use cost-benefit analysis to make business decisions.
6. Use reasonable standards to make ethical judgments.

CHAPTER REVIEW

Objective 1 - Distinguish financial accounting from management accounting.

Financial accounting leads to financial statements that allow stockholders and creditors—both parties external to the business—to make investment and credit decisions. The financial statements we have discussed are the income statement, balance sheet, statement of stockholders' equity and statement of cash flows. **Management accounting** provides information to the individuals inside a business—the managers—to assist them in making decisions related to running the business. Managers have two main responsibilities:

1. **Planning** by choosing goals and deciding how to achieve them. A **budget** is a quantitative expression of the plan that helps managers coordinate their efforts to achieve the goal.
2. **Controlling** by evaluating the results of business operations by comparing the actual results to the plan.

Exhibit 19-2 in your textbook summarizes the differences between financial and management accounting.

The weighing of costs against benefits to aid decision-making is called **cost-benefit analysis**. For planning and control purposes, managers must know the costs of the products and services provided. For service businesses, the most significant cost is labor. For merchandising companies, the most significant cost will be inventory. For manufacturers, the cost of the finished product will include raw materials, labor, and all the costs related to the conversion of the raw materials into a finished good. (See Exhibit 19-3 in your text.)

Objective 2 - Describe service, merchandising, and manufacturing companies and classify their costs by value-chain element.

Service companies provide intangible services rather than tangible products. Labor makes up the largest cost for service businesses in addition to costs to develop new services, marketing costs and costs of providing customer service.

Merchandising companies resell a tangible product that they buy from suppliers. Inventory makes up the largest cost for merchandising businesses in addition to costs to research new products and locations for new stores, marketing costs, and costs of providing customer service.

Manufacturing companies use labor, plant, and equipment to convert raw materials into new, finished products. Manufacturers have three kinds of inventory:

- **Materials inventory** consists of the basic materials required to produce a finished good.
- **Work in process inventory** consists of those goods that have begun the manufacturing process, but are still in the process of being converted into a finished product.
- **Finished goods inventory** refers to those products that have been completed and are ready for sale.

The **value chain** refers to those business activities that result in value being added to a company's product. There are six elements of the value chain:

1. **Research and development:** Researching and developing new or improved products or services, or the processes for producing them.
2. **Design:** Detailed engineering of products and services, or the processes for producing them.
3. **Production or purchases:** Resources used to produce a product or service, or to purchase finished merchandise.
4. **Marketing:** Promotion of products or services.
5. **Distribution:** Delivery of products or services.
6. **Customer service:** Support provided for customers after the sale.

Review Exhibit 19-4 in your text to become familiar with the elements of the "value chain."

Objective 3 - Distinguish among (a) direct costs and indirect costs; and (b) full product costs, inventoriable product costs, and period costs.

Controlling costs throughout the entire chain is of primary importance to managers. In manufacturing, the term "cost" has a variety of meanings, determined by the context in which it is used.

Direct costs are costs which can be traced to cost objects, whereas **indirect costs** are costs which cannot be traced to cost objects. A **cost object** can be anything for which a separate measurement of cost is desired. Therefore, the important consideration in distinguishing direct from indirect costs is the specific cost object. Consider the calculator you use in this accounting course. If it is the cost object, then some of the direct costs will be its plastic casing, the container and packing material in which it was sold, the components inside which make it work, and batteries (if they were included when you purchased it). In other words, each of the costs mentioned can be traced directly to the calculator. However, these are not the only costs involved in the calculator's manufacture. For instance, the building in which the calculator was produced is also a cost, but its cost cannot be traced directly to the calculator. Therefore, the building is an indirect cost. Obviously, if the cost object changes, the assignment of costs as direct or indirect will also change.

The term **product costs** refers to the costs of producing or purchasing goods intended for sale. The two types of product costs are:

- **Full product costs** that include *all* the costs of all resources used throughout the value chain.
- **Inventoriable product costs** refer to only those costs that GAAP requires companies to treat as assets for external reporting purposes. These costs are not expensed until the product is sold.

For a merchandiser, inventoriable product costs are only those included as Inventory (an asset) until the product is sold, at which time they become part of Cost of Goods Sold. Therefore, inventoriable product costs for a merchandiser would include the actual price paid for the product plus the freight costs. Any other related costs (advertising, sales salaries, etc.) are not inventoriable. These "other" related costs are classified as **period costs**—ones that are expensed immediately and appear on the income statement in the period in which they are incurred. They never become part of the asset account Inventory. Exhibit 19-5 illustrates full product costs, inventoriable product costs and period costs for a merchandising business.

For a manufacturing company, the inventoriable product costs are more complex. This is due to the manufacturing process of taking raw materials and converting them into a finished product.

The inventoriable product costs for a manufacturing business include:

Direct materials 1) must become a physical part of the finished product and 2) their costs must be separately and conveniently traceable to the finished product.

Direct labor is the compensation of the employees who physically convert materials into finished goods.

Manufacturing overhead includes all manufacturing costs other than direct materials and direct labor. Manufacturing overhead costs include:

- **Indirect materials** are materials used to manufacture a product but are not conveniently traceable to specific finished products.
- **Indirect labor** consists of the wages and salaries of all factory workers who are not directly involved in converting material into finished goods.
- **Other indirect manufacturing overhead costs** such as plant rent, insurance, and property taxes.

Prime costs are the sum of direct materials plus direct labor.
Conversion costs are the sum of direct labor plus manufacturing overhead.

(Review carefully Exhibit 19-6 in your text.)

Objective 4 - Prepare the financial statements of a manufacturing company.

Computing cost of goods manufactured:

1) Cost of goods manufactured = Beginning work in process inventory + Total manufacturing costs - Ending work in process inventory

2) Total manufacturing costs = Direct materials used + Direct labor + Manufacturing overhead

3) Direct materials used = Beginning materials inventory + Purchases - Ending materials inventory

Familiarize yourself with Exhibit 19-11 to be sure you understand how to compute cost of goods manufactured. Study the diagram below. It will help you to understand the flow of inventory costs through a manufacturing company.

DIRECT MATERIALS (DM)	WORK IN PROCESS (WIP)	FINISHED GOODS (FG)

Beginning inventory-DM
+ Purchases
	Beginning inventory-WIP
	+ Direct material used
	    Direct labor
	    Manufacturing overhead
		Beginning inventory-FG
		+ Cost of goods manufactured

Direct materials
  available for use
- Ending inventory-DM
	Total manufacturing costs
	  to account for
	- Ending inventory-WIP
		Goods available for sale
		- Ending inventory-FG

Direct materials
  used
	Cost of goods
	  manufactured
		Cost of goods sold

All of the costs that flow through manufacturing inventories are **inventoriable costs**. **Period costs** are not traced through the inventory accounts. They are accounted for as operating expenses and include selling expenses and general and administrative expenses.

Study the Decision Guidelines titled *Building Blocks of Management Accounting* to further your understanding of the concepts introduced through Objective 4.

Objective 5 – Identify trends in the business environment, and use cost-benefit analysis to make business decisions.

Business operations and management accounting are being influenced by the following trends in the business environment:

1. A shift towards a service economy
2. Competing in the global marketplace
3. Time-based competition (including electronic commerce and just-in-time management)
4. Total quality management

As the economy becomes more service oriented, managers will need increasing amounts of information about the costs of providing services thereby enabling the companies to more competitively price those services.

Global markets provide a more competitive business environment requiring companies to possess more accurate information for decision-making. Companies must decide whether to expand into foreign countries and consider the costs of manufacturing their products domestically versus the costs of manufacturing abroad.

Time-based competition refers to meeting the demands of consumers who demand quality and want the products they order delivered quickly. The Internet, electronic commerce (e-commerce), email and express delivery have enhanced the speed at which business is conducted. **Supply chain management** is the exchange of information between suppliers and customers in an effort to reduce costs, improve quality, and speed delivery of goods and services from suppliers, through the company itself, and on to customers. The **just-in-time (JIT) management philosophy** has been adopted by many companies. Originally developed in Japan by Toyota, JIT emphasizes scheduling production precisely to meet demands thereby eliminating the costs associated with excess raw materials and finished goods inventory. Doing so means the **throughput time** (the length of time from the purchase of raw materials to the actual sale of a finish product) is drastically reduced. Obviously, the shorter the time commitment, the lower the costs. Careful analysis, frequently using present value tables, can assist managers in analyzing the costs and benefits of adopting JIT.

As competition becomes global, customers will be attracted to those products providing the highest quality. **Total quality management** is a philosophy whereby employees not only strive for top quality, but also attempt to insure their success through a program of continuous improvement. Ethical behavior is a key indicator of quality.

Objective 6 – Use reasonable standards to make ethical judgments.

Everyone is faced with ethical dilemmas. Occasionally, the correct decision (i.e., the ethical decision) is not always clear-cut, particularly when there might be adverse consequences to your decisions. Both the Institute of Management Accountants (IMA) and the American Institute of Certified Public Accountants (AICPA) have adopted Standards of Ethical Conduct that serve as guidelines for accounting professionals. The IMA Standards of Ethical Conduct for Management Accountants include competence, confidentiality, integrity and objectivity.

TEST YOURSELF

All the self-testing materials in this chapter focus on information and procedures that your instructor is likely to test in quizzes and examinations.

I. Matching   *Match each numbered term with its lettered definition.*

_____ 1. Budget
_____ 2. Direct labor
_____ 3. Direct materials
_____ 4. Manufacturing overhead
_____ 5. Indirect materials
_____ 6. Indirect labor
_____ 7. Continuous improvement
_____ 8. Cost-benefit analysis
_____ 9. Period costs
_____ 10. Inventoriable product cost

_____ 11. Supply chain management
_____ 12. Materials inventory
_____ 13. Conversion costs
_____ 14. Just-in-time production
_____ 15. Total quality management
_____ 16. Value chain
_____ 17. Work in process inventory
_____ 18. Finished goods inventory
_____ 19. Prime costs
_____ 20. Cost object

A. Companies exchange of information between suppliers and customers in an effort to reduce costs, improve quality, and speed deliver of goods and services from suppliers, through the company itself, and on to customers.
B. Sequence that adds value to a firm's products or services
C. Direct labor plus manufacturing overhead
D. The weighing of costs against benefits to aid in decision making
E. All manufacturing costs other than direct materials and direct labor
F. A philosophy requiring employees to continually look for ways to improve performance
G. All costs of a product that are regarded as an asset for financial reporting
H. Quantitative expression of a plan of action that helps managers to coordinate and implement that plan
I. Completed goods that have not yet been sold
J. Cost of salaries and wages for the employees who physically convert materials into the company's products
K. Costs that are never traced through the inventory accounts
L. Manufacturing labor costs which are difficult to trace to specific products
M. Goods that are in production but not complete at the end of the period
N. Manufacturing materials whose costs cannot easily be traced to a particular finished product
O. Material that becomes a physical part of a finished product and whose cost is separately and conveniently traceable through the manufacturing process to finished goods
P. Materials on hand to be used in the manufacturing process
Q. A system in which a company schedules production just in time to satisfy needs
R. A philosophy of satisfying customers by providing them with superior products and services
S. Anything for which a separate measurement of costs is desired
T. Direct materials plus direct labor

II. Multiple Choice   *Circle the best answer.*

1. If cost of goods manufactured exceeds total manufacturing costs, which of the following must be true?

   A. Finished goods inventory has increased
   B. Finished goods inventory has decreased
   C. Work in process inventory has decreased
   D. Work in process inventory has increased

2. If finished goods inventory has increased, which of the following must be true?

   A. Total manufacturing costs are more than cost of goods manufactured
   B. Total manufacturing costs are less than cost of goods manufactured
   C. Cost of goods sold is less than cost of goods manufactured
   D. Cost of goods sold is more than cost of goods manufactured

3. Which inventory account reflects the costs of products that have been started but not completed?

   A. Materials inventory
   B. Work in process inventory
   C. Finished goods inventory
   D. Manufacturing overhead

4. Total manufacturing costs equals:

   A. direct materials used plus direct labor plus manufacturing overhead.
   B. beginning finished goods inventory plus cost of goods manufactured.
   C. beginning work in process plus direct materials plus direct labor plus manufacture overhead.
   D. beginning finished goods plus cost of goods manufactured less ending finished goods inventory.

5. Which of the following would not be included in manufacturing overhead?

   A. Factory utilities
   B. Repairs to manufacturing equipment
   C. Property taxes on the factory
   D. Supplies used in the warehouse

6. If beginning finished goods inventory is $55,000, ending finished goods inventory is $40,000, and cost of goods sold is $385,000, then cost of goods manufactured must be:

   A. $480,000
   B. $400,000
   C. $370,000
   D. Cannot be determined

7. Which of the following is not an inventoriable product cost?

   A. Indirect labor
   B. Direct labor
   C. Sales commissions
   D. Direct materials

8. Which of the following accounts would not be found in a merchandiser's records?

   A. Supplies
   B. Merchandise Inventory
   C. Work in Process Inventory
   D. Depreciation Expense

9. Which of the following is a period cost?

   A. Materials used   C. Depreciation expense - manufacturing
   B. Office salary expense   D. Manufacturing wages expense

10. Throughput time refers to:

   A. the time between selling a product and collecting the receivable.
   B. the time between purchasing raw materials and completing the finished product.
   C. the time between purchasing raw materials and placing those materials into production.
   D. the time between purchasing raw materials and selling the finished product.

III. Completion   *Complete each of the following.*

1. The two primary responsibilities of managers are_____ and
   _____.
2. The inventory accounts of a manufacturing firm will include _____,
   _____, and _____ inventories.
3. _____ are a physical part of the finished product and their cost is
   separately and conveniently traceable through the manufacturing process.
4. Indirect materials and indirect labor are part of _____.
5. _____ are also called inventoriable costs.
6. _____ are never traced through the inventory accounts.
7. A reduction in throughput time is a feature of _____ management
   philosophy.
8. Prime costs include _____ and _____.
9. Conversion costs include _____ and _____.
10. The philosophy of delighting customers by providing them with superior products and services is
    referred to as _____.

IV. Daily Exercises

1. If cost of goods manufactured was $240,000, and beginning and ending Work in Process Inventories
   were $18,000 and $21,000 respectively, what were total manufacturing costs?

2. Work in Process Inventory increased $4,000 during the year for a manufacturing company. Total
   manufacturing costs were $305,000. What was Cost of Goods Manufactured?

3. Given the following information, calculate total Manufacturing Overhead:

Factory Building Depreciation	$ 50,000
Sales Office Expense	4,400
Factory Equipment Depreciation	21,900
Advertising Expense	51,000
Administrative Salaries	202,000
Property Taxes - Manufacturing	42,000
Depreciation on Delivery Equipment	17,000
Office Utilities Expense	8,200
Indirect Materials	2,700
Factory Equipment Repair Expense	6,600
Indirect Labor	12,500
Utilities Expense - Manufacturing	9,100

4. Given the following information, determine the amount of direct materials used.

Raw Material Inventory, 12/31	$ 15,000
Freight-In	1,200
Materials Returns	10,300
Raw Materials Inventory, 1/1	17,800
Discounts on Materials Purchases	3,480
Raw Material Purchases	109,740

5. Review the information in Daily Exercise #4 above and calculate total manufacturing costs, assuming direct labor was $67,580 and manufacturing overhead was $71,065.

6. Review the information in Daily Exercises #4 and #5 above and calculate cost of goods manufactured assuming Beginning Work in Process Inventory was $23,810 and Ending Work in Process Inventory was $19,770.

V. Exercises

1. The following information pertains to Ace Manufacturing, Inc., for 20X9:

Cost of Goods Sold	$425,000
Direct Materials Purchased	170,000
Direct Materials Used	158,000
Beginning Work in Process Inventory	6,000
Net increase in Work in Process Inventory	18,000

Finished Goods Inventory did not change.
Manufacturing Overhead is twice direct labor cost.

A. Compute Ending Work in Process Inventory.

B. Compute Cost of Goods Manufactured.

C. Compute Total Manufacturing Costs.

D. Compute Direct Labor and Manufacturing Overhead.

2. Using a check mark, indicate if the following list of accounts would appear in the records of a service, merchandising, or manufacturing business. Some of the accounts may appear in more than one business.

Accounts	Service	Merchandising	Manufacturing
Fees Earned			
Cost of Goods Sold			
Merchandise Inventory			
Freight-In			
Sales Discounts			
Advertising Expense			
Raw Materials Inventory			
Purchase Discounts			
Factory Wages			
Insurance Expense			
Prepaid Rent			
Work in Process Inventory			
Sales Returns			
Finished Goods Inventory			
Office Salary Expense			
Payroll Tax Expense			
Purchase Discounts			
Manufacturing Overhead			

3. Novis Company wants to adopt several quality improvement programs related to the manufacturing of electrical components. To implement the new programs, Novis expects to incur a cost of $5,750,000. A review of their current traditional system compared with the new programs indicates Novis could expect an initial cost savings of $5,000,000. Novis managers further predict they will yield additional benefits (cost savings) with a present value of a $1,867,250 that has a 70% probability of resulting while a lesser-cost savings with a present value of $1,387,100 has a 30% probability of occurring. Given this information, what are the total benefits expected from adopting the additional quality improvement programs?

Beyond the Numbers

Using the information provided in Exercise #3, was Novis' decision to implement additional quality improvement programs worthwhile?

_____

_____

_____

_____

_____

Demonstration Problems

Demonstration Problem #1

Lifestyle Liquids manufactures a variety of organic vegetable and fruit juice blends, all sold exclusively in health-food stores. During the current period, the following amounts were recorded:

Freight-In	$ 650
Insurance Expense – Delivery Trucks	1,400
Depreciation Expense – Manufacturing Equipment	2,770
Payroll Tax Expense – Manufacturing Wages	14,215
Utilities Expense – Manufacturing	9,970
Sales Salaries Expense	124,000
Advertising Expense	72,440
Fresh Organic Vegetables	189,600
Manufacturing Wage Expense – Direct	204,114
Research and Development Expenses	71,265
Miscellaneous Selling Expense	820
Fresh Organic Fruits	161,970
Sales Discounts	2,775
Fresh Vegetable/Fruit Returns	3,545
Manufacturing Supervisor Salaries	51,150
Product Design Expenses	81,735
Consumer Hotline Expense	36,000
Sales	1,937,400
Purchase Discounts	2,030
Sales Returns/Allowances	8,990
Fresh Herbs/Spices/Flavoring	810
Maintenance Expense – Manufacturing	14,930
Property Tax Expense – Manufacturing	28,790
Container Expense	104,720
Delivery Wages Expense	80,205

Requirement 1 – Using the format that follows, classify the above costs according to their place in the value chain. When you have finished, total each column.

| | Research | Design | Production | | | Marketing | Distribution | Customer Service |
			DM	DL	MO			
Freight-In								
Insurance Expense – Delivery Trucks								
Depreciation Expense – Manufacturing Equipment								
Payroll Tax Expense – Manufacturing Wages								
Utilities Expense – Manufacturing								
Sales Salaries Expense								
Advertising Expense								
Fresh Organic Vegetables								
Manufacturing Wage Expense – Direct								
Research and Development Expenses								
Miscellaneous Selling Expense								
Fresh Organic Fruits								
Sales Discounts								
Fresh Vegetable/Fruit Returns								
Manufacturing Supervisor Salaries								
Product Design Expenses								
Consumer Hotline Expense								
Sales								
Purchase Discounts								
Sales Returns/Allowances								
Fresh Herbs/Spices/Flavoring								
Maintenance Expense – Manufacturing								
Property Tax Expense – Manufacturing								
Container Expense								
Delivery Wages Expense								
Totals								

200

Requirement 2 – Calculate the following

a. Total full product costs

b. Total inventoriable product costs

c. Total prime costs

d. Total conversion costs

e. Total period costs

Demonstration Problem #2

Lifestyle Liquids had the following inventories for the period ended December 31, 20X8:

Raw Materials, 1/1	$18,680
Work in Process, 1/1	8,225
Finished Goods, 1/1	30,005
Raw Materials, 12/31	14,130
Work in Process, 12/31	7,830
Finished Goods, 12/31	34,375

Requirement 1 – In the space provided, present the annual Schedule of Cost of Goods Manufactured for Lifestyle Liquids for the year ended December 31, 20X8 using the appropriate amounts from both Demonstration Problem #1 and the inventory values listed above.

Requirement 2 – In the space provided, present the annual Income Statement for the year ended December 31, 20X8 for Lifestyle Liquids using the appropriate amounts above and from Demonstration Problem #1.

SOLUTIONS

Matching

1. H	5. N	9. K	13. C	17. M
2. J	6. L	10. G	14. Q	18. I
3. O	7. F	11. A	15. R	19. T
4. E	8. D	12. P	16. B	20. S

Multiple Choice

1.   C Recall:

                Beginning Work in Process Inventory (WIP)
        +   Total Manufacturing Costs
        -   <u>Ending Work in Process Inventory (WIP)</u>
        =   Cost of Goods Manufactured

    If cost of goods manufactured exceeds total manufacturing costs, then the net effect of Work in Process (WIP) inventory in the formula must be positive. Accordingly, beginning WIP Inventory must be greater than ending WIP Inventory. If the ending balance is smaller than the beginning balance, the inventory has decreased.

2.   C Recall:

                Beginning Finished Goods Inventory
        +   <u>Cost of Goods Manufactured</u>
        =   Goods Available for Sale
        -   <u>Ending Finished Goods Inventory</u>
        =   Cost of Goods Sold

    If Finished Goods Inventory has increased, the net effect of Finished Goods Inventory on the above formula is negative. Accordingly, Cost of Goods Sold would be less than Cost of Goods Manufactured. Answers A and B are incorrect because they do not relate to the calculation of Cost of Goods Sold.

3.   B Materials Inventory reflects the cost of the materials needed to produce a product. Finished Goods Inventory reflects the cost of goods that have been completed. Manufacturing Overhead is one of the components of the total cost of Work In Process Inventory to include the cost of indirect materials, indirect labor, and other manufacturing overhead costs.

4.   A Manufacturing costs is synonymous with inventoriable costs, i.e., direct materials, direct labor plus manufacturing overhead.

5.   D Warehouse supplies are a cost incurred after the product has been manufactured and would not be included in manufacturing overhead.

6.   C The formula is beginning finished goods inventory + cost of goods manufactured − ending finished goods inventory = cost of goods sold. $55,000 + X - $40,000 = $385,000; so X = $370,000.

7. C Inventoriable product costs = direct materials + direct labor + manufacturing overhead. Indirect labor is a component of manufacturing overhead. Sales commissions are a period cost, not a product cost.

8. C The Work in Process Inventory account relates to a manufacturer, not a merchandiser.

9. B Of those listed, only office salaries is a period cost. Materials, manufacturing depreciation, and manufacturing wages are all inventoriable costs.

10. D Throughput time refers to the time it takes a manufacturer to purchase raw materials, convert them into a finished product, and sell the finished product to the customer. Companies adopting the just-in-time system seek to decrease the throughput time on their products.

Completion

1. planning, control
2. materials, work in process, finished goods
3. Direct materials
4. manufacturing overhead
5. Product costs
6. Period costs
7. just-in-time (JIT)
8. direct materials, direct labor
9. direct labor, manufacturing overhead
10. total quality management (TQM)

Daily Exercises

1.
	Beginning Work in Process Inventory	$ 18,000
+	Total Manufacturing Costs	?
-	Ending Work in Process Inventory	21,000
=	Cost of Goods Manufactured	240,000

Total Manufacturing Costs = $243,000

2.
	Beginning Work in Process Inventory	$ X
+	Total Manufacturing Costs	305,000
-	Ending Work in Process Inventory	X + 4,000
=	Cost of Goods Manufactured	$?

X + $305,000 – (X + $4,000) = $301,000

3.

Factory Building Depreciation	$ 50,000
Factory Equipment Depreciation	21,900
Property Taxes – Manufacturing	42,000
Indirect Materials	2,700
Factory Equipment Repair Expense	6,600
Indirect Labor	12,500
Utilities Expense – Manufacturing	9,100
Total Manufacturing Overhead	$144,800

4.

Beginning Raw Materials Inventory			$17,800
Add: Raw Materials Purchases		109,740	
Freight-In		1,200	
		110,940	
Less: Returns	10,300		
Discounts	3,480	13,780	
Net Raw Materials Purchases			97,160
Raw Materials Available for Use			114,960
Less: Ending Raw Materials Inventory			15,000
Raw Materials Used			$99,960

> **Study Tip:** This format is identical to the one you learned in the Chapter 5 Appendix for cost of goods sold.

5.

Total Manufacturing Costs = Direct Materials + Direct Labor + Manufacturing Overhead

Direct Materials Used	$ 99,960
Direct Labor	67,580
Manufacturing Overhead	71,065
Total Manufacturing Costs	$238,605

6.

Cost of Goods Manufactured = Beginning Work in Process + Total Manufacturing Costs – Ending Work in Process

Beginning Work in Process Inventory	$ 23,810
Total Manufacturing Costs	238,605
	262,415
Less: Ending Work in Process Inventory	19,770
Cost of Goods Manufactured	$242,645

> **Study Tip:** Remember, "Total Manufacturing Costs" and "Cost of Goods Manufactured" are NOT synonymous terms.

Exercises

1.
A.

Ending Work in Process Inventory = Beginning Work in Process Inventory + Net increase in Work in Process Inventory

$6,000 + $18,000 = $24,000 Ending Work in Process Inventory

B.

Beginning Finished Goods (FG) Inventory + Cost of Goods Manufactured – Ending FG Inventory= COGS

Beginning FG Inventory= Ending FG Inventory

Cost of Goods Manufactured = COGS = $425,000

C.

	Beginning Work in Process Inventory	$ 6,000
+	Total Manufacturing Costs	X
-	Ending Work in Process Inventory	24,000
=	Cost of Goods Manufactured	$425,000

Total Manufacturing Costs = $443,000

D.

	Direct Materials Used	$158,000
+	Direct Labor	X
+	Manufacturing Overhead	2X
=	Total Manufacturing Costs	$443,000

3X = $285,000

 X = $95,000 (Direct Labor)

2X = $190,000 (Manufacturing Overhead)

2.

Accounts	Service	Merchandising	Manufacturing
Fees Earned	√		
Cost of Goods Sold		√	√
Merchandise Inventory		√	
Freight-In		√	√
Sales Discounts		√	√
Advertising Expense	√	√	√
Raw Materials Inventory			√
Purchase Discounts		√	√
Factory Wages			√
Insurance Expense	√	√	√
Prepaid Rent	√	√	√
Work in Process Inventory			√
Sales Returns		√	√
Finished Goods Inventory			√
Office Salary Expense	√	√	√
Payroll Tax Expense	√	√	√
Purchase Discounts		√	√
Manufacturing Overhead			√

3.

$1,867,250 × .7	=	1,307,075
$1,387,100 × .3	=	416,130
		$1,723,205 Expected Value of Additional Benefits
		5,000,000 Initial Benefit
		$6,723,205 Total benefits expected from adopting JIT

VI. Beyond the Numbers

The total benefits expected of $6,723,205 exceed the $5,750,000 cost by $973,205; therefore suggesting that the quality improvement efforts were worthwhile.

VII. Demonstration Problems

Demonstration Problem #1 Solved and Explained

Requirement 1

Item	Research	Design	Production			Marketing	Distribution	Customer Service
			DM	DL	MO			
Freight-In			$ 650					
Insurance Expense – Delivery Trucks							$ 1,400	
Depreciation Expense – Manufacturing Equipment					$ 2,770			
Payroll Tax Expense – Manufacturing Wages				$ 14,215				
Utilities Expense – Manufacturing					9,970			
Sales Salaries Expense						$124,000		
Advertising Expense						72,440		
Fresh Organic Vegetables			189,600					
Manufacturing Wage Expense – Direct				204,114				
Research and Development Expenses	$71,265							
Miscellaneous Selling Expense						820		
Fresh Organic Fruits			161,970					
Sales Discounts								
Fresh Vegetable/Fruit Returns			(3,545)					
Manufacturing Supervisor Salaries					51,150			
Product Design Expenses		$81,735						
Consumer Hotline Expense								$36,000
Sales								
Purchase Discounts			(2,030)					
Sales Returns/Allowances								
Fresh Herbs/Spices/Flavoring					810			
Maintenance Expense – Manufacturing					14,930			
Property Tax Expense – Manufacturing					28,790			
Container Expense			104,720					
Delivery Wages Expense							80,205	
Totals	$71,265	$81,735	$452,175	$218,329	$107,610	$197,260	$81,605	$36,000

209

Requirement 2

a. Total full product costs = all costs associated with the value chain

Research	$ 71,265
Design	81,735
Production – DM	452,175
Production – DL	218,329
Production – MO	107,610
Marketing	197,260
Distribution	81,605
Customer Service	36,000
Total Full Product Costs	$1,245,979

b. Total inventoriable product costs = total production costs

Direct Materials	$452,175
Direct Labor	218,329
Manufacturing Overhead	107,610
	$778,114

c. Total prime costs = direct materials + direct labor

Direct Materials	$452,175
Direct Labor	218,329
Total	$670,504

d. Total conversion costs = direct labor + manufacturing overhead

Direct Labor	$218,329
Manufacturing Overhead	107,610
Total	$325,939

e. Total period costs = total full product costs less total inventoriable product costs

Total full product costs	=	$1,245,979 (from (a) above)
Total inventoriable product costs	=	778,114 (from (b) above)
Total period costs	=	$ 467,865

210

Demonstration Problem #2 Solved

Requirement 1

Lifestyle Liquids
Schedule of Cost of Goods Manufactured
For the Year Ended December 31, 20X8

Beginning Work in Process Inventory			$ 8,225
Add: Direct Materials			
Beginning Inventory Direct Materials		$ 18,680	
Add: Purchases		457,100	
Freight-In		650	
Total		476,430	
Less: Discounts	$2,030		
Returns	3,545	5,575	
Net Direct Material Available		470,855	
Less: Ending Direct Material Inventory		14,130	
Direct Material Used			456,725
Direct Labor			218,329
Manufacturing Overhead:			
Depreciation Expense – Manufacturing Equipment		2,770	
Utilities Expense		9,970	
Supervisor Salaries		51,150	
Maintenance Expense		14,930	
Property Taxes		28,790	107,610
Total Manufacturing Costs Incurred			782,664
Total Manufacturing Costs to Account for			790,889
Less: Ending Work in Process Inventory			7,830
Cost of Goods Manufactured			$783,059

Requirement 2

Lifestyle Liquids
Income Statement
For the Year Ended December 31, 20X8

Revenues:			
Sales			$ 1,937,400
Less: Sales Discounts	$ 2,775		
Sales Returns/Allowance	8,990	11,765	
Net Sales			1,925,635
Cost of Goods Sold:			
Beginning Inventory Finished Goods		30,005	
Add: Cost of Goods Manufactured		783,059	
Goods Available for Sale		813,064	
Less: Ending Inventory Finished Goods		34,375	
Cost of Goods Sold			778,689
Gross Profit			1,146,946
Less: Operating Expenses			
Research		71,265	
Design		81,735	
Marketing		197,260	
Distribution		81,605	
Customer Service		36,000	
Total Operating Expenses			467,865
Net Income			$ 679,081

Chapter 20 - Job Costing

CHAPTER OVERVIEW

In Chapter 19, you were introduced to Management Accounting and some topics unique to manufacturing operations. We now apply that information to a specific type of cost accounting system—job costing. A second type of cost accounting system will be introduced in the next chapter —process costing. The learning objectives for this chapter are to

1. Distinguish between job costing and process costing.
2. Trace materials and labor in a manufacturer's job costing system.
3. Allocate manufacturing overhead in a manufacturer's job costing system.
4. Account for completion and sales of finished goods and adjust for under- or overallocated manufacturing overhead.
5. Assign noninventoriable costs in job costing.

CHAPTER REVIEW

Objective 1 – Distinguish between job costing and process costing.

The two major types of costing systems are **job costing and process costing**. Both types share common characteristics. For instance, both systems accumulate the same type of costs – direct materials, direct labor, and manufacturing overhead. Also, both systems average these accumulated costs over the number of units produced. The major distinguishing characteristic between the two is the cost object. As the names imply, the cost object in job costing is a job (from raw materials to finished good) whereas the cost object in process costing is a specific process, for example, blending, baking, finishing, or packaging. Review Exhibit 20-3 in your text for a comparison between the two systems. Generally, job costing requires less averaging because the output is usually less – frequently only a single unit (a large construction project, for instance) or a small number of units. Process costing, in contrast, usually results in a high number of units being "processed" so costs are averaged over a larger base. In both systems, the per unit cost is calculated the same, as follows:

$$\frac{\text{Total Costs}}{\text{Total Units}} = \text{Cost per unit}$$

Also, both job and process costing can be found in service and merchandising businesses, in addition to manufacturers. Review Exhibit 20-2 in your text that presents a matrix comparing job and process costing in service, merchandising, and manufacturing businesses.

In job costing, a job cost record is used to accumulate costs for each job. Remember that manufacturing "costs" include direct materials, direct labor, and manufacturing overhead. The job cost record continues to accumulate direct materials and direct labor until the job is complete, at which time manufacturing overhead is allocated.

Objective 2 – Trace materials and labor in a manufacturer's job costing system.

A manufacturer acquires materials by sending a purchase order to a supplier. When the materials are received, a receiving report is prepared and a journal entry is recorded:

Materials Inventory	XX	
Accounts Payable		XX

A **subsidiary materials ledger** is maintained which tracks the receipt, usage, and the balance of each materials inventory item. See Exhibit 20-6.

When a job is entered into production, a **materials requisition** is prepared to have materials transferred from inventory storage to the factory floor. See Exhibit 20-7.

The cost of direct materials is debited to Work in Process Inventory, while the cost of any indirect materials is debited to Manufacturing Overhead:

Work in Process Inventory (direct materials)	XX	
Manufacturing Overhead (indirect materials)	XX	
Materials Inventory (total materials requisitioned)		XX

This entry records the transfer of both direct and indirect materials from materials inventory to the manufacturing process. At the same time, the cost of the direct materials is entered on the job cost record. See Exhibit 20-8.

A **labor time record** (Exhibit 20-9 in your text) is used to identify the employee, accumulate the time spent on a particular job and the labor cost associated with the job.

Manufacturing wages are recorded with this entry:

Manufacturing Wages	XX	
Wages Payable		XX

Based on the information from the labor time record, the balance in the Manufacturing Wages account is allocated to direct labor and indirect labor, and recorded with this entry:

Work in Process Inventory (direct labor)	XX	
Manufacturing Overhead (indirect labor)	XX	
Manufacturing Wages (total manufacturing wages)	XX	

The direct labor costs associated with each job are posted to the appropriate job cost records. Exhibit 20-10 in your text summarizes accounting for materials and labor in job costing. Also, see the Decision Guidelines titled *Job Costing: Tracing direct materials and direct labor*.

Objective 3 - Allocate manufacturing overhead in a manufacturer's job costing system.

During the year, actual overhead costs are debited to Manufacturing Overhead as they are incurred:

Manufacturing Overhead	XX	
Various Accounts		XX

At year-end, the Manufacturing Overhead account contains all the actual overhead costs of the period. Now, we must determine how to assign these overhead costs to the products that were produced. In addition, applying overhead costs to production cannot wait until the end of each year. To enable accountants to assign manufacturing overhead costs throughout the year, a **predetermined manufacturing overhead rate** is used:

$$\text{Predetermined manufacturing overhead rate} = \frac{\text{Estimated manufacturing overhead costs}}{\text{Estimated quantity of the manufacturing overhead allocation base}}$$

To allocate manufacturing overhead accurately, the allocation base should be the primary cost driver of those overhead costs. Historically, direct labor (expressed as either dollars or hours) has been the primary cost driver in many manufacturing operations. While this remains the case in some industries, increasingly the use of a different cost driver, such as machine hours, may become the primary cost driver, especially in highly automated processes. Obviously, selecting the primary cost driver accurately will insure the most realistic total cost for each job. The steps to develop a predetermined overhead rate and allocate overhead are as follows:

1. Estimate the total overhead cost for the planning period.
2. Identify the manufacturing overhead (cost) allocation base.
3. Estimate the total quantity of the overhead allocation base.
4. Compute the predetermined manufacturing overhead rate.
5. Obtain actual quantities of the overhead allocation base used by individual jobs.
6. Allocate manufacturing overhead to jobs by multiplying the *predetermined* manufacturing overhead rate by the *actual* quantity of the allocation base used by each job.

The entry to record the allocation of overhead is:

Work in Process Inventory	XX	
Manufacturing Overhead		XX

Once overhead is allocated to a job, we can compute unit cost:

$$\frac{\text{unit}}{\text{cost}} = \frac{\text{direct materials + direct labor + overhead allocated}}{\text{number of units produced}}$$

See Exhibit 20-11 for the manufacturing overhead entry on the job cost record.

Objective 4 – Account for completion and sales of finished goods, and adjust for under- or overallocated manufacturing overhead.

As jobs are completed, they are transferred to finished goods inventory:

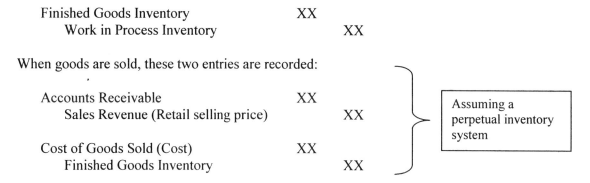

Note: The difference in these two entries represents gross profit.

Consider this T-account:

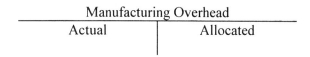

If allocated overhead is less than actual overhead (a debit balance remains), then overhead is **underallocated**. If allocated overhead is greater than actual overhead (a credit balance remains), then overhead is **overallocated**.

Insignificant amounts of over- or underallocated overhead are closed to Cost of Goods Sold at year-end. Significant amounts of over- or underallocated overhead are distributed to Work in Process Inventory, Finished Goods Inventory, and Cost of Goods Sold.

The process for distributing a significant amount of over- or under allocated overhead is called **proration**. Proration spreads the remaining debit balance (representing an underallocation) or credit balance (representing an overallocation) to the three accounts in proportion to the balance in each.

Whether significant or insignificant, the balance of the Manufacturing Overhead account should be zero at the end of the accounting period.

Review Exhibit 20-12 in your text for a summary of job costing.

Objective 5– Assign noninventoriable costs in job costing.

Recall from Chapter 19 that inventoriable costs refer to only manufacturing costs (direct materials, direct labor, and manufacturing overhead) and not to the costs incurred in other elements of the value chain. However, these non-inventoriable costs can also be traced and allocated to jobs using the same principles introduced in the preceding sections of this chapter.

As illustrated in Exhibit 20-1, both job and process costing systems can also be used by service and merchandising businesses.

Obviously, a service business will not have any direct materials assigned to particular jobs (a lawyer advising a client, a CPA preparing a tax return, or a physician examining a patient, etc.); however, direct labor can constitute a significant portion of the fee charged for the service. In addition, every service business will incur many indirect costs (rent, utilities, insurance, salaries for support staff, etc.) and these costs need to be accurately allocated to jobs if the business owner is going to have a realistic picture of business operations.

TEST YOURSELF

All the self-testing materials in this chapter focus on information and procedures that your instructor is likely to test in quizzes and examinations.

I. Matching   *Match each numbered term with its lettered definition.*

_____ 1. Predetermined manufacturing overhead rate
_____ 2. Job cost record
_____ 3. Cost driver
_____ 4. Cost allocation base
_____ 5. Cost allocation
_____ 6. Cost assignment
_____ 7. Labor time record

_____ 8. Materials requisition
_____ 9. Overallocated overhead
_____ 10. Underallocated overhead
_____ 11. Cost tracing
_____ 12. Job costing
_____ 13. Process costing
_____ 14. Time record

A. A common denominator for systematically linking indirect costs to products
B. Any factor that affects costs
C. Document used to accumulate the costs of a job
D. Request for materials, prepared by manufacturing personnel
E. Source document used primarily by employees engaging in service activities, to trace direct labor to specific jobs
F. A credit balance in manufacturing overhead after overhead has been allocated to jobs
G. System for assigning costs to large numbers of identical units that usually proceed in a continuous fashion through a series of uniform production processes
H. Estimated manufacturing overhead rate computed at the beginning of the year
I. Source document manufacturing firms commonly use to trace direct labor to specific job cost records
J. Assigning indirect costs to cost objects
K. Assigning direct costs to cost objects
L. A general term that covers both tracing direct costs and allocating indirect costs
M. A remaining debit balance in manufacturing overhead after overhead has been allocated to jobs
N. A system for assigning costs to specific units or to a small batch of products

II. Multiple Choice   *Circle the best answer.*

1. When manufacturing labor costs are incurred, the account credited is:

   A. Manufacturing Wages.
   B. Wages Payable.
   C. Manufacturing Overhead.
   D. Work In Process Inventory.

2. Which of the following is not an inventoriable cost?

   A. Manufacturing Overhead
   B. Indirect Materials
   C. Delivery Expense
   D. Direct Labor

3. Which of the following manufacturers would be most likely to use process costing?

   A. Oil refinery
   B. Contractors
   C. Aircraft
   D. Furniture

4. When indirect materials are used in production:

    A. Work In Process Inventory is debited. C. Manufacturing Overhead is debited.
    B. Manufacturing Overhead is credited. D. Materials Inventory is debited.

5. When direct materials are used in production:

    A. Work In Process Inventory is credited. C. Materials Inventory is debited.
    B. Manufacturing Overhead is debited. D. Work In Process Inventory is debited.

6. When manufacturing wages are allocated, indirect labor is:

    A. Debited to Work In Process Inventory. C. Credited to Manufacturing Overhead.
    B. Debited to Manufacturing Overhead. D. Credited to Work In Process Inventory.

7. The entry to debit Cost of Goods Sold and credit Finished Goods Inventory as sales are made is recorded in:

    A. a periodic inventory system
    B. a perpetual inventory system
    C. when goods have completed the production process
    D. both B. and C.

8. Underallocated overhead implies:

    A. a credit balance in the Manufacturing Overhead account.
    B. too little overhead was applied to production.
    C. too much overhead was applied to production.
    D. Cost of Goods Sold is overstated.

9. In a service business, which of the following is an appropriate allocation base for indirect costs?

    A. Labor hours   C. Direct materials
    B. Machine hours   D. None of the above

10. An insignificant amount of under/over allocated manufacturing overhead should be:

    A. carried forward to the next accounting period.
    B. closed to Cost of Goods Sold.
    C. reported as an "Other expenses and revenues" on the income statement.
    D. allocated proportionately to Work In Process Inventory, Finished Goods Inventory, and Cost of Goods Sold.

III. Completion   *Complete each of the following.*

1. In a job costing system, unit cost is determined by dividing _____ by _____.

2. The document used to accumulate all the costs for each job is the _____.

3. _____ are a physical part of the finished product and their cost is separately and conveniently traceable through the manufacturing process.

4. Indirect materials and indirect labor are part of _____.

5. _____ are also called inventoriable costs.

6. _____ are never traced through the inventory accounts.

7. There are two main types of accounting systems for product costing: _____ and _____.

8. The purpose of a Materials Ledger is to _____.

9. Generally, the difference between direct and indirect labor is _____.

10. Job costing is used by companies that manufacture products _____.

IV. Daily Exercises

1. Place the following in correct sequence (use 1 through 6).

    _____ A. Compute the predetermined manufacturing overhead rate
    _____ B. Estimate the total overhead cost for the planning period
    _____ C. Obtain actual quantities of the overhead allocation base used by individual jobs
    _____ D. Select a cost allocation base
    _____ E. Allocate manufacturing overhead to jobs
    _____ F. Estimate the total quantity of the overhead allocation base

2. Raw Material XX had a balance of $56,500. During November, the following requisitions were processed for XX and charged to:

Job 243	$11,550
Job 256	8,210
Job 261	14,925
Factory Maintenance	775

    Record the entry assigning Raw Material XX.

3. During November, the following manufacturing labor costs were incurred and the following time tickets were assigned:

Job 243	$ 6,250
Job 256	2,340
Job 261	5,980
Factory Maintenance	16,810

Record the entry to assign November's labor costs.

4. Review the information in Daily Exercises #2 and #3 above and assume $53,200 in manufacturing overhead costs have been incurred and recorded, exclusive of indirect materials and indirect labor. If Manufacturing Overhead is allocated at a rate of 200% of Direct Materials cost, allocate Manufacturing Overhead to Jobs 243, 256, and 261. Is Manufacturing Overhead over- or underallocated?

5. Review the information in Daily Exercises #2, #3, and #4 above but assume overhead is allocated at the rate of 450% of direct labor costs. Determine the amount of manufacturing overhead to allocate to Jobs 243, 256, and 261. Is Manufacturing Overhead over- or underallocated?

V. Exercises

1. Review the information in Daily Exercises #2, #3 and #4, assuming the number of units produced for each job were:

Job 243	200 units
Job 256	120 units
Job 261	350 units

    A. Calculate the total cost and the per unit cost for each job.

    B. Record the journal entry for the completed jobs.

2. At the end of the year, the Manufacturing Overhead account appears as follows:

    Manufacturing Overhead

280,000	292,000

    A. Was overhead under- or overallocated for the year?

    B. Assuming the balance in the overhead account is not significant, record the journal entry to close the account.

3. Given the following information, calculate total Manufacturing Overhead:

Factory Building Depreciation	$ 50,000
Sales Office Expense	4,400
Factory Equipment Depreciation	21,900
Advertising Expense	51,000
Administrative Salaries	202,000
Property Taxes - Manufacturing	42,000
Depreciation on Delivery Equipment	17,000
Office Utilities Expense	8,200
Indirect Materials	2,700
Factory Equipment Repair Expense	6,600
Indirect Labor	12,500
Utilities Expense - Manufacturing	9,100

4. Record the following journal entries in the space provided.
   a. $62,000 of direct materials was requisitioned for jobs.
   b. Direct labor costs of $32,600 were assigned to jobs.
   c. Manufacturing overhead of $18,000 was allocated to jobs.
   d. Three jobs with a total cost of $87,000 were completed.

5. Using the information in Exercise #4 above, reconstruct the Work in Process Inventory T-account and calculate the ending balance in the account, assuming a beginning balance of $12,575.

VI. Beyond the Numbers

Review the information in Daily Exercises #2 though #5 and comment on the appropriateness of direct materials or direct labor as the manufacturing overhead cost allocation base.

_____
_____
_____
_____
_____
_____
_____
_____
_____
_____
_____

VII. Demonstration Problems

Demonstration Problem #1

Pat's Pottery had the following inventory balances on January 1, 20X9:

Materials Inventory	$28,000
Work in Process Inventory	41,250
Finished Goods Inventory	62,425

The Work in Process and Finished Goods Inventory accounts consisted of the following:

Work in Process:

		Direct Materials	Direct Labor	Manufacturing Overhead	Total
Job	420	$13,280	$7,100	$3,984	$24,364
Job	423	2,700	4,860	810	8,370
Job	424	5,640	1,184	1,692	8,516
				Total	$41,250

Finished Goods:

		Cost of job:
Job	419	$24,215
Job	421	21,910
Job	422	16,300
		$62,425

During the month of January 20X9, the following transactions occurred:

A. Pat purchased 900 tons of clay (materials) for $35 per ton.

B. Workers requisitioned $38,000 of direct materials for the following jobs:

420	$4,000
423	3,200
424	2,450
425	7,100
426	14,700
427	4,300
428	2,250
	$38,000

C. $4,050 of indirect materials was used.

D. The total manufacturing wages, $10,125, were incurred and assigned to production. 80% of total manufacturing wages was direct labor. (2 entries)

Time cards indicated the direct labor cost should be assigned to the jobs as follows:

420	$ 925
423	860
424	1,270
425	1,020
426	3,110
427	585
428	330
	$ 8,100

E. The following additional overhead costs were incurred: $1,600 in depreciation on manufacturing equipment and $3,765 in miscellaneous other costs (credit Accounts Payable).

F. Overhead is allocated to production at the rate of 30% of direct materials cost.

G. Jobs 420, 423, 424, 425 and 427 were completed.

H. Jobs 419, 420, 421, 422, 424, and 425 were sold on account. The total sales price for the jobs was $186,000. Assume a perpetual inventory system.

I. The balance in Manufacturing Overhead was considered insignificant.

Required:

1. Place the January 1 balances in the inventory accounts and the Work In Process Inventory and Finished Goods Inventory subsidiary ledgers.

2. Record the transactions in the general journal and post to the job T-accounts.

3. Calculate the ending balances in the inventory accounts, the job T-accounts, and manufacturing overhead.

4. Was Manufacturing Overhead overallocated or underallocated?

5. What will be the amount of Cost of Goods Sold on the January income statement?

Requirements 1, 2 & 3 (T-accounts)

Materials Inventory	Work in Process Inventory	Finished Goods Inventory

Work in Process Inventory Subsidiary Ledger

Job 420	Job 423	Job 424

Job 425	Job 426	Job 427

Job 428

Finished Goods Inventory Subsidiary Ledger

Job 419

Job 420

Job 421

Job 422

Requirement 2 (record transactions)

Date	Accounts and Explanation	PR	Debit	Credit

Requirement 3 (overhead)

Manufacturing Overhead account:

Manufacturing Overhead

Requirement 4 (overhead)

Manufacturing overhead is _____.

Requirement 5 (cost of goods sold)

Cost of Goods Sold

Demonstration Problem #2

Review your solution to Demonstration Problem #1 and present a Schedule of Cost of Goods Manufactured for Pat's Pottery for the month ended January 31, 20X9.

SOLUTIONS

I. Matching

1. H	5. J	9. F	13. G
2. C	6. L	10. M	14. E
3. B	7. I	11. K	
4. A	8. D	12. N	

II. Multiple Choice

1. B   Manufacturing Wages is debited when direct labor is *incurred* and Wages Payable is credited. When Manufacturing Wages are *assigned* to jobs, Manufacturing Overhead is debited for indirect labor Work in Process Inventory is debited for direct labor and Manufacturing Wages is credited.

2. C   Delivery Expense is a non-inventoriable cost.

3. A   Manufacturers producing a continuous flow of the same product use process costing. Of the manufacturers listed, the oil refinery is most likely to produce the same product in a continuous flow.

4. C   The use of indirect materials requires Materials Inventory to be reduced and Manufacturing Overhead to be increased. The journal entry is:

Manufacturing Overhead	XX	
Materials Inventory		XX

5. D   The journal entry for the use of direct materials is:

Work in Process Inventory	XX	
Materials Inventory		XX

6. B   Recall that manufacturing wages are cleared through a clearing account so that direct labor and indirect labor can be allocated properly. In recording the payroll allocation, Work in Process Inventory is debited for direct labor and Manufacturing Overhead is debited for indirect labor.

7. B   Only a perpetual inventory system has a Cost of Goods Sold account.

8. B   If overhead is underallocated, actual overhead costs were greater than overhead allocated to Work in Process Inventory. Accordingly, the debits to Manufacturing Overhead are greater than the credits, and Manufacturing Overhead will have a debit balance.

9. A   Labor hours are used to allocate indirect costs in a service businesses. Machine hours would be more appropriate allocation base in a manufacturing business.

10. B   When the amount of under/overallocated manufacturing overhead is insignificant it is closed to Cost of Goods Sold.

III. Completion

1. total costs assigned to a job, number of units completed (order important)
2. job cost record
3. direct materials
4. manufacturing overhead
5. Product costs
6. Period costs
7. job costing, process costing
8. maintain accurate records for each raw material
9. direct labor can be traced directly to the units being manufactured
10. as individual units or in small batches

IV. Daily Exercises

1. A. 4   D. 2
   B. 1   E. 6
   C. 5   F. 3

2.
Work in Process Inventory	34,685	
Manufacturing Overhead	775	
Raw Materials Inventory		35,460

3.
Work in Process Inventory	14,570	
Manufacturing Overhead	16,810	
Manufacturing Wages		31,380

4.

Total manufacturing overhead (MOH) incurred =	$53,200 + $775 (from Daily Exercise #2) + $16,810 (from Daily Exercise #3) = $70,785

Manufacturing Overhead allocated to jobs:
Job 243   = $11,550 × 200% = $23,100
Job 256   = $ 8,210 × 200% = 16,420
Job 261   = $14,925 × 200% = 29,850
                           $69,370 Allocated to Work in Process Inventory

Total MOH incurred –Total MOH allocated to production = Over- or Underallocated Overhead
$70,785 - $69,370 = $1,415 Underallocated

4. Total manufacturing (MOH) overhead incurred = $70,785 (from Daily Exercise #4)

Manufacturing Overhead allocated to jobs:
Job 243   = $6,250 × 450% = $28,125
Job 256   = $2,340 × 450% = 10,530
Job 261   = $5,980 × 450% = 26,910
                           $65,165

Total MOH incurred –Total MOH allocated to production = Over- or Underallocated Overhead
$70,785 - $65,165 = $5,620 Underallocated

V. Exercises

1. A.

	Job 243	Job 256	Job 261
Direct Materials	$11,550	$8,210	$14,925
Direct Labor	6,250	2,340	5,980
Manufacturing Overhead	23,571	16,755	30,459
Total Costs	$41,371	$27,305	$51,364
Divided by units	÷ 200	÷ 120	÷ 350
Unit Cost	$206.86	$227.54	$146.75

B. Finished Goods Inventory   120,040

    Work in Process Inventory   120,040

This could also be recorded as separate entries for each of the three jobs.

2. A. Overallocated

Study Tip:	debit balance	=	underallocated overhead
	credit balance	=	overallocated overhead

B. Manufacturing Overhead   12,000

    Cost of Goods Sold   12,000

Study Tip: Because too much overhead was allocated to jobs throughout the year, the cost of goods sold account contains more overhead than was actually incurred. Therefore, it needs to be reduced by the amount of the overallocation.

3.

Factory Building Depreciation	$ 50,000
Factory Equipment Depreciation	21,900
Property Taxes - Manufacturing	42,000
Indirect Materials	2,700
Factory Equipment Repair Expense	6,600
Indirect Labor	12,500
Utilities Expense - Manufacturing	9,100
Total Manufacturing Overhead	$144,800

4.

a. Work in Process Inventory	62,000	
Materials Inventory		62,000
b. Work in Process Inventory	32,600	
Manufacturing Wages		32,600
c. Work in Process Inventory	18,000	
Manufacturing Overhead		18,000
d. Finished Goods Inventory	87,000	
Work in Process Inventory		87,000

5.

```
                    Work in Process Inventory
              Bal. 12,575 |
                 (a) 62,000 |      87,000   (d)
                 (b) 32,600 |
                 (c) 18,000 |
              Bal 38,175   |
```

VI. Beyond the Numbers

In many respects, the question is unfair because one would need a great deal of additional information before one could determine if direct materials or direct labor are the appropriate cost drivers to use as the manufacturing overhead allocation base. However, as you were given just the two choices, it should be apparent that direct materials is the more appropriate of the two. Why? First, a comparison of the two total amounts reveals the cost of direct materials is over twice the amount of direct labor. Second, the total direct labor charged to the jobs is even less than the indirect labor charged to manufacturing overhead. Therefore, between the two, direct materials would appear to be the more appropriate cost driver.

VII. Demonstration Problems

Demonstration Problem #1 Solved and Explained

Requirements 1, 2 & 3 (T-accounts)

Materials Inventory			Work in Process Inventory			Finished Goods Inventory		
1/1 28,000	38,000	B.	1/1 41,250	73,275	G.	1/1 63,425	116,135	H.
A. 31,500	4,050	C.	B. 38,000			G. 73,275		
Bal. 17,450			D. 8,100			Bal.19,565		
			F. 11,400					
			Bal. 25,475					

Work in Process Inventory Subsidiary Ledger

Job 420			Job 423			Job 424		
1/1 24,364	30,489	G.	1/1 8,370	13,390	G.	1/1 8,516	12,971	G.
B. 4,000			B. 3,200			B. 2,450		
D. 925			D. 860			D. 1,270		
F. 1,200			F. 960			F. 735		

Job 425			Job 426			Job 427		
B. 7,100	10,250	G.	B. 14,700			B. 4,300	6,175	G.
D. 1,020			D. 3,110			D. 585		
F. 2,130			F. 4,410			F. 1,290		
			Bal. 22,220					

Job 428	
B. 2,250	
D. 330	
F. 675	
Bal. 3,255	

Finished Good Inventory Subsidiary Ledger

Job 419		Job 420		Job 421	
1/1 24,215	24,215 H.	1/1 30,489	30,489 H.	1/1 21,910	21,910 H.

Job 422		Job 423		Job 424	
1/1 16,300	16,300 H.	G. 13,390		G. 12,971	12,971 H.

Job 425		Job 427	
G. 10,250	10,250 H.	G. 6,175	

Requirement 2 (record transactions)

		Accounts and Explanation	PR	Debit	Credit
A.		Material Inventory		31,500	
		Accounts Payable			31,500
B.		Work in Process Inventory		38,000	
		Materials Inventory			38,000
C.		Manufacturing Overhead		4,050	
		Materials Inventory			4,050
D.		Manufacturing Wages		10,125	
		Wages Payable			10,125
		Work in Process Inventory (.80 × $10,125)		8,100	
		Manufacturing Overhead (.20 × $10,125)		2,025	
		Manufacturing Wages			10,125
E.		Manufacturing Overhead		5,365	
		Accumulated Depreciation-Manufacturing Equip.			1,600
		Accounts Payable			3,765
F.		Work in Process Inventory (.30 × $38,000)		11,400	
		Manufacturing Overhead			11,400
G.		Finished Goods Inventory		73,275	
		Work in Process Inventory			73,275
H.		Accounts Receivable		186,000	
		Sales Revenue			186,000

	Cost of Goods Sold		116,135	
	Finished Goods Inventory			116,135
I.	Cost of Goods Sold		40	
	Manufacturing Overhead			40

Points to Remember

In transaction D, it is important to distinguish between direct labor and indirect labor. Direct labor is 80% of the total manufacturing wages of $10,125, or $8,100. The remaining amount is indirect labor.

In transaction F, it is important to note that overhead is allocated based on *direct materials*. The only direct materials in this problem are the $38,000 of direct materials in transaction B.

To prepare the entry for item I, it is necessary to know the balance in the Manufacturing Overhead account:

```
          Manufacturing Overhead
        (C) 4,050   |
        (D) 2,025   |
        (E) 5,365   |  (F) 11,400
        ───────────────────────────
        Bal.   40   |  (I)     40
        Bal.    0   |
```

Since the account has a debit balance, we credit it in order to bring its balance to zero, and transfer the balance to Cost of Goods Sold.

Requirement 3 See T-account for Manufacturing Overhead above.

Requirement 4 (overhead)

A debit balance in the Manufacturing Overhead account indicates that Manufacturing Overhead is underallocated. The T-account in requirement 3 indicates that Manufacturing Overhead had a debit balance of $40 prior to closing the account.

Requirement 5 (cost of goods sold)

```
              Cost of Goods Sold
        (H) 116,135   |
        (I)      40   |
        ──────────────────────────
        Bal. 116,175  |
```

Demonstration Problem #2 Solved and Explained

Pat's Pottery
Schedule of Cost of Goods Manufactured
Month Ended January 31, 20X9

Beginning work in process inventory			$41,250
Direct materials			
Beginning inventory	$28,000		
(A) Purchases of direct materials	27,450		
Materials available for use	55,450		
Less: Ending inventory	17,450		
Direct materials used		$38,000	
Direct labor		8,100	
Manufacturing overhead			
Indirect materials	4,050		
Indirect labor	2,025		
Depreciation - factory equipment	1,600		
Miscellaneous	3,765		
(B) Total manufacturing overhead		11,440	
Total manufacturing costs incurred			57,540
Total manufacturing costs to account for			98,790
Less: Ending work in process inventory			25,475
(C) Cost of goods manufactured			$73,315

A. Because we only include 'direct materials purchased' in this section, the total materials purchased ($31,500) have been reduced by the amount of indirect materials used ($4,050).

B. Total manufacturing overhead includes the actual costs *incurred*, not the actual amount allocated.

C. The cost of goods manufactured shown on the schedule ($73,315) differs from the amount recorded in entry (G) ($73,275) for the following reasons:

$73,275 is the amount which includes the *allocated* manufacturing overhead, not the actual overhead incurred. After entry (I) is recorded and posted, the Cost of Goods sold account is increased because manufacturing overhead was underallocated (i.e. too little was allocated to production).

Study Tip: Remember, Finished Goods Inventory does not appear on this schedule. They are reported on the Income Statement and used to calculate Cost of Goods Sold.

Chapter 21 - Process Costing

CHAPTER OVERVIEW

In Chapter 20 you were introduced to job costing. Now, we turn our attention to a second system found in many manufacturing operations—process costing. Process costing is more complex than job costing, and both systems assume an understanding of manufacturing accounting. Therefore, it is important that you are familiar with the material in Chapters 19 and 20 in order to master these concepts. The learning objectives for this chapter are to

1. Distinguish between the flow of costs in process costing and job costing.
2. Compute equivalent units of production.
3. Use process costing to assign costs to units completed and to units in ending Work in Process Inventory inventory.
4. Use the weighted-average method to assign costs to units completed and to units in ending work in process inventory in a second department.

Appendix to Chapter 21: The FIFO Costing Method

CHAPTER REVIEW

Objective 1 - Distinguish between the flow of costs in process costing and job costing.

Process costing assigns costs to goods produced in a continuous sequence of steps called processes. With process costing, costs are accumulated for a period of time, such as a week or a month. This contrasts with a **job cost system**, which accumulates costs for a specific job or specific batches of product.

With process costing, a product typically passes through several departments. For each department, there is a separate Work in Process Inventory account. (In a job costing system, there is one Work in Process Inventory account supported by job cost records for the various jobs.) Review Panels A and B in Exhibit 21-1 for a summary of the differences between process and job cost systems. Exhibit 21-3 illustrates the flow of costs in a process costing system.

Objective 2 - Compute equivalent units of production.

The objective in process costing is to allocate the costs of production between the cost of goods that have been completed and the cost of incomplete units. As we have seen before, the cost of completed goods is found in Finished Goods Inventory and the cost of incomplete units is found in Work in Process Inventory. Companies that use process costing use two categories of manufacturing costs:

1. Direct materials
2. Conversion costs (direct labor plus manufacturing overhead)

When a company has Work in Process Inventory that consists of partially completed goods, **equivalent units of production** are used to measure the amount of work done during a period in terms of fully complete units of output.

To calculate equivalent units, you must know whether direct materials are added at the beginning or the end of the production process, and you must assume that conversion costs are incurred evenly throughout the production process. Then, multiply the number of partially completed units by their percentage of completion. Equivalent units must be determined for both direct materials and conversion costs.

The **steps in process costing accounting for the first process when there is no beginning inventory** may be summarized as follows:

Step 1: Summarize the flow of physical units.

Total **physical units <u>to account</u> for** = Beginning Work in Process Inventory + Production started during the period.

Total **physical units <u>accounted</u> for** = Units completed and transferred out during the period + Ending Work in Process Inventory.

Units <u>to account</u> for must equal units <u>accounted</u> for.

Step 2: Compute output in terms of equivalent units.

Compute equivalent units separately for direct materials and conversion costs. Remember that this is necessary because the percentage of completion may be different for materials and conversion costs. Exhibit 21-5 in your text reviews Steps 1 and 2.

Step 3: Summarize total costs to account for.

Total costs to account for = Cost of Beginning Work in Process Inventory + Direct materials + Direct labor + Manufacturing overhead. Review Exhibit 21-7.

Objective 3 - Use process costing to assign costs to units completed and to units in ending work in process inventory inventory.

Step 4: Compute the cost per equivalent unit.

Compute separate unit costs for direct materials and conversion costs: (i.e., make two separate calculations):

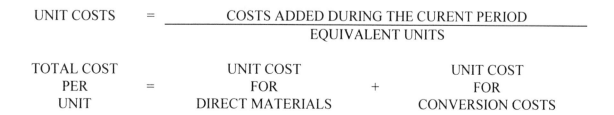

241

Review Exhibit 21-8.

Step 5: Assign costs to units completed and to units in ending Work in Process Inventory Inventory.

The unit costs from Step 4 are applied to units completed and to units in ending Work in Process Inventory. Cost of units completed and transferred out = units completed and transferred out times total unit costs.

Cost of Ending Work in Process Inventory = (equivalent units of ending Work in Process Inventory for direct materials × unit cost for direct materials) + (equivalent units of ending Work in Process Inventory for conversion costs × unit cost for conversion costs).

Review Exhibit 21-9. Note that the total costs accounted for in Step 5 must agree with the total costs from Step 3.

Process costing typically accounts for **direct materials** and **conversion costs**. Recall that conversion costs represent the sum of direct labor plus manufacturing overhead. The journal entries used for process costing are very similar to those used for job costing.

To record current period costs:

Work in Process Inventory - Dept. 1	XXX	
Materials Inventory		XX
Manufacturing Wages		XX
Manufacturing Overhead		XX

To record the transfer to the next department:

Work in Process Inventory - Dept. 2	XX	
Work in Process Inventory - Dept. 1		XX

Additional materials and conversion costs may be added in subsequent departments.

> **Helpful hint:** You may find it helpful to trace through the mid-chapter review problem in your text.

Objective 5 - Use the weighted-average method to assign costs to units completed and to units in ending work in process inventory in a second department.

When working with multiple departments, it is important to distinguish between costs from the prior department and costs in the current department. Remember that the costs follow the units from one department to the next.

All costs in a department that were incurred in a prior department are called **transferred-in costs**. Only costs in the current department are accounted for as material or conversion costs in that department. Let's see what happens when beginning Work in Process Inventory exists and the weighted-average method is used to assign costs to units completed and to units in ending Work in Process Inventory in a second processing department.

Step 1: Summarize the flow of physical units.

With a second department, rather than units started in production we use units transferred in. This follows the flow of production in physical units.

Total units <u>to account</u> for = Beginning Work in Process Inventory + Units transferred in.

Total units <u>accounted</u> for = Units completed and transferred out + Ending Work in Process Inventory.

Note that total units to account for must equal total units accounted for.

Step 2: Compute output in terms of equivalent units.

When computing equivalent units for a second department, there are three categories: transferred-in equivalent units, direct materials equivalent units, and conversion costs equivalent units. For each category, equivalent units are computed for 1) units completed and transferred out, and 2) units in ending inventory.

Study Exhibits 21-11 and 21-12 in your text to be sure you understand equivalent unit computations in a multiple department process costing system.

Steps 3 and 4: Summarize total costs to account for and compute cost per equivalent unit.

These steps are similar to what is done for a single department with no beginning inventory. To calculate the total cost per category take the costs related to the Beginning Inventory plus any costs added during the current period. The cost per equivalent unit is calculated by taking the total cost per category and dividing by the respective equivalent units per category.

Review Exhibit 21-13.

Step 5: Assign costs to units completed and to units in ending Work in Process Inventory Inventory.

The unit costs from Step 4 are applied to units completed and to units in ending Work in Process Inventory. Cost of units completed and transferred out = units completed and transferred out times total unit costs.

Cost of Ending Work in Process Inventory = (equivalent units for units transferred in × unit cost for units transferred in) + (equivalent units of ending Work in Process Inventory for direct materials × unit cost for direct materials) + (equivalent units of Ending Work in Process Inventory for conversion costs × unit cost for conversion costs).

Review Exhibit 21-14. Note that the total costs accounted for in Step 5 must agree with the total costs from Step 3.

The journal entries to record costs in a second department are:

Work in Process Inventory - Dept. 2	XX	
Materials Inventory		XX

Manufacturing Wages	XX	
Manufacturing Overhead	XX	

The entry to record the transfer of completed units to Finished Goods Inventory (or to a subsequent department) is:

Finished Goods Inventory (or Work in Process Inventory - Dept. 3)	XX	
Work in Process Inventory - Dept. 2		XX

A **production cost report** summarizes the operations in a department during the period. Exhibit 21-16 in your text presents a production cost report incorporating all the information contained in the five steps outlined above. Study it carefully.

BY THIS POINT IN YOUR STUDY OF THIS CHAPTER YOU SHOULD HAVE THE FIVE STEPS COMMITTED TO MEMORY:

Step 1: Compute physical units.

Step 2: Compute equivalent units.

Step 3: Summarize total costs.

Step 4: Compute equivalent unit cost.

Step 5: Assign total cost to units completed and units in ending inventory.

Appendix to Chapter 21: The FIFO Costing Method

Objective 5 - Account for a second processing department by the FIFO method.

When working with multiple departments, it is important to distinguish between costs from the prior department and costs in the current department. Remember that the costs follow the units from department to department.

All costs in a department that were incurred in prior department are called **transferred-in costs**. Only costs in the current department are accounted for as material or conversion costs in that department.

When beginning Work in Process Inventory exists and the FIFO (first-in, first-out) method is used, certain changes occur in the five steps used in the application of process costing:

Step 1: Flow of production in physical units.

With a second department, units transferred in replace units started. This follows the flow of production in physical units.

Total units to account for = Beginning Work in Process Inventory + Units transferred in.

Total units accounted for = Units from beginning Work in Process Inventory completed and transferred out + units transferred in, completed and transferred out during the current period + ending Work in Process Inventory.

Note that total units to account for must equal total units accounted for. *Note also that the FIFO method requires the separation of completed units into units from beginning inventory and units started and completed during the period.*

Review Exhibits 21A-1 and 21A-2.

Step 2: Equivalent units of production.

When computing equivalent units, there are three categories: transferred-in equivalent units, direct materials equivalent units, and conversion costs equivalent units. For each category, equivalent units are computed for 1) units from beginning inventory that were completed and transferred out, 2) units started (transferred in) and completed during the period, and 3) units in ending inventory.

Note that equivalent unit computation for units completed from beginning inventory is equal to the percentage of work done during the current month (subtract the percentage completed during the prior month from 100%).

Study Exhibit 21A-2 in your text to be sure you understand equivalent unit computations using FIFO in a multiple department process costing system.

Step 3 and 4: Summarize total costs to account for and compute cost per equivalent unit.

These steps are similar to what is done for a single department with no beginning inventory. When performing Step 4, remember that costs associated with beginning Work in Process are NOT included in the unit cost calculation.

Review Exhibit 21A-3

Step 5: Assign costs to units completed and to units in ending work in process.

The unit costs from Step 4 are applied to units completed and to units in ending Work in Process Inventory.

Cost of units completed and transferred out = (cost of Beginning Work in Process Inventory) + (equivalent units of Beginning Work in Process Inventory for direct materials × unit cost for direct materials) + (equivalent units of Beginning Work in Process Inventory for conversion costs s × unit cost for conversion costs) + the units started and completed times total unit costs.

Cost of Ending Work in Process Inventory = (equivalent units of Ending Work in Process Inventory for direct materials × unit cost for direct materials) + (equivalent units of Ending Work in Process Inventory for conversion costs × unit cost for conversion costs).

The journal entries to record costs in a second department are:

Work in Process Inventory - Dept. 2   XX
    Materials Inventory   XX
    Manufacturing Wages   XX
    Manufacturing Overhead   XX

The entry to record the transfer of completed units to Finished Goods Inventory (or to a subsequent department) is:

    Finished Goods Inventory (or Work in Process Inventory - Dept. 3)   XX
        Work in Process Inventory - Dept. 2   XX

Review Exhibit 21A-4.

TEST YOURSELF

All the self-testing materials in this chapter focus on information and procedures that your instructor is likely to test in quizzes and examinations.

I. Matching   *Match each numbered term with its lettered definition.*

_____ 1. FIFO
_____ 2. Equivalent units
_____ 3. Process costing
_____ 4. Weighted-average
_____ 5. Conversion costs

_____ 6. Physical units
_____ 7. Production cost report
_____ 8. Equivalent costs per unit
_____ 9. Transferred-in costs

A. A costing method which considers both the current and previous period's costs
B. Measure of the number of complete units that could have been manufactured from start to finish
C. A costing method which considers only the current period's costs
D. The actual number of units processed without regard to their percent of completion
E. Summary of the activity in a processing department for a period
F. The sum of direct labor and manufacturing overhead
G. Used to account for the manufacture of goods that are mass-produced in a continuous sequence of steps
H. The result of dividing equivalent units into total costs
I. Costs incurred in a previous process that are carried forward as part of the product's cost when it moves to the next department

II. Multiple Choice   *Circle the best answer.*

1. The purpose of process costing is to:

   A. calculate how many units have been completed for a period
   B. allocate the costs of production between the cost of goods that have been completed and the cost of incomplete units

   C. determine the ending balance of the Materials Inventory account
   D. determine the ending balance of the Finished Goods Inventory account.

2. All of the following businesses are likely to use a process costing system except:

   A. industrial chemicals.
   B. paint.

   C. residential construction.
   D. soft drinks .

3. When summarizing the flow of production in physical units for the first department, the physical units to account for equals

   A. Beginning Work in Process Inventory + Transferred In
   B. Beginning Work in Process Inventory + Production started
   C. Units completed and transferred out + Beginning Work in Process Inventory
   D. Units completed and transferred out + Ending Work in Process Inventory

4. When summarizing the flow of production in physical units for the second department, the physical units to account for equals

   A. Beginning Work in Process Inventory + Transferred In
   B. Beginning Work in Process Inventory + Production started
   C. Units completed and transferred out + Beginning Work in Process Inventory
   D. Units completed and transferred out + Ending Work in Process Inventory

5. Which of the following systems will usually have more than one Work in Process Inventory account?

   A. Job costing
   B. Process costing
   C. Both job costing and process costing
   D. Job costing and process costing both have only one Work in Process Inventory account

6. Direct materials in the second department refer to:

   A. materials added in the first department.
   B. materials added in the second department.
   C. materials added in both departments.
   D. materials added in departments other than the first or second.

7. Which of the following is not a category used to calculate the cost per equivalent unit:

   A. Direct Materials
   B. Direct Labor
   C. Conversion Costs
   D. Transferred In

8. The first step in process cost accounting is:

   A. the production cost report.
   B. determining physical units.
   C. determining equivalent units.
   D. determining equivalent unit costs.

9. If Carlton Manufacturing Group has completed and transferred out 10,000 units and has 3,000 units in ending Work in Process Inventory that have incurred 45% of their conversion costs and 100% of their materials, how many equivalent units are there with respect to direct materials and conversion costs?

	Direct Materials	Conversion Costs
A.	10,000	3,000
B.	4,500	1,350
C.	13,000	13,000
D.	13,000	11,350

10. The journal entry transferring costs from Department A to Department B in a process costing system would:

A. debit Work in Process Inventory-Department A.
B. credit Work in Process Inventory-Department B.
C. credit Work in Process Inventory-Department A.
D. not be required.

III. Completion *Complete each of the following.*

1. A manufacturer who produces custom goods uses a _____cost system.
2. A manufacturer with a continuous mass production of identical units through a sequence of steps uses a _____cost system.
3. Conversion costs refer to _____ and _____.
4. Ending Work in Process Inventory of 5,000 units 25% complete would represent_____ equivalent units.
5. After the physical units have been determined, the next step in process cost accounting is _____.
6. The "Costs to be accounted for" is calculated as _____ + _____ + _____ + _____.
7. Costs that flow with the goods from one department to another are called_____ _____ costs.
8. Under the _____ process costing method, the cost per equivalent unit for all equivalent units of work are determined using a weighted average of that period's and the previous period's costs per equivalent unit.
9. If a production process has two processing departments, when a unit is completed in Department 2, the costs are transferred to _____.
10. The _____ summarizes a processing department's operations for a period.

IV. Daily Exercises

1. Using the numbers 1 to 6, place the following steps in correct sequence.

_____ A. Determine equivalent units

_____ B. Determine equivalent unit costs

_____ C. Determine the costs to be accounted for

_____ D. Determine physical units

_____ E. Production Cost Report

_____ F. Apply total cost to units completed and units in ending inventory

2. An assembly department has no units in process at the beginning of the current period. During the period, 25,000 units were started in production. At the end of the current period, 4,500 units remained in the assembly department. Calculate the physical units for the assembly department for the current period.

3. Using the information in Daily Exercise 2 above, calculate the equivalent units for conversion costs assuming the units remaining in Work in Process Inventory are 40% complete.

4. A processing department has the following amounts charged to it during the current period:

Beginning Work in Process Inventory	$ 12,000
Direct Materials	109,000
Direct Labor	45,000
Manufacturing Overhead	60,000

Assuming the Work in Process Inventory account has an ending balance of $27,500, determine the costs transferred out to the next department.

5. Using the information in Daily Exercise 4 above, present the journal entry assuming (a) the units were transferred to the Packing Department and (b) the units were transferred to Finished Goods Inventory.

a)		
b)		
		.

V. Exercises

1. The following information is for Department 2 of Atlas Electroplating Co. for the month of April:

Beginning Work in Process Inventory	10,000
Units completed and transferred to Department 3	60,000
Units in ending Work in Process Inventory (20% complete as to conversion costs)	15,000

All materials are added at the beginning of Department 2, and Atlas uses the weighted-average method, determine the number of units started into production in April.

2. Refer to the information in Exercise 1, determine:

    1. The number of equivalent units for materials for April.

    2. The number of equivalent units for conversion costs for April.

3. Marliss Corporation prepared the following production cost report for Department A for September:

	Physical Units	Total Costs
Beginning Work in Process Inventory	-	-
Started into production in September (costs include $102,000 for materials and $82,350 for conversion costs)	26,000	$184,350
Total to account for	26,000	$184,350
Completed and transferred to Department B during September	20,000	?
Ending Work in Process Inventory, Sept. 30 (100% complete as to materials and 40% complete as to conversion)	6,000	?
	26,000	$184,350

A. What is the cost per equivalent unit for materials?

B. What is the cost per equivalent unit for conversion costs?

C. What costs are transferred to Department B at the end of September?

D. What costs remain in Ending Work in Process Inventory - Department A?

4. Marliss Corporation prepared the following production cost report for Department A for September:

	Physical Units	Total Costs
Work in Process Inventory Sept. 1 (100% complete as to materials and 20% complete as to conversion)	2,000	$ 11,150
Started into production in September (costs include $102,000 for materials and $82,350 for conversion)	24,000	184,350
Total to account for	26,000	$195,500
Completed and transferred to Department B during September	20,000	?
Work in Process, Sept. 30 (100% complete as to materials and 40% complete as to conversion)	6,000	?
	26,000	$195,500

Note that Marliss has Beginning Work in Process Inventory of 2,000 units with costs of $11,150. The balance in beginning work in process consists of $9,540 in materials cost and $1,610 in conversion costs.

Assuming Marliss uses the weighted-average method, answer the following questions:

A. What is the cost per equivalent unit for materials?

B. What is the cost per equivalent unit for conversion costs?

C. What costs are transferred to Department B at the end of September?

D. What costs remain in Ending Work in Process Inventory - Department A?

VI. Beyond the Numbers

Refer your answers in Exercise 3 (A and B). On which of the financial statements would the cost for units completed and transferred out and Ending Work in Process Inventory appear? When do product costs appear on the income statement?

_____

_____

_____

_____

_____

VII. Demonstration Problems

Demonstration Problem #1 (Weighted-Average)

Flush Manufacturing Corporation produces plumbing fixtures. The following is a summary of activity and costs for the enameling department for the month of November:

Enameling Department
For the Month Ended November 30, 20X4

Units:
 Beginning Work in Process Inventory
  (20% complete as to materials; 40% complete as
   to conversion)   22,500
 Transferred in from the Fabricating Department   105,000
 Total units completed   90,000
 Ending Work in Process Inventory
  (40% complete as to materials; 50% complete as
   to conversion)   37,500

Costs:
 Beginning Work in Process Inventory (Transferred in cost,
  $34,800; Materials cost, $650; Conversion cost, $ 54,000
   $18,550)
 Transferred in costs from the Fabricating Department   157,500
 Materials added   14,070
 Conversion costs added   205,485

Required:

Show the application of total costs to units completed and units in ending Work in Process Inventory for the Enameling Department for the month of November, assuming a weighted-average cost flow assumption.

<u>Steps 1 & 2</u>

Flow of Production in Physical Units				
and Equivalent Units of Production				
Enameling Department				
For the Month Ended November 30, 20X4				
		Equivalent Units		
Flow of Production	**Flow of Physical Units**	**Transferred In**	**Materials**	**Conversion Costs**

<u>Steps 3 & 4</u>

Computation of Unit Cost				
Enameling Department				
For the Month Ended November 30, 20X4				
	Transferred In	**Materials**	**Conversion Costs**	**Total**

Step 5

	Transferred In	Materials	Conversion Costs	Total
Application of Total Cost to Units Completed and Units in Ending Work in Process Inventory — Enameling Department — For the Month Ended November 30, 20X4				

Demonstration Problem #2 (The FIFO Process Costing Method from Appendix)

Flush Manufacturing Corporation produces plumbing fixtures. The following is a summary of activity and costs for the enameling department for the month of November:

Enameling Department
For the Month Ended November 30, 20X4

Units:
Beginning Work in Process Inventory (20% complete as to materials; 40% complete as to conversion)	22,500
Transferred in from the Fabricating Department	105,000
Total units completed	90,000
Ending Work in Process Inventory (40% complete as to materials; 50% complete as to conversion)	37,500

Costs:
Beginning Work in Process Inventory	$ 54,000
Transferred in costs from the Fabricating Department	157,500
Materials added	14,070
Conversion costs added	205,485

Required:

Show the application of total cost to units completed and units in ending Work in Process Inventory for the Enameling Department for the month of November, assuming a first-in, first-out (FIFO) cost flow assumption.

Steps 1 & 2

Flow of Production in Physical Units				
and Equivalent Units of Production				
Enameling Department				
For the Month Ended November 30, 20X4				
		Equivalent Units		
Flow of Production	**Flow of Physical Units**	**Transferred In**	**Materials**	**Conversion Costs**

Steps 3 & 4

	Transferred In	Materials	Conversion	Total
Computation of Unit Cost				
Enameling Department				
For the Month Ended November 30, 20X4				

Step 5

	Transferred In	Materials	Conversion	Total
Application of Total Cost to Units Completed and Units in Ending Work in Process Inventory				
Enameling Department				
For the Month Ended November 30, 20X4				

SOLUTIONS

I. Matching

1. C	6. D
2. B	7. E
3. G	8. H
4. A	9. I
5. F	

II.   Multiple Choice

1. B   The purpose of process costing is to allocate the costs of production between the cost of goods that have been completed and the cost of incomplete units.

2. C   Since residential construction tends to be of identifiable units, job costing would be appropriate for it. Process costing is appropriate for the others listed.

3. B   In the first department, the physical units to account for is calculated as Beginning Work in Process Inventory + Production started.

4. A   In the second (and subsequent) department(s), the physical units to account for is calculated as Beginning Work in Process Inventory + Transferred In

5. B   Job cost systems maintain only one Work in Process Inventory account. The job cost record for each incomplete job in such a system comprises the job cost or Work in Process Inventory subsidiary ledger for the control account. In a process cost system, with more than one department, each department has its own Work in Process Inventory account.

6. B   Materials added in the first department and transferred to the second department are referred to as Transferred-in Costs. Accordingly, only materials added in the current department are called direct materials.

7. B   All are categories except Direct Labor. The direct labor cost is added to manufacturing overhead costs and referred to as Conversion Costs in a process costing system.

8. B   The first of the five steps in process cost accounting is determining physical units.

9. D

	Beginning Inventory	-
+	Completed and transferred out	10,000
+	Ending Inventory	3,000
	Equivalent units for direct materials	13,000

	From Beginning Inventory	-
+	Completed and transferred out	10,000
+	Ending Inventory (.45 × 3,000)	1,350
	Equivalent units for conversion costs	11,350

10.   C   To record the transfer to the next department:

Work in Process Inventory - Dept. B	XX	
Work in Process Inventory - Dept. A		XX

III. Completion

1. job
2. process
3. direct labor, manufacturing overhead
4. .25 × 5,000 units =1,250
5. to calculate the equivalent units of production
6. Cost of Beginning Work in Process Inventory + Direct materials + Direct labor + Manufacturing overhead
7. transferred in
8. weighted-average
9. Department 3 (the next department)
10. production cost report

IV. Daily Exercises

1.   A. 2
      B. 4
      C. 3
      D. 1
      E. 6
      F. 5

2.   Units to account for = Beginning Work in Process Inventory + units started in production
      = 0 + 25,000 = 25,000

      Units accounted for   = units completed and transferred out + Ending Work in Process
                   = 20,500 + 4,500 = 25,000
      Units completed and transferred out = units started in production – ending inventory

3.

Beginning Work in Process Inventory	=	0
Units completed and transferred out	=	20,500
Ending Work in Process Inventory	=	1,800 *
Equivalent units for conversion costs		22,300

*4500 units × 40% complete

261

4.

Work in Process Inventory -Processing Department

Bal.	12,000		
	109,000		
	45,000		
	60,000	198,500	costs transferred to next department
Bal.	27,500		

5.

a) Work in Process Inventory- Packing	198,500	
Work in Process Inventory- Processing		198,500
b) Finished Goods Inventory	198,500	
Work in Process Inventory- Processing		198,500

V. Exercises

1. Units completed and transferred out + Ending inventory = Units accounted for

    60,000 + 15,000 = 75,000

    Beginning inventory - Units started in production = Units to account for

    10,000 - X = 75,000

    Units started = 65,000

2. 1.

Completed and transferred out	60,000
Ending Work in Process Inventory (100% complete)	15,000
Equivalent units for materials	75,000

   2.

Completed and transferred out	60,000
Ending Work in Process Inventory (20% complete)	3,000
Equivalent units for conversion costs	63,000

3. A. Equivalent units for materials = 26,000

    Cost per equivalent unit for materials = \$102,000/26,000 = \$3.92 (rounded)

   B. Equivalent units for conversion = $20,000 + (6,000 \times .40) = 22,400$

    Cost per equivalent unit = \$82,350/22,400 = \$3.68 (rounded)

   C.

Units completed and transferred out	
$[20,000 \times (\$3.92 + \$3.68)]$	
Cost transferred out	152,000

D.

Materials (6,000 × 100% × 3.92)	$23,520
Conversion (6,000 × 40% × $3.68))	8,832
Cost of ending Work in Process Inventory	$32,352

4. A. Equivalent units for materials = 26,000 (20,000 + 6,000)
   Cost per equivalent unit for materials:
     $9,540 + $102,000 = $111,540/26,000 = $4.29

   B. Equivalent units for conversion costs= 22,400 (20,000 + 2,400)
      Cost per equivalent unit for conversion costs:
        $1,610 + $82,350 = $83,960/22,400 = $3.748 (rounded)

   C.

Units completed and transferred out	
[20,000 × ($4.29 + $3.748)]	
Cost transferred out	160,760

   D.

Materials (6,000 × 100% × 4.29)	$25,740
Conversion (6,000 × 40% × $3.75 * (rounded))	9,000
Cost of Ending Work in Process Inventory	$34,740

   *Rounded to nearest dollar for computation in D. so that the sum of costs transferred out and the cost of Ending Work in Process Inventory will equal the total costs to account for of $195,500.

VI. Beyond the Numbers

The costs of units completed and transferred out will either appear in the next processing Department's Work in Process Inventory account, or the Finished Goods Inventory account. Either way, both accounts are current asset accounts that will appear on the balance sheet. Product costs appear on the income statement as cost of goods sold in the period in which the goods are sold.

VII. Demonstration Problems

Demonstration Problem #1 Solved and Explained

<u>Steps 1 & 2</u>

Flow of Production in Physical Units
and Equivalent Units of Production
Enameling Department
For the Month Ended November 30, 20X4

		Equivalent Units		
Flow of Production	Flow of Physical Units	Transferred In	Materials	Conversion Costs
Units to account for:				
Work in Process Inventory, October 31	22,500			
Transferred in	105,000			
Total units to account for	127,500			
Units accounted for:				
Completed and transferred out in November	90,000[1]	90,000	90,000	90,000
Ending inventory	37,500	37,500	15,000[2]	18,750[3]
Total units accounted for	127,500	127,500	105,000	108,750

[1] A total of 90,000 units were transferred out according to the problem. Since these are completed units, each completed unit equals one equivalent unit, and the completed units are carried across to the equivalent unit computation.

[2] The problem states that 40% of the direct materials had been added during November to the physical units remaining in ending inventory.

$$.40 \times 37,500 = 15,000 \text{ equivalent units}$$

[3] The problem states that 50% of the conversion had been performed during November to the physical units remaining in ending inventory.

$$.50 \times 37,500 = 18,750 \text{ equivalent units}$$

<u>Steps 3 & 4</u>

Computation of Unit Cost
Enameling Department
For the Month Ended November 30, 20X4

	Transferred In	Materials	Conversion Costs	Total
Work in Process Inventory, October 31	$34,800	$650	$18,550	$ 54,000
Costs added in November	157,500	14,070	205,485	377,055
Total cost	192,300	14,720	224,035	431,055
Divide by equivalent units	127,500	105,000	108,750	
Cost per equivalent unit	$1.508235	$0.14019	$2.06009	

Total cost to account for:		$431,055

Points to Remember:

When computing unit costs using the weighted-average method, the costs from the prior period are included in the computation of unit costs. The unit cost for each cost category is the sum of the current period's cost plus the amounts incurred last period and divided by equivalent units.

<u>Step 5</u>

Application of Total Cost to Units Completed
and Units in Ending Work in Process Inventory
Enameling Department
For the Month Ended November 30, 20X4

	Transferred In	Materials	Conversion Costs	Total
Units completed and transferred out to Finished Goods Inventory: $90,000 \times (1.508235 + 0.14019 + 2.06009)$				$333,766[†]
Work in Process Inventory, November 30:				
Transferred-in costs	$37,500 \times \$1.508235$			$56,559
Direct materials		$15,000 \times \$0.14019$		2,103
Conversion costs			$18,750 \times \$2.06009$	38,627
Total Work in Process Inventory, November 30				97,289
Total costs accounted for				$431,055

[†]Adjusted for rounding

Points to Remember:

The Step 5 procedure above is less complicated using weighted-average because all 90,000 units transferred out are assigned the unit cost amounts calculated in Step 4. Unlike the FIFO method, there is no need to distinguish between those units in process at the beginning of the period and those units transferred-in and completed during the period.

Like the FIFO method however, the ending Work in Process Inventory amounts are determined by multiplying equivalent units (from Step 2) times unit cost (Step 4).

Once the costs have been applied, you should compare total costs accounted for in Step 5 with the total cost to account for from Step 3. In both cases the amount in this problem is $431,055.

Demonstration Problem #2 Solved and Explained

Steps 1 & 2

Flow of Production in Physical Units
and Equivalent Units of Production
Enameling Department
For the Month Ended November 30, 20X4

		Equivalent Units		
Flow of Production	Flow of Physical Units	Transferred In	Materials	Conversion Costs
Units to account for:				
Work in Process Inventory, October 31	22,500			
Transferred in	105,000			
Total units to account for	127,500			
Units accounted for:				
Completed and transferred out in November:				
From beginning inventory	22,500		18,000[2]	13,500[3]
Transferred-in and completed	67,500[1]	67,500	67,500	67,500
Total transferred out	90,000			
Ending inventory	37,500	37,500	15,000[4]	18,750[5]
Total units accounted for	127,500	105,000	100,500	99,750

266

¹ A total of 90,000 units were transferred out according to the problem. Since 22,500 of those units were from beginning inventory, the balance of 67,500 was transferred-in and completed during the period. Since these are completed units, each completed unit equals one equivalent unit, and the completed units are carried across to the equivalent unit computation.

Total transferred out	-	Beginning inventory	=	Transferred in and completed
90,000	-	22,500	=	67,500 units

² The Beginning Work in Process Inventory was 20% complete with respect to direct materials. Therefore, 80% of the direct materials were added during November to the physical units in beginning inventory (100% - 20%).

$$.80 \times 22,500 = 18,000 \text{ equivalent units}$$

³ The Beginning Work in Process Inventory was 40% complete with respect to conversion. Therefore, 60% of the conversion was performed on Beginning Work in Process Inventory during November (100% - 40%).

$$.60 \times 22,500 = 13,500 \text{ equivalent units}$$

⁴ The problem states that 40% of the direct materials had been added during November to the physical units remaining in ending inventory.

$$.40 \times 37,500 = 15,000 \text{ equivalent units}$$

⁵ The problem states that 50% of the conversion had been performed during November to the physical units remaining in ending inventory.

$$.50 \times 37,500 = 18,750 \text{ equivalent units}$$

Steps 3 & 4

Computation of Unit Cost
Enameling Department
For the Month Ended November 30, 20X4

	Transferred In	Materials	Conversion Costs	Total
Work in Process Inventory, October 31 (costs for work done before November)				$ 54,000
Costs added in November	$157,500	$14,070	$205,485	377,055
Divide by equivalent units	105,000	100,500	99,750	
Cost per equivalent unit	$1.50	$0.14	$2.06	
Total cost to account for:				$431,055

Points to Remember:

When computing unit costs, the costs from the prior period are *not included* in the computation of unit costs. The unit cost for each cost category is equal to the costs added to that category during the period divided by the equivalent units for that category, which were computed in Step 2.

Step 5

Application of Total Cost to Units Completed
and Units in Ending Work in Process Inventory
Enameling Department
For the Month Ended November 30, 20X4

	Transferred In	Materials	Conversion Costs	Total
Units completed and transferred out to Finished Goods Inventory:				
From Work in Process Inventory, October 31				$ 54,000
Costs added during November				
Direct materials		18,000 × $0.14		2,520
Conversion costs			13,500 × $2.06	27,810
Total completed from beginning inventory				84,330
Units transferred in and completed during November	67,500 × ($1.50 + $0.14 + $2.06)			249,750
Total costs transferred out				$334,080
Work in Process Inventory, November 30:				
Transferred-in costs	37,500 × $1.50			$ 56,250
Direct materials		15,000 × $0.14		2,100
Conversion costs			18,750 × $2.06	38,625
Total Work in Process Inventory, November 30				96,975
Total costs accounted for				$431,055

Points to Remember:

Units Completed and Transferred Out

Units from Work in Process Inventory, October 31:

The problem states that $54,000 of costs was associated with the October 31 Work in Process Inventory balance. The FIFO process costing method *always* assumes that costs associated with beginning Work in Process Inventory are the *first* costs to be transferred out in the next period.

Costs added during November:

Whenever beginning Work in Process Inventory exists, it is necessary to compute the balance of costs incurred to complete the work. According to the problem, additional materials and conversion were needed to complete the beginning Work in Process Inventory. The equivalent units were computed in Step 2, and the unit costs for each category was determined in Step 4. The amount of cost to complete beginning Work in Process Inventory is the equivalent units times the unit cost. A separate computation is made for (1) direct materials and (2) conversion costs.

Units Transferred-In and Completed during November:

Since transferred-in and completed units are 100% complete, separate computations for each of the cost categories are not necessary. The cost associated with units transferred-in and completed in the same period will equal the number of units times the sum of the unit costs of 1) transferred-in costs, 2) direct materials, and 3) conversion.

Ending Work in Process Inventory, November 30:

To compute the balance of ending Work in Process Inventory, it is necessary to make a separate computation for 1) transferred-in costs, 2) direct materials, and 3) conversion. For each of the costs, the balance in ending Work in Process Inventory will equal the equivalent units of production from Step 2 times the unit cost from Step 4.

Once the costs have been applied, you should compare the total costs accounted for in Step 5 with the total cost to account for from Step 3. In both cases the amount in this problem is $431,055.

Chapter 22 - Cost-Volume-Profit Analysis

CHAPTER OVERVIEW

In Chapters 20 and 21 you learned about a particular type of management accounting concerned with manufacturing businesses wherein direct materials are converted into finished goods. We now turn our attention to Cost-Volume-Profit (CVP) analysis to more closely examine "costs" and how they change relative to changes in output. The interaction of costs and volume results in changes in profits (or losses). The learning objectives for this chapter are to

1. Identify how changes in volume affect costs.
2. Use CVP analysis to compute breakeven points.
3. Use CVP analysis for profit planning, and graph the cost-volume-profit relations.
4. Use CVP methods to perform sensitivity analyses.
5. Compute income using variable costing and absorption costing

CHAPTER REVIEW

Objective 1 - Identify how changes in volume affect costs.

Cost behavior is the way that costs change as volume changes. A **cost driver** is any factor that affects costs. You were introduced to cost drivers in Chapter 19. The three patterns of cost behavior are:

1. **Total variable costs** change in direct proportion to changes in volume or level of activity. However, on a per unit basis, variable costs are constant. Examples of variable costs include direct materials, sales commissions, and delivery expense. Suppose CDs have a cost of $6 per disk when purchased for resale. If a retailer sells 1,000 CDs, cost of goods sold will be $6,000. However, if 2,000 CDs are sold, cost of goods sold will be $12,000. Thus, the more CDs the retailer sells, the higher the cost of goods sold will be; thus, the cost of goods sold is variable in total, and constant at the $6 variable cost per unit.

2. **Total fixed costs** do not change in total despite wide changes in volume. Examples of fixed costs include expenses such as rent and depreciation. Suppose the rent for a store is $5,000 per month. The storeowner will pay $5,000 per month whether sales increase, decrease, or remain the same. However, on a per unit basis, fixed costs will vary. If the rent is $5,000 per month and the retailer sells 1,000 CDs, then the fixed cost per CD is $5 per unit. If the retailer sells 2,000 CDs, then the fixed cost per unit is $2.50. Notice as the number of CDs sold increases, the fixed cost of $5,000 is spread over more units, thus decreasing the cost per unit. Therefore, we can see that the fixed cost per unit is inversely proportional to volume.

3. **Mixed costs** are costs that have both a variable and fixed component. The monthly telephone bill, for example, is based both on local service and long distance service. The amount for local (unlimited) service is a fixed cost, while the amount for long distance service is a variable cost. Therefore, the total telephone bill is a mixed cost.

Study the graphs in your text that illustrate cost behavior patterns (Exhibits 22-1, 22-2, and 22-3). The variable cost graph begins at the origin (zero volume, zero cost) and increases in a straight line, whose slope equals the variable cost per unit. As the slope of the line gets steeper, the more the variable cost per unit increases. The fixed cost graph is a horizontal line that intersects the cost (vertical) axis at the fixed cost level. The mixed cost graph intersects the cost axis at the level of the fixed cost component, and its slope equals the variable cost per unit.

When budgeting costs, companies use the **relevant range concept**. Relevant range is the band of volume where total fixed costs remain constant and the variable cost per unit remains constant. These relationships will be different in other ranges. See Exhibit 22-4 in your text.

Objective 2 - Use CVP analysis to compute breakeven points.

Cost-volume-profit analysis is often called **breakeven analysis**. The **breakeven point** is the sales level at which operating income is zero. If sales are below the breakeven point, the result is a loss. If sales are above the breakeven point, the result is a profit. Decision-makers use cost-volume-profit analysis to answer questions such as, "How much do we need to sell to breakeven?" or "If our sales are some specific amount, what will our profit be?"

CVP analysis assumes the following:
1. The only factor that affects costs is changes in volume.
2. Managers can classify each cost (or the components of mixed costs) as either variable or fixed.
3. Both costs and revenues are linear throughout the relevant range of volume.
4. Inventory levels will not change.
5. The sales mix of products will not change. **Sales mix** is the combination of products that make up total sales.

There are two approaches used in CVP analysis:

1. **The Income Statement Approach:**

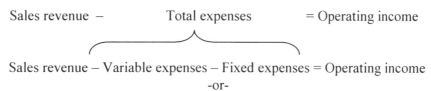

Sales revenue −   Total expenses   = Operating income

Sales revenue − Variable expenses − Fixed expenses = Operating income

-or-

(Sale price per unit × units sold) − (Variable cost per unit × units sold) − Fixed expenses = Operating income

To calculate the breakeven point, operating income in the formula will always be zero. This is because operating income is always zero at breakeven. The equation shows how many units must be sold (and the total dollar amount of the sales) in order to breakeven.

2. The Contribution Margin Approach:

The contribution margin receives its name because it represents the excess of sales revenue over variable costs that contributes to covering fixed expenses and providing operating income.

Breakeven sales in units is computed by dividing fixed expenses plus operating income, where operating income is zero ($0) by the contribution margin per unit:

Contribution Margin Per Unit = Sales Price Per Unit - Variable Expense Per Unit

$$\text{Breakeven Sales in Units} = \frac{\text{Fixed expenses} + \text{Operating income}}{\text{Contribution Margin Per Unit}}$$

Breakeven sales in dollars is computed by dividing fixed expenses by the contribution margin ratio:

$$\text{Contribution Margin Ratio} = \frac{\text{Contribution margin}}{\text{Sales revenue}}$$

$$\text{Breakeven Sales in Dollars} = \frac{\text{Fixed expenses} + \text{Operating income}}{\text{Contribution Margin Ratio}}$$

Objective 3 - Use CVP analysis for profit planning, and graph the cost-volume-profit relations.

Managers of business are also interested in the sales level needed to earn a target profit. We use the same formula as we did to calculate the breakeven point, except instead of setting operating income to zero, use the target operating income. The profit that a business wishes to earn is called the **target operating income**.

$$\text{Target Sales In Units} = \frac{\text{Fixed Expenses} + \text{Target Operating Income}}{\text{Contribution Margin Per Unit}}$$

$$\text{Target Sales In Dollars} = \frac{\text{Fixed Expenses} + \text{Target Operating Income}}{\text{Contribution Margin Ratio}}$$

Notice that the only difference between computing breakeven sales and target sales is that with target sales, the target operating income amount is added to fixed expenses.

Managers are also interested in knowing the amount of operating income or operating loss to expect at various levels of sales. One convenient way to provide this information is to prepare a **cost-volume-profit graph**.

In order to familiarize yourself with the components of the CVP graph, study these steps and review Exhibit 22-7 in your text:

Step 1: Draw the sales revenue line from the origin through a preselected sales volume.

Step 2: Draw the fixed expense line.

Step 3: Draw the total expense line by computing the variable expenses at your preselected sales volume (Step 1) and then plot them beginning at your fixed expense line.

Step 4: Identify the breakeven point (where sales revenue and total expenses intersect).

Step 5: Identify the operating income and operating loss areas.

Objective 4 - Use CVP methods to perform sensitivity analyses.

Sensitivity analysis is a "what if" technique that managers use to ask what a result will be if a predicted amount is not achieved or if an underlying assumption changes. For example, managers may want to determine answers to the following questions:

- If a special "25% off" sale is held, what is the new breakeven point in units and in sales dollars?
- If a supplier notifies the company of an increase in a key raw material, what will be the new breakeven point?
- If the cost of renting a sales office doubles, how much must our sales increase to cover the new rent expense and not affect operating income?

Each of these scenarios can be analyzed using the breakeven formulas.

The **margin of safety** is the excess of expected or actual sales over breakeven sales. It tells a business how much sales can drop before an operating loss is incurred. The margin of safety may be computed in terms of either dollars or units:

Margin of safety in units = Expected sales in units - Breakeven sales in units
Margin of safety in dollars = margin of safety in units × sale price per unit

Objective 5 – Compute income using variable costing and absorption costing.

GAAP requires that both variable and fixed manufacturing costs be assigned to products. This approach is called **absorption costing** because products "absorb" fixed manufacturing costs as well as variable manufacturing costs. Absorption costing has been used in the financial statements presented throughout this discussion because it conforms to GAAP requirements. However, managers prefer to use an alternative approach called **variable costing** for planning and decision-making. Variable costing assigns variable manufacturing costs to products, but fixed manufacturing costs (property taxes on the factory, depreciation on the building, etc.) are treated as period costs and reported on the income statement when incurred. The argument for the variable costing approach is that fixed manufacturing costs will be incurred regardless of production levels and should therefore be treated as period costs.

Carefully review Exhibit 22-8 in your text. Notice that the only difference between these two approaches is the treatment of fixed manufacturing costs. However, this difference will affect net income, as illustrated in Exhibits 22-9 and 22-10 in your text. Because absorption costing assigns fixed manufacturing costs to inventory, these costs will not appear on the income statement until the units are actually sold, whereas under variable costing all fixed manufacturing costs are included on the income statement when they are incurred. The general rule is that when inventories are increasing, absorption costing income will be higher than variable costing income. The reverse is true when inventories are declining.

TEST YOURSELF

All the self-testing materials in this chapter focus on information and procedures that your instructor is likely to test in quizzes and examinations.

Matching *Match each numbered term with its lettered definition.*

_____ 1. Cost behavior	_____ 8. Margin of safety
_____ 2. Variable cost	_____ 9. Relevant range
_____ 3. Fixed cost	_____ 10. Variable costing
_____ 4. Mixed cost	_____ 11. Sales mix
_____ 5. Breakeven point	_____ 12. CVP analysis
_____ 6. Contribution margin	_____ 13. Absorption costing
_____ 7. Target operating income	_____ 14. Period costs

A. The amount of unit sales or dollar sales at which revenues equal expenses
B. A costing method that assigns only variable manufacturing costs to products
C. The description of how costs change in response to a shift in the volume of business activity
D. The excess of sales price over variable expenses
E. A band of activity where total fixed costs remain constant and where the variable cost per unit remains constant.
F. A cost that does not change in total as volume changes
G. The excess of expected (or actual) sales over breakeven sales
H. A cost that is part variable and part fixed
I. A cost that changes in total in direct proportion to changes in volume or activity
J. The desired operating income a business wishes to earn
K. Costs reported on the income statement as they are incurred
L. The combination of products that make up total sales
M. A costing method that assigns all manufacturing costs to products
N. A part of the budgeting system that helps managers predict the outcome of their decisions by analyzing relationships among costs, volume, and profit or loss.

II. Multiple Choice *Circle the best answer.*

Use the following information for Questions 1 through 4:

Movie Mania, Inc. sells DVDs. Last year Movie Mania sold 5,500 cases at $24 per case. The variable cost per case was $14.40 and fixed costs amounted to $28,800.

1. The breakeven point in cases of tapes was:

    A. 1,200.   C. 3,000.
    B. 2,000.   D. 5,500.

2. The breakeven point in sales dollars was:

   A. $66,000.
   B. $72,000.

   C. $24,000.
   D. $14,400.

3. The margin of safety in dollars was:

   A. $60,000.
   B. $48,000.

   C. $51,000.
   D. $-0-.

4. If Movie Mania wished to earn an operating income of $34,800, how many cases of tapes would have to be sold?

   A. 3,600.
   B. 4,400.

   C. 5,500.
   D. 6,625.

5. Dividing breakeven point in sales dollars by the unit selling price results in the:

   A. variable cost per unit.
   B. breakeven point in dollars.

   C. breakeven point in units.
   D. variable cost ratio.

6. Which of the following will decrease the breakeven point?

   A. Decreasing fixed costs
   B. Increasing fixed costs

   C. Increasing variable costs per unit
   D. Decreasing selling price

7. Which of the following will increase the breakeven point?

   A. Decreasing fixed costs
   B. Increasing selling price

   C. Decreasing variable cost per unit
   D. Decreasing selling price

Use the following graph to answer questions 8 through 10:

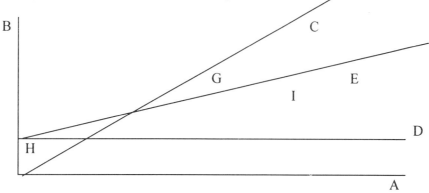

8. Line D must be:

   A. the sales line.
   B. total expense line.

   C. fixed expense line.
   D. cannot be determined.

275

9. If E is the total expense line then I must be:

A. operating income area.
B. variable expense area.
C. operating loss area.
D. cannot be determined.

10. If C is the sales line and E is the total expense line then F must be:

A. breakeven point.
B. total units.
C. total dollars.
D. cannot be determined.

III. Completion   *Complete each of the following.*

1. The _____ is equal to the sales price per unit minus the variable expenses per unit.

2. A convenient way to determine operating income or loss at various levels of sales is to prepare a _____.

3. _____ and _____ are examples of costs that change proportionately with sales.

4. The_____ is the combination of products that make up total sales.

5. Two approaches used in CVP analysis are the _____ approach and the _____ approach.

6. _____ tells a decision maker how much sales can drop before an operating loss is incurred.

For questions 7 through 10, complete the sentence with **increase, decrease,** or **not affect**.

7. An increase in direct material cost will _____ the contribution margin.

8. An increase in direct labor cost will _____ the breakeven point.

9. A decrease in direct materials costs will _____the breakeven point.

10. An increase in fixed plant insurance will _____the breakeven point.

11. Absorption costing reports all _____ costs as _____ costs on the income statement.

12. Variable costing reports only _____ costs as _____ costs on the income statement.

IV. Daily Exercises

1. Classify each of the following costs as fixed, variable, or mixed. (Assume sales volume is within the relevant range for the current period.)

Cost	Classification
a) Property taxes	_____
b) Direct materials	_____
c) Depreciation on office equipment	_____
d) Advertising expense	_____
e) Office salaries expense	_____
f) Direct labor	_____
g) Manufacturing overhead	_____
h) Rent expense	_____
i) Insurance expense	_____
j) Supplies expense	_____

2. Bola's Basketry has fixed costs of $420,000. Variable costs are 30% of sales. Assuming each basket sells for $10, what is their breakeven point in unit sales?

3. Manuel's Manufacturing sells a product for $8 per unit. If the variable cost is $4.25 per unit, and breakeven is 48,000 units, what are Manuel's fixed costs?

4. If variable costs are 60% of sales and fixed costs are $230,000 what is the breakeven point in sales dollars?

V. Exercises

1. A monthly income statement for Bijan's Burritos appears as follows:

Sales		$280,000
Cost of Goods Sold		120,000
Gross Margin		160,000
Operating Expenses:		
Marketing Expense	$35,000	
General Expense	70,000	105,000
Operating Income		$ 55,000

Cost of Goods Sold is a variable expense. Marketing expense is 70% variable and 30% fixed. General Expense is half fixed and half variable. In the space below, present a contribution margin income statement for the month.

2. Review the information in Exercise 1 above, and calculate the following:

a. Contribution margin ratio

b. Breakeven point in sales

c. If the frozen burritos sell for $2 per package, what is the breakeven point in units?

d. By what amount would operating income decrease if sales dropped by 20%?

3. Using the form below and the information in Exercise 1 above, graph Bijan's Burritos total expense (both fixed and variable) and sales, showing clearly the breakeven point calculated in Exercise 2 above.

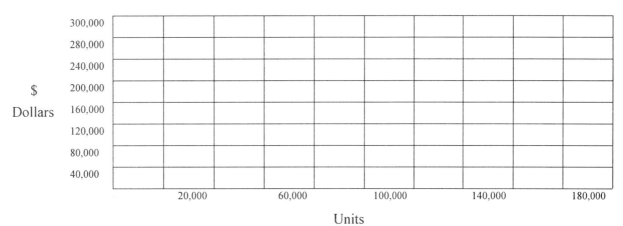

4. A manufacturer of rubber exercise balls provides the following cost information:

Variable cost per ball	$ 9.50
Fixed monthly expenses	$15,000
Selling price per ball	$ 20.00

a. What is the manufacturer's contribution margin per ball and contribution margin ratio?

b. What is the manufacturer's breakeven point in units and dollars?

c. Prove the accuracy of your answers in (b) above by presenting an income statement at breakeven.

d. Assuming the manufacturer's targeted net income is $12,000 per month, and the company is subject to a 40% tax rate, calculate the sales necessary to achieve the targeted net income (after tax).

5. Review the information in Exercise 4 above, assuming the manufacturer achieves the $12,000 targeted net income, after tax. The owner is considering an advertising campaign to increase sales. The cost of the ads would be $5,000 per month. By what amount, expressed in units and dollars, would sales need to increase to justify the advertising expenditure?

VI. Beyond the Numbers

Review Daily Exercise 1. How would your answers change if output remains within the relevant range but the costs listed are classified over a long period?

Cost	Classification
a) Property taxes	_____
b) Direct materials	_____
c) Depreciation on office equipment	_____
d) Advertising expense	_____
e) Office salaries expense	_____
f) Direct labor	_____
g) Manufacturing overhead	_____
h) Rent expense	_____
i) Insurance expense	_____
j) Supplies expense	_____

VII. Demonstration Problems

Demonstration Problem #1

The Gentry Game Corporation is planning to introduce a new table game. The relevant range of output is between 10,000 and 40,000 units. Within this range, fixed expenses are estimated to be $325,000 and variable expenses are estimated at 35% of the $30 selling price.

Required:

1. Using the contribution margin approach, calculate breakeven sales in units and in dollars.

2. If targeted net operating income (pretax) is $120,000, how many games must be sold?

3. Prepare a graph showing operating income and operating loss areas from 0 to 40,000 games, assuming a selling price of $30. Identify the breakeven sales level and the sales level needed to earn operating income of $120,000.

4. If the corporation increases the selling price to $36, how many games must be sold to earn operating income of $60,000? Assume variable costs are 35% of the new selling price.

Requirement 1 (Breakeven sales in units and dollars)

Requirement 2 (Targeted operating income)

Requirement 3 (Graph)

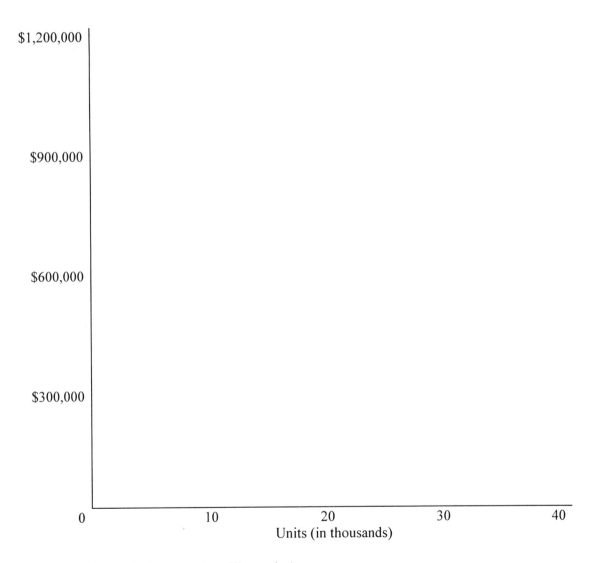

Requirement 4 (Effect of change in selling price)

281

SOLUTIONS

I. Matching

1. C	3. F	5. A	7. J	9. E	11. L	13. M
2. I	4. H	6. D	8. G	10. B	12. N	14. K

II. Multiple Choice

1.   C $28,800 / ($24.00 - $14.40) = 3,000$

2.   B $28,800 / [($24.00 - $14.40) / $24.00] = $72,000$

3.   A   (5,500 boxes - 3,000 boxes) $\times$ $24.00 = $60,000$

4.   D   ($28,800 + $34,800) / ($24.00 - $14.40) = $63,600 / $9.60 = 6,625$

5.   C   BE$ = Breakeven sales dollars. BEu = Breakeven in units.
            $Pu = unit selling price.
            BE$ = BEu $\times$ $Pu
            BE$ / $Pu = BEu

6.   A   BE$ = Breakeven sales dollars. BEu = Breakeven in units.
            $Pu = unit selling price. FC = Fixed Cost
            VCu = Variable cost per unit.

            Recall that BEu = FC /($Pu - VCu)

            Of the answers listed, only A "Decreasing fixed costs" will decrease the breakeven point.

7.   D   Refer to 6 above. Note that answer D, "Decreasing selling price," will decrease the contribution margin and increase the breakeven point.

Study tip: If you have difficulty with 5 through 7, consider the formula for the breakeven point in units:

Fixed Expenses / Contribution Margin Per Unit = Breakeven in Units

If the numerator increases, or the denominator decreases, the breakeven point increases. If the numerator decreases, or the denominator increases, the breakeven point decreases.

---

8.   C   The sales and total expense line slope upward; only the fixed expense line is flat.

9.   B   The variable expense area is the difference between the total expense line and the fixed expense line.

10.   A   Total units and total dollars are the A and B axis. F is the breakeven point where sales intersect total expenses.

III. Completion

1. contribution margin per unit
2. cost-volume-profit graph
3. Cost of goods sold, selling commission (other answers may be acceptable)
4. sales mix
5. income statement approach, contribution margin approach
6. The margin of safety
7. decrease (An increase in direct materials is an increase in the variable cost per unit. This decreases the contribution margin.)
8. increase (An increase in direct labor cost is an increase in the variable cost per unit. This decreases the contribution margin. As the contribution margin decreases, the breakeven point increases.)
9. decrease (A decrease in direct materials cost is a decrease in variable cost per unit. This increases the contribution margin. As the contribution margin increases, the breakeven point decreases. Contrast with #8.)
10. increase (An increase in plant insurance is an increase in fixed costs. An increase in fixed costs increases the breakeven point.)
11. manufacturing, product (order important)
12. variable, product (order important)

IV. Daily Exercises

1.

Cost	Classification
a) Property taxes	Fixed
b) Direct materials	Variable
c) Depreciation on office equipment	Fixed
d) Advertising expense	Fixed
e) Office salaries expense	Fixed
f) Direct labor	Variable
g) Manufacturing overhead	Mixed (because some are fixed, such as rent, depreciation, etc., whereas others are variable—indirect materials, utilities, for instance)
h) Rent expense	Fixed
i) Insurance expense	Fixed
j) Supplies expense	Variable

2. If VC = 30% of sales, then CM = 70% of sales, or $7 per unit.

$$\frac{\text{Fixed expenses}}{\text{Contribution margin}} = \text{Breakeven point}$$

$$\frac{\$420,000}{\$7} = 60,000 \text{ units}$$

3.

$$\frac{\text{Fixed expenses (FE)}}{\text{Contribution margin}} = \text{Breakeven point}$$

$$\frac{\text{FE}}{\$3.75} = 48,000$$

$$\text{FE} = \$180,000$$

4. If VC = 60% of sales, then CM = 40% of sales.

$$\frac{\text{Fixed expenses}}{\text{Contribution margin ratio}} = \text{Breakeven in sales}$$

$$\frac{\$230,000}{40\%} = \$575,000$$

V. Exercises

1.

Sales		$280,000
Less: Variable Expenses		
Cost of Goods Sold	$120,000	
Marketing Expense	24,500	
General Expense	35,000	179,500
Contribution Margin		100,500
Less: Fixed Expenses		
Marketing Expense	10,500	
General Expense	35,000	45,500
Operating Income		$ 55,000

2.

  a. Contribution margin ratio = contribution margin / sales
                                  = 100,500 / 280,000 = 35.9% (rounded)

  b. Breakeven point in sales   = $0 operating income
                                   = fixed expense / contribution margin ratio
                                   = $45,500 / 35.9% = $126,741

  c. $126,741 / $2 each = 63,371 packages

d.

Sales [($280,000 – 20%($280,000)]		$224,000
Less: Variable Expenses		
Cost of Goods Sold	$96,000	
Marketing Expense	19,600	
General Expense	28,000	143,600
Contribution Margin		80,400
Less: Fixed Expenses		*45,500
Operating Income		$ 34,900

*Fixed expenses remain the same, regardless of sales level (assuming no change in the relevant range). If sales drop 20%, operating income decreases by $20,100 ($55,000-$34,900).

3.

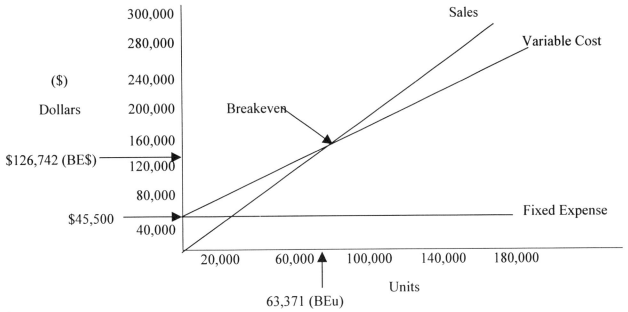

4.
a. Contribution margin   =   sales – variable costs
                           = $20 - $9.50 = $10.50

    Contribution ratio   =   contribution margin / sales
                           = $10.50 / $20.00 = 52.5%

b. Breakeven (units)   =   fixed expenses / contribution margin
                           = $15,000 / $10.50 = 1,428.5714 units

    Breakeven (sales)   =   fixed expenses / contribution margin ratio
                           = $15,000 / 52.5% = $28,571 (rounded)

285

c.

Sales	$28,571	
Less: Variable Costs (1,428.5714 units × $9.50 ea)	13,571	(rounded)
Contribution Margin	15,000	(rounded)
Less: Fixed Expenses	15,000	
Operating Income	-0-	

d. Since the targeted net income ($12,000) is after-tax, first we have to calculate the pre-tax target income.

pre-tax target income　　　=　$12,000 / 60% = $20,000
targeted sales　　=　(fixed expenses + net income) / contribution margin ratio
　　　=　($15,000 + $20,000) / 52.5%
　　　=　$35,000 / 52.5% = $66,667 (rounded)

5. The advertising cost is a fixed expense so replace the $15,000 amount with $20,000, then solve as follows:

Target sales (dollars)　　=　($20,000 + $20,000) / 52.5% = $76,190 (rounded)

Target sales (units)　　=　($20,000 + $20,000) / $10.50 = 3,810 units

Sales need to increase $9,523 ($76,190 - $66,667) or 476 units (3,810-3,334).

VI. Beyond the Numbers

a) Fixed (while property taxes will probably rise over the long run, they still are a fixed cost)
b) Variable
c) Fixed
d) Mixed (the business will always advertise, but the amount will vary over the long run)
e) Fixed
f) Variable
g) Variable
h) Mixed
i) Possibly mixed (a portion fixed regardless of output with add-ons to reflect changes in output)
j) Variable

VII. Demonstration Problems

Demonstration Problem #1 Solved and Explained

Requirement 1

To compute breakeven in dollars and in units, we need to find the contribution margin per unit and the contribution margin ratio:

$$\text{Contribution Margin Per Unit} = \text{Sales Price Per Unit} - \text{Variable Cost Per Unit}$$

$$\text{Contribution Margin Percentage or Ratio} = \frac{\text{Contribution Margin}}{\text{Sales Price Per Unit}}$$

Since the variable costs are 35% (0.35) of sales, the contribution margin per unit is:

$$\$30 - (.35 \times 30) = \$30 - \$10.50 = \$19.50$$

The contribution margin ratio is:

$$\$19.50 / 30 = .65$$

The computation of breakeven sales in units is:

$$\text{Breakeven Sales in Units} = \frac{\text{Fixed Expenses}}{\text{Contribution Margin Per Unit}}$$

$$\$325,000 / \$19.50 = 16,667 \text{ games}$$

The breakeven point in units is 16,667 games.

The computation of breakeven sales in dollars is:

$$\text{Breakeven Sales in Dollars} = \frac{\text{Fixed Expenses}}{\text{Contribution Margin Percentage}}$$

$$\$325,000 / .65 = \$500,000$$

The breakeven point in dollars is $500,000.

Requirement 2

The target operating income is given as $120,000. The number of games that must be sold to earn a target income of $120,000 is:

$$\text{Target Sales in Units} = \frac{\text{Fixed Expenses} + \text{Target Operating Income}}{\text{Contribution Margin Per Unit}}$$

$$(\$325,000 + \$120,000) / \$19.50 = 22,821 \text{ games}$$

To achieve the target operating income of $120,000, 22,821 games must be sold.

Requirement 3 (Graph)

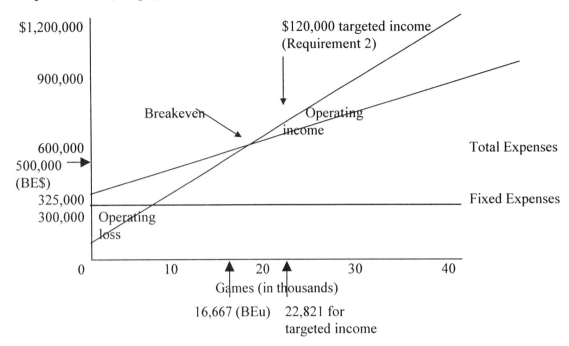

Requirement 4

To find the solution to Requirement 4, you must first determine exactly what item changes. No change in fixed expenses is indicated, and the target operating income of $60,000 remains the same. However, the selling price increases from $30 to $36, an increase of $6. Since variable expenses are 35% of the selling price, the new variable cost is $12.60 (35% × $36). Since the selling price of the game has changed, we must find the new contribution margin per unit in order to use the formula for target sales in Requirement 2. The new contribution margin per unit is:

$$\$36 - \$12.60 = \$23.40$$

Since the contribution margin per unit has increased to $23.40, the new target sales in units will be:

$$(\$325,000 + \$60,000) / \$23.40 = 16,453 \text{ games}$$

Target sales in units has decreased to 16,453 units. This is due to the increase in the selling price and the resulting increase in the contribution margin per unit.

Chapter 23 - The Master Budget and Responsibility Accounting

CHAPTER OVERVIEW

In the last chapter you learned more about costs—specifically how CVP analysis is used to predict outcomes. We now turn our attention to some of the ways managers plan and control their organization's activities using budgets. The learning objectives for this chapter are to

1. Learn why managers use budgets.
2. Prepare an operating budget.
3. Prepare a financial budget.
4. Use sensitivity analysis in budgeting.
5. Prepare performance reports for responsibility centers.

CHAPTER REVIEW

Objective 1 – Learn why managers use budgets.

A **budget** is a quantitative expression of a plan of action that helps managers to coordinate and implement the plan. The benefits of budgeting are:

1. **Planning** - budgets require managers to make plans, set goals, and design strategies for achieving those goals.
2. **Coordination and communication** - since the master budget is an overall company plan, it requires managers to work with other departments to achieve organizational goals and to communicate a consistent set of plans throughout the company.
3. **Benchmarking** - the budget can be used to evaluate performance by comparing actual results with the budgeted ones.

The **performance report** compares actual figures with budgeted figures in order to identify areas that need corrective action. The performance report also serves as a guide for the next period's budget.

The **master budget** is the set of budgeted financial statements and supporting schedules for the entire organization. A master budget has three components:

1) the **operating budget** projects sales revenue, cost of goods sold, and operating expenses leading to the budgeted income statement that projects operating income for the period.
2) the **capital expenditures budget** is the company's plan for the purchase of property, plant, and equipment, and other long-term assets.
3) the **financial budget** projects cash inflows and outflows—the cash budget—the budgeted period-end balance sheet, and the statement of cash flows.

You should study Exhibit 23-5 to understand the flow of information in preparation of the master budget.

Objective 2 - Prepare an operating budget for a company.

The **operating budget** starts with preparation of the sales budget; followed by the inventory, purchases and cost of goods sold budget, and then the operating expenses budget and culminates with the budgeted income statement. The budgeted income statement contains budgeted amounts rather than actual amounts. The steps in preparing the operating budget are as follows:

Step 1. Prepare the **sales budget** (Exhibit 23-7 in your text). Remember that there is no way to accurately plan for inventory purchases or inventory levels without a sales budget. The sales budget will generally schedule sales for each month, and present a total for the entire budget period.

Step 2. Prepare a schedule of the **inventory, purchases, and cost of goods sold, budget** (Exhibit 23-8, in your text). Remember that you need to buy enough inventory to meet both expected sales levels and the desired ending inventory levels. If there is a beginning inventory, it reduces the amount of inventory you need to purchase.

Study Tip: PURCHASES = COST OF GOODS SOLD + ENDING INVENTORY − BEGINNING INVENTORY

Step 3. Calculate **budgeted operating expenses** (Exhibit 23-9 in your text). Remember that some expenses vary with sales, such as sales commissions, while other expenses, such as rent, are fixed amounts from month to month.

The schedules prepared for the operating budget are now used to prepare **the budgeted income statement** (Exhibit 23-10 in your text). Budgeted sales on the income statement were determined by preparation of the sales budget. Budgeted cost of goods sold was determined by the preparation of the inventory, purchases, and cost of goods sold budget. The gross margin is equal to sales minus cost of goods sold. Operating expenses were scheduled on the operating expenses budget. Operating income is equal to the gross margin minus the operating expenses. The one remaining part of the budgeted income statement is interest expense, which is determined from the cash budget. Remember, all of these are budgeted amounts.

Objective 3 - Prepare a financial budget.

Once the operating budget is complete, the second part of the master budget is the **financial budget**. The financial budget includes:

Step 1: Prepare the **cash budget** (also called the **statement of budgeted cash receipts and disbursements**) (see Exhibit 23-14 in your text) details how the business expects to go from the beginning cash balance to the desired ending balance. The cash budget has four major parts:
1) **Budgeted cash collections from customers** (Exhibit 23-11 in your text) requires that you estimate 1) cash sales and 2) cash collections from credit sales. These amounts should be determined for each period contained in the budget.
2) **Budgeted cash payments for purchases** (Exhibit 23-12 in your text) uses the inventory, purchases, and cost of goods sold budget from the preparation of the operating budget.
3) **Budgeted cash payments for operating expenses** (Exhibit 23-13 in your text) uses the operating expenses budget from the preparation of the operating budget.
4) **Budgeted cash payments for capital expenditures**, if any. The budgeted acquisition of long-term assets appears in the **capital expenditures budget**, which is discussed in more detail in Chapter 26.

290

Step 2: Prepare the **budgeted balance sheet** (Exhibit 23-15 in your text) to project each asset, liability, and owner's equity account based on the plans outlined in the previous schedules.

Step 3: Prepare the **budgeted statement of cash flows** (Exhibit 23-16 in your text). Information for the cash flow budget is obtained from the previously completed budgets; specifically the cash collections and cash disbursements schedules, the cash budget, and the beginning balance of cash. These amounts are organized into the standard cash flow format: operating, investing, and financing activities.

Objective 4 - Use sensitivity analysis in budgeting.

Remember that the master budget models the company's *planned* activities. What happens if actual results differ from the plan? **Sensitivity analysis** is a "what-if" technique that asks what a result will be if a predicted amount is not achieved or if an underlying assumption changes.

Computer spreadsheets are particularly useful in answering many of the questions that arise when there is a difference in an assumption or an actual result because their speed permits managers to react and adjust more quickly.

Objective 5 - Prepare performance reports for responsibility centers.

Responsibility accounting is a system for evaluating the performance of each responsibility center and its manager. A **responsibility center** can be any part or subunit of an organization whose manager is accountable for specific activities. Responsibility accounting performance reports compare budgets with actual results for each center.

Four common types of responsibility centers are:
1) **Cost centers:** Generate no revenue and managers are accountable only for controlling costs.
2) **Revenue centers:** Exist where managers are primarily accountable for generating revenues, although, they may also have some responsibility for controlling costs.
3) **Profit centers:** Exist where managers are responsible for both revenues and expenses, and therefore, profits.
4) **Investment centers:** Such as a single department store in a chain where managers are responsible for generating sales, controlling expenses, and managing the amount of investment required to earn income.

Management by exception is a strategy in which management investigates important deviations from budgeted amounts. Responsibility and authority are delegated to lower-level employees; management does not become involved unless necessary. Exhibit 23-20 in your text illustrates a **performance report** that stresses variances. The format of a performance report is a matter of personal preference of the users. Basically, the report compares actual and budgeted performance at different levels of the organization.

TEST YOURSELF

All the self-testing materials in this chapter focus on information and procedures that your instructor is likely to test in quizzes and examinations.

I. Matching   *Match each numbered term with its lettered definition.*

_____ 1. Master budget
_____ 2. Responsibility center
_____ 3. Sales budget
_____ 4. Cash budget
_____ 5. Sensitivity analysis
_____ 6. Operating budget

_____ 7. Financial budget
_____ 8. Capital expenditures budget
_____ 9. Responsibility accounting
_____ 10. Management by exception
_____ 11. Cash collections from customers budget

A. A company's plan for purchases of property, plant, equipment, and other long-term assets
B. Details how the business expects to go from the beginning cash balance to the desired ending balance
C. Directs management's attention to important differences between actual and budgeted amounts.
D. A system for evaluating the performance of each responsibility center and its managers
E. Projects cash inflows and outflows, the period ending balance sheet, and budgeted cash flow statement
F. Requires an estimate of 1) cash sales and 2) cash collections from credit sales.
G. Consists of the sales budget, inventory, purchases, and cost of goods sold budget, and operating expenses budget.
H. The cornerstone of the master budget.
I. A part, segment, or subunit of an organization whose manager is accountable for specified activities
J. A "what if" technique that asks what a result will be if a predicted amount is not achieved or if an underlying assumption changes
K. The comprehensive budget that includes the operating budget, the capital expenditures budget, and the financial budget

II. Multiple Choice   *Circle the best answer.*

1. A variance occurs when

   A. actual results exceed budgeted amounts.
   B. actual result is less than budgeted amounts.
   C. actual results differ from budgeted amounts.
   D. none of the above.

2. Which of the following is a cost center?

   A. The men's department in a retail store
   B. The West coast division of a large oil refinery
   C. The administrative division of a corporation
   D. The local branch of a statewide chain store

3. When preparing the master budget, the first step is the

   A. financial budget.
   B. operating budget.
   C. the cash budget.
   D. the capital expenditures budget.

4. When preparing the operating budget, the first step is

   A. the purchase budget.
   B. the sales budget.
   C. the operating expense budget.
   D. the inventory budget.

5. An example of a profit center is:

   A. the housewares department in a department store.
   B. the accounting department in a hardware store.
   C. both of these.
   D. neither of these.

6. An example of an investment center is:

   A. a department store in a chain of stores.
   B. the delivery department of an auto parts store.
   C. the shipping department of a manufacturer.
   D. both B and C.

7. Which factor is important in an effective responsibility accounting system?

   A. Control over operations
   B. Access to information
   C. Both of these
   D. Neither of these

8. Responsibility accounting systems are used for:

   A. finding fault.

   B. placing blame for failure to meet goals.

   C. determining who can explain specific variances.

   D. both finding fault and placing blame for failure to meet goals.

9. Which of the following is a analytical technique that asks what a result will be if a predicted amount is not achieved or if an underlying assumption changes?

   A. Management by exception
   B. Responsibility accounting
   C. Responsibility center
   D. Sensitivity analysis

10. Which of the following compares actual amounts with budgeted amounts in order to identify areas that need corrective action?

   A. The master budget
   B. Performance report
   C. The operating budget
   D. The budgeted statement of cash flows

III. Completion *Complete each of the following statements.*

1. The benefits of budgeting are 1) _____ 2) _____ and 3) _____ .

2. The budgeted income statement can be prepared after the _____ has been completed.

3. _____ are primarily evaluated by their ability to generate revenues.

4. The three components of the master budget are _____ , _____ , and _____ .

5. To determine what might happen if predicted outcomes are not achieved or underlying assumptions change, managers use _____ .

6. _____ are evaluated on their ability to control costs.

7. Budgeted purchases for long-term assets are included in the _____ budget.

8. The financial budget consists of the _____ , the _____ , and the _____ .

9. A _____ results when actual results differ from projected results.

10. The _____ compares actual results with budgeted figures.

IV. Daily Exercises

1. Assuming Inventory increased by $9,000 during the period and Cost of Goods Sold was $245,000, what were purchases?

2. If ending Accounts Receivable is 50% greater than beginning Accounts Receivable, cash receipts from customers are $400,000 and credit sales are $500,000, calculate the beginning and ending Accounts Receivable balances.

3. Susana's Shoes has three locations in Anytown, USA. The owner received the following data for the third quarter of the current year:

	Revenues			Expenses	
	Budget	Actual		Budget	Actual
West Store	$220,000	$250,000		$210,000	$198,000
Center Store	187,000	175,000		146,000	150,000
East Store	713,000	874,000		706,000	696,000

Arrange the data in a performance report, showing third quarter results in thousands of dollars.

V. Exercises

1. Kay's Cameras sells disposable, recyclable cameras for use underwater. The units cost $3 each and are sold for $6 a piece. At the end of the first quarter, 200 cameras were on hand. Projected sales for the next four months are 700 units, 900 units, 1,200 units, and 1,000 units, respectively. Kay wants to maintain inventory equal to 40% of the next month's sales.

Prepare a sales budget and the inventory, purchases, and cost of goods sold budget for the next quarter.

Sales Budget - 2nd Quarter

1st month	2nd month	3rd month	Total

Inventory, Purchases, and Cost of Goods Sold Budget

	1st month	2nd month	3rd month	Total

2. Using the following information, present an income statement for the year ended December 31, 20X5.

a) Consulting Fees Earned were $850,000.

b) Salaries: the staff consists of two full-time consultants, one half-time consultant and an office assistant. The consultants are paid a base salary, plus a 30% commission on fees earned. The base for full-time consultants is $40,000 while the half-time consultant receives a base of $20,000. The office assistant's salary is $35,000.

c) Office rent was $5,500/month for 1/1 – 6/30 at which time it was raised to $6,000 for the remainder of the year.

d) Depreciation on office equipment, computed on the straight-line basis, was $15,000 for the year.

e) Office expenses were $20,000 plus 5% of consulting fees.

f) Travel expenses were 4% of consulting fees.

g) Miscellaneous expenses were 1% of consulting fees.

3. Review the information in Exercise 2 above and the following information, and present a budgeted income statement in the space provided. You may want to first compare your answer for Exercise 2 with the solution.

a) Revenues are expected to increase by 25%.
b) The office assistant will receive a 10% salary increase at the beginning of the year.
c) On 7/1 the lease for the office will be renewed. It is expected to increase by 15%/month.
d) Depreciation will remain unchanged for the year.

4. Review the information from Exercise 3 above and present, in the space provided, a performance report for the year, considering the following additional information.

a) Revenues increased by 40%.
b) The growth in revenues required an expansion of the staff by one additional full-time consultant, who was hired on April 1. Also on April 1, base salaries for full-time consultants (including the new hire) were increased to $50,000 while the half-time consultant's base was increased to $25,000. The commission rate remained unchanged.
c) The July 1 rent increase was 25%.
d) Travel expenses were 6% of revenues.

	Actual	Budgeted	Variance

5. The Jones-Jackson Partnership owns and operates a sporting goods store specializing in trekking equipment. Sales for the first two quarters of the current year are as follows:

January	$343,200
February	386,000
March	408,000
April	440,900
May	501,800
June	527,100

The partnership's sales are 15% cash and 85% credit. Collections from credit customers are 20% the month of sale, 45% the month following sale, 30% two months following sale, and 4% three months after sale. 1% of credit sales become uncollectible and are written off.

Using the following format, prepare a schedule for budgeted cash collections for April, May and June (round to the whole dollar amounts).

	April	May	June
Cash Sales			
Collections from January			
Collections from February			
Collections from March			
Collections from April			
Collections from May			
Collections from June			
Monthly Totals			
Total for the Quarter			

VI. Beyond the Numbers

Refer to Exercises 3 & 4. The budgeted income statement prepared in Exercise 3 was based on the projection that revenues would increase by 25%. At that projection, the company was still budgeted to generate net income of $386,600. Explain how the actual increase in revenues was 40%, yet the net income fell short of the projected amount by $7,150.

VII. Demonstration Problems

Demonstration Problem #1

Tele-data Communication's cash budget for the first three quarters of 20X8 is given below (note that some of the data is missing and must be calculated). The company requires a minimum cash balance of at least $40,000, and owes $4,000 on a note payable from a previous quarter. (Ignore interest.)

Tele-data Communications
Quarterly Cash Budget
For the Quarter Ended March 31, 20X8

	1	2	3
Beginning cash balance	$ 64,000	$ D	$ 52,000
Add collections from customers	A	280,000	268,000
Cash available	$ B	$ E	$320,000
Deduct disbursements			
Inventory purchases	$124,000	$ F	$ 92,000
Operating expenses	100,000	88,000	120,000
Equipment purchases	40,000	44,000	116,000
Dividends	0	24,000	J
Total disbursements	$264,000	$G	$ K
Excess (deficiency) in cash	$ 28,000	$ 68,000	($ 8,000)
Financing			
Add borrowing	$ C	-	$ 48,000
Deduct repayments	-	H	0
Ending cash balance	$ 40,000	$ I	$ 40,000

Required:

Find the missing value represented by each letter. (Hint: it may not be possible to solve this problem in sequence i.e. A. first, B. second, and so on.)

A.

B.

C.

D.

E.

F.

G.

H.

I.

J.

K.

Demonstration Problem #2

The Baguette Bakery has two departments, wholesale and retail. The company's income statement for the year ended December 31, 20X7 appears as follows:

Net Sales		$1,130,000
Cost of Goods Sold		548,000
Gross Margin		582,000
Operating expenses:		
Salaries	$310,000	
Depreciation	45,000	
Advertising	18,000	
Other	30,000	403,000
Operating income		$ 179,000

Cost of goods sold is distributed $226,000 for wholesale and $322,000 for retail. Salaries are allocated to departments based on sales: wholesale, $472,000; retail $658,000. Advertising is evenly allocated to the two departments. Depreciation is allocated based on square footage: wholesale, 4,000 square feet; retail, 6,000 square feet. Other expenses are allocated based on sales.

Prepare a departmental income statement showing revenue, expenses, and operating income for two departments.

The Baguette Bakery			
Departmental Income Statement			
For the Year Ended December 31, 20X7			
		Department	
	Total	Wholesale	Retail
Net sales	$1,130,000		
Cost of goods sold	548,000		
Gross margin	582,000		
Operating expenses:			
Salaries	310,000		
Depreciation	45,000		
Advertising	18,000		
Other	30,000		
Total operating expenses	403,000		
Operating income	$ 179,000	$	$

SOLUTIONS

I. Matching

1. K	3. H	5. J	7. E	9. D	11. F
2. I	4. B	6. G	8. A	10. C	

II. Multiple Choice

1. C A variance does not imply direction, only a difference.

2. C The men's department is a profit center, while choices B and D are investment centers.

3. B The order is operating budget, the capital expenditures budget, and financial budget (which includes the cash budget).

4. B The operating budget always begins with the sales budget - the others are prepared after the sales budget is completed.

5. A The accounting department is a cost center.

6. A Both choices B and C are cost centers.

7. C Both the control over operations and access to information are important factors in an effective responsibility accounting system.

8. C Responsibility accounting systems are not intended to find fault or place blame.

9. D Sensitivity analysis is a "what-if" technique that asks what a result will be if a predicted amount is not achieved or if an underlying assumption changes.

10. B The performance report compares actual figures with budgeted figures in order to identify areas that need corrective action.

III. Completion

1. planning; coordination and communication; benchmarking
2. operating budget
3. Revenue centers
4. operating budget, capital expenditures budget, financial budget
5. sensitivity analysis
6. Cost centers
7. capital expenditures
8. cash budget, budgeted balance sheet, budgeted statement of cash flows
9. variance
10. performance report

IV. Daily Exercises

1. Beginning inventory + Purchases - Ending inventory = Cost of goods sold
   X + Purchases - (X + $9,000) = $245,000
   Purchases   = $254,000

2. Beginning Accounts Receivable = X
   Ending Accounts Receivable = 150%X
   Credit Sales = $500,000

   Beginning Accounts Receivable + Credit Sales – Receipts from customers =
   Ending Accounts Receivable
        X   + $500,000 - $400,000   = 150%X
   Beginning Accounts Receivable = $200,000
   Ending Accounts Receivable = 150% × $200,000 = $300,000

3.

Operating income by location	Budgeted Income	Actual Income	Variance Favorable (Unfavorable)
West Store			
(220-210)	10		
(250-198)		52	42
Center Store			
(187-146)	41		
(175-150)		25	(16)
East Store			
(713-706)	7		
(874-696)		178	171
	$58	$255	$197

V. Exercises

1.

Sales Budget – 2nd Quarter

1st month	2nd month	3rd month	Total
$4,200	$5,400	$7,200	$16,800

Multiply number of units by unit cost.

Purchases, Cost of Goods Sold, and Inventory Budget

		1st month	2nd month	3rd month	Total
	Cost of Goods Sold[1]	$2,100	$2,700	$3,600	$8,400
+	Desired Ending Inventory[2]	1,080	1,440	1,200[5]	1,200
	Subtotal	3,180	4,140	4,800	9,600
-	Beginning Inventory[3]	600[4]	1,080	1,440	600
=	Purchases	$2,580	$3,060	$3,360	$9,000

[1] Cost of Goods Sold is 50% of budgeted sales: $3/$6 = 50%

[2] Desired Ending Inventory is 40% of the following month's Cost of Goods Sold.

[3] Beginning Inventory is 40% of current month's Cost of Goods Sold (or simply last month's Ending Inventory!)

[4] Beginning Inventory is 200 units × $3 ea = $600

[5] The next month's projected Cost of Goods Sold = 1,000 units × $3 ea = $3,000; Ending Inventory = 40% × $3,000 = $1,200

2.

Consulting Fees Earned		$850,000
Less: Operating Expenses		
Salaries and Commissions Expense	$390,000	
Rent Expense	69,000	
Depreciation Expense	15,000	
Office Expense	62,500	
Travel Expense	34,000	
Miscellaneous Expense	8,500	579,000
Net Income		$271,000

Calculations:

Salaries and Commissions	
2 Full-time Consultants	$ 80,000
1 Half-time Consultant	20,000
30% of Consulting Fees	255,000
Office Assistant	35,000
Total	$390,000

Rent Expense = 6 × $5,500 + 6 × $6,000	=	69,000
Office Expense = $20,000 + .05 × $850,000	=	62,500
Travel Expense = .04 × $850,000	=	34,000
Miscellaneous Expense = .01 × $850,000	=	8,500

3.

Budgeted Income Statement

Consulting Fees Earned		$1,062,500
Less: Operating Expenses		
Salaries and Commissions Expense	$457,250	
Rent Expense	77,400	
Depreciation Expense	15,000	
Office Expense	73,125	
Travel Expense	42,500	
Miscellaneous Expense	10,625	675,900
Net Income		$ 386,600

Calculations:

Salaries and Commissions	
Consultants Base	$100,000
30 % of Consulting Fee	318,750
Office Assistant	38,500
Total	$457,250

Rent Expense = 6 × $6,000 + 6 × $6,900	=	77,400
Office Expense = $20,000 + .05 × $1,062,500	=	73,125
Travel Expense = .04 × $1,062,500	=	42,500
Miscellaneous Expense = .01 × $1,062,500	=	10,625

4.

Performance Report

	Actual	Budgeted	Variance
Consulting Fees Earned	$1,190,000	$1,062,500	$127,500
Salaries and Commissions	551,750	457,250	(94,500)
Rent Expense	81,000	77,400	(3,600)
Depreciation Expense	15,000	15,000	0
Office Expense	79,500	73,125	(6,375)
Travel Expense	71,400	42,500	(28,900)
Miscellaneous Expense	11,900	10,625	(1,275)
Net Income	$ 379,450	$ 386,600	$ (7,150)

Calculations:
Salaries and Commissions
2 Full-time Consultants:

$40,000 \times 2 \times 3/12$	=	$ 20,000
$50,000 \times 2 \times 9/12$	=	75,000

1 Full-time Consultant:

$50,000 \times 9/12$	=	37,500

1 Half-time Consultant

$20,000 \times 3/12$	=	5,000
$25,000 \times 9/12$	=	18,750
30% Commission		357,000
Office Assistant		38,500
		$551,750

Rent Expense = $6 \times \$6,000 + 6 \times \$7,500 = 81,000$
Office Expense = $\$20,000 + .05 \times \$1,190,000 = 79,500$
Travel Expense = $.06 \times \$1,190,000 = 71,400$
Miscellaneous Expense = $.01 \times \$1,190,000 = 11,900$

5.

	April	May	June
Cash Sales	$ 66,135	$ 75,270	$ 79,065
Collections from January	11,669		
Collections from February	98,430	13,124	
Collections from March	156,060	104,040	13,872
Collections from April	74,953	168,644	112,430
Collections from May		85,306	191,939
Collections from June			89,607
Monthly Totals	$407247	$446,384	$486,913
Total from Quarter			$1,340,544

VI. Beyond the Numbers

Even though the company had an actual increase of 40% in revenues rather than the projected 25%, total operating expenses had only been expected to increase approximately 16.7% ($675,900/$579,000), when they actually increased 40.0% ($810,550/$579,000). So, while revenues increased 15% over budget, the expenses increased 23.3% over budget, thus resulting in a lower net income for the year.

VII. Demonstration Problems

Demonstration Problem #1 Solved and Explained

The solution is given in the order in which the exercise may be worked.

B. Cash available - Total disbursements = Excess (deficiency)
    B - $264,000 = $28,000
    B = $292,000

A. Beginning cash balance + Cash collections = Cash available
    $64,000 + A = $292,000
    A = $228,000

C. Excess + Borrowing = Ending cash balance
    $28,000 + C = $40,000
    C = $12,000

D. $40,000; the beginning cash balance for any quarter is the ending cash balance from the previous quarter.

E. Beginning cash balance + Cash collections = Cash available
    $40,000 + $280,000 = E
    E = $320,000

I. $52,000; the ending cash balance for any quarter is the beginning cash balance for the next quarter.

H. Excess - Repayments = Ending cash balance
    $68,000 - H = $52,000
    H = $16,000

G. Cash available - Total disbursements = Excess
    $320,000 - G = $ 68,000
    G = $252,000

F. Inventory purchases + Operating expenses + Equipment purchases + Dividends = Total disbursements
    F + $88,000 + $44,000 + $24,000 = $252,000
    F = $96,000

K. Cash available - Total disbursements = (deficiency)
    $320,000 - K = ($8,000)
    $320,000 + $8,000 = K
    K = $328,000

J. Inventory purchases + Operating expenses + Equipment purchases + Dividends = Total disbursements
    $92,000 + $120,000 + $116,000 + J = $328,000
    $328,000 + J = $328,000
    J = $0

Demonstration Problem #2 Solved and Explained

	Total	Department Wholesale	Retail
The Baguette Bakery			
Departmental Income Statement			
For the Year Ended December 31, 20X7			
Net sales	$1,130,000	$472,000	$658,000
Cost of goods sold	548,000	226,000	322,000
Gross margin	582,000	246,000	336,000
Operating expenses:			
Salaries	310,000	129,487	180,513
Depreciation	45,000	18,000	27,000
Advertising	18,000	9,000	9,000
Other	30,000	12,531	17,469
Total operating expenses	403,000	169,018	233,982
Operating income	$ 179,000	$ 76,982	$102,018

Calculations:

Salaries:
- Wholesale: $[(\$472,000 \div \$1,130,000)] \times \$310,000 = \$129,487$
- Retail: $[(\$658,000 \div \$1,130,000)] \times \$310,000 = \$180,513$

Depreciation:
- Wholesale: $[4,000 \div (4,000 + 6,000)] \times \$45,000 = \$18,000$
- Retail: $[6,000 \div (4,000 + 6,000)] \times \$45,000 = \$27,000$

Advertising:
- Wholesale: $\$18,000 \div 2 = \$9,000$
- Retail: $\$18,000 \div 2 = \$9,000$

Other:
- Wholesale: $(\$472,000 \div \$1,130,000) \times \$30,000 = \$12,531$
- Retail: $(\$658,000 \div \$1,130,000) \times \$30,000 = \$17,469$

Chapter 24 - Flexible Budgets and Standard Costs

CHAPTER OVERVIEW

In Chapter 23 you were introduced to the master budget and its components. In addition, you learned how budgeted amounts are compared with actual results as one means of evaluating performance. The topics in the previous chapter provide a foundation for those covered in this chapter—flexible budgets and standard costs. The learning objectives for this chapter are to

1. Prepare a flexible budget for the income statement.
2. Use the flexible budget to show why actual results differ from the static budget.
3. Identify the benefits of standard costs and learn how to set standards.
4. Compute standard cost variances for direct materials and direct labor.
5. Analyze manufacturing overhead in a standard cost system.
6. Record transactions at standard cost and prepare a standard cost income statement.

CHAPTER REVIEW

Objective 1 – Prepare a flexible budget for the income statement.

As you learned in previous chapters, **cost behavior** may be fixed or variable. Mixed costs have both variable and fixed components. Cost behaviors are valid only for a relevant range of activity.

The master budget is a **static budget** that is prepared for only one level of sales volume. Once developed, the static budget does not change. In Chapter 23, you studied the **performance report** that compares actual with budgeted results to show **variances** (differences). A variance is labeled as favorable if it increases operating income and unfavorable if it decreases operating income.

In contrast to the static budget, a **flexible budget** is a summarized budget that managers can easily compute for several different volume levels. Flexible budgets separate variable costs from fixed costs. Generally, the flexible budget is prepared for the actual volume achieved (that is, when actual volume is known). Review Exhibit 24-2 in your text.

To prepare a flexible budget, we use the **flexible budget formula for total cost**:

Flexible budget total cost = (number of output units × variable cost per output unit) + Total fixed cost

Note, it is the variable costs that put the "flex" in the flexible budget, because budgeted total fixed costs remain constant within the relevant range.

Study Exhibit 24-3 in your text to understand the preparation of a flexible budget income statement.

The flexible budget cost line can be graphed for further analysis. The vertical axis of the budget graph shows total expenses and the horizontal axis shows the level of volume. Both budgeted and actual results can be graphed. Remember that the only valid portion of the graph is the area within the relevant range. Refer to Exhibit 24-4 and 24-5 in your text for a graph of a flexible budget and a graph of actual and budgeted total expenses.

Objective 2 – Use the flexible budget to show why actual results differ from the static budget.

Managers must examine why a variance occurred to identify any problems and to take corrective action. To analyze variances, managers begin by using the flexible budget for the number of units actually sold to divide the static budget variance into two broad categories:

- **Sales volume variance**—arises when the number of units actually sold differs from the static budget sales. This equals the difference between a *static* budget amount and a *flexible* budget amount.
- **Flexible budget variance**—arises when the company actually earned more or less revenue, or incurred more or less cost, than expected for the actual level of output. This equals the difference between the *actual* amount and a *flexible* budget amount.

See Exhibit 24-6 in your text.

Objective 3 - Identify the benefits of standard costs and learn how to set standards.

A **standard cost** is a budget for a single unit. When using a standard cost system, each input has both a price standard and a quantity standard.

Price standards are established for direct materials, direct labor, and manufacturing overhead. Accountants work with managers and suppliers to set the price standards for direct materials; with human resource managers to set direct labor cost standards; and with production managers to estimate variable and fixed manufacturing overhead expenses.

Engineers and production managers set quantity standards for direct materials and direct labor.

The benefits to an organization of standard costs are:

1. Providing the unit amounts needed for budgeting
2. Help management control operations by setting target levels of operating performance
3. Motivating employees by setting goals against which performance will be evaluated
4. Providing a unit cost basis for establishing selling prices
5. Reducing clerical costs

See Exhibit 24-8 in your text

Objective 4 - Compute standard cost variances for direct materials and direct labor.

Variances between actual and standard costs are separated into **price variances** and **efficiency variances** for direct materials and direct labor.

Direct Materials:

The total flexible budget variance for direct materials is separated into the price variance and the efficiency variance. The **direct materials price variance** measures the difference between the actual and the standard price of materials for the amount of materials used.

$$\text{MATERIALS PRICE VARIANCE} = \left[\begin{array}{c}\text{DIFFERENCE BETWEEN}\\\text{ACTUAL AND STANDARD}\\\text{PRICES PER INPUT UNIT}\end{array}\right] \times \begin{array}{c}\text{ACTUAL QUANTITY OF}\\\text{INPUTS}\end{array}$$

$$\text{MATERIALS PRICE VARIANCE} = \left[\begin{array}{cc}\text{ACTUAL PRICE} & \text{STANDARD PRICE}\\\text{PER INPUT UNIT} & - \ \text{PER INPUT UNIT}\end{array}\right] \times \begin{array}{c}\text{ACTUAL}\\\text{QUANTITY OF}\\\text{INPUTS}\end{array}$$

If the actual unit price is less than the standard unit price, the variance is favorable. If the actual unit price is greater than the standard unit price, the variance is unfavorable.

The **direct materials efficiency variance** measures whether the quantity of materials actually used to make the actual number of outputs is within the standard allowed for that number of outputs. This is computed as the difference between the actual quantity of inputs used and the standard quantity of inputs allowed for the actual number of outputs multiplied by the standard price per unit of the input.

$$\text{MATERIALS EFFICIENCY VARIANCE} = \left[\begin{array}{c}\text{DIFFERENCE BETWEEN}\\\text{ACTUAL QUANTITY OF}\\\text{INPUTS USED AND THE}\\\text{STANDARD QUANTITY OF}\\\text{INPUTS THAT SHOULD}\\\text{HAVE BEEN USED FOR THE}\\\text{ACTUAL NUMBER OF}\\\text{OUTPUTS}\end{array}\right] \times \begin{array}{c}\text{STANDARD}\\\text{PRICE PER}\\\text{INPUT UNIT}\end{array}$$

$$\text{MATERIALS EFFICIENCY VARIANCE} = \left[\begin{array}{cc}\text{ACTUAL} & \text{STANDARD}\\\text{QUANTITY} - & \text{QUANTITY}\\\text{OF INPUTS} & \text{OF INPUTS}\end{array}\right] \times \begin{array}{c}\text{STANDARD}\\\text{PRICE PER}\\\text{INPUT UNIT}\end{array}$$

Note that INPUTS THAT SHOULD HAVE BEEN USED FOR ACTUAL OUTPUT is equal to standard input per unit times actual units produced. If inputs actually used are less than the inputs that should have been used, the variance is favorable. If inputs actually used are greater than the inputs that should have been used, the variance is unfavorable.

Exhibit 24-13 in your text summarizes the direct materials variance computations.

311

Direct Labor:

The **direct labor price variance** measures the difference between the actual rate per labor hour and the STANDARD rate per labor hour.

$$\text{LABOR PRICE VARIANCE} = \left[\text{DIFFERENCE BETWEEN ACTUAL AND STANDARD UNIT PRICES OF INPUTS} \right] \times \text{ACTUAL QUANTITY OF INPUTS}$$

$$\text{LABOR PRICE VARIANCE} = \left[\text{ACTUAL PRICE PER INPUT UNIT} - \text{STANDARD PRICE PER INPUT UNIT} \right] \times \text{ACTUAL QUANTITY OF INPUTS}$$

The **direct labor efficiency variance** measures the difference between the hours actually used and hours that should have been used for the output achieved.

$$\text{LABOR EFFICIENCY VARIANCE} = \left[\text{ACTUAL QUANTITY OF INPUTS} - \text{STANDARD QUANTITY OF INPUTS} \right] \times \text{STANDARD PRICE PER INPUT UNIT}$$

Note that these equations are identical to the direct materials variance equations. Exhibit 24-14 in your text summarizes direct labor variance computations.

The advantage to the company of calculating these variances is that management can investigate when the variances are significant.

In addition to direct materials and direct labor, variances are also calculated for manufacturing overhead as one means of evaluating performance.

Objective 5 – Analyze manufacturing overhead in a standard cost system.

As you learned in Chapter 20, manufacturing overhead is allocated to production using a predetermined overhead rate. The first step in accounting for manufacturing overhead is to calculate the predetermined overhead rate. This rate is based on the amounts from the static (master) budget, which provides known amounts at the beginning of the year. See Exhibit 24-16. Once the standard predetermined manufacturing overhead rate is calculated, the next step is to identify the standard quantity of the allocation base allowed for the actual number of outputs, and then allocate the manufacturing overhead. To allocate manufacturing overhead (MOH) to production, you use the formula:

$$\text{MOH ALLOCATED TO PRODUCTION} = \text{STANDARD PREDETERMINED MOH RATE} \times \text{STANDARD QUANTITY OF THE ALLOCATION BASE ALLOWED FOR THE ACTUAL NUMBER OF OUTPUTS}$$

Overhead variances are computed differently from material and labor variances. The **total manufacturing overhead variance** is the difference between actual overhead cost, which is accumulated as costs are incurred, and the standard manufacturing overhead allocated to production. Manufacturing overhead variances are commonly separated into the:

- **Overhead flexible budget variance**, which is the difference between the actual overhead cost and the flexible budget overhead for the actual number of outputs.
- **Production volume variance**, which is the difference between the manufacturing overhead cost in the flexible budget for actual outputs, and the standard overhead allocated to production. The production volume variance is favorable when actual output exceeds expected output.

Exhibit 24-17 in your text summarizes this two-variance approach.

Objective 6 - Record transactions at standard cost and prepare a standard cost income statement.

To record purchases of direct materials:

Materials Inventory	XX		
Direct Materials Price Variance	X	or	X
Accounts Payable			XX

To record direct materials used:

Work in Process Inventory	XX		
Direct Materials Efficiency Variance	X	or	X
Materials Inventory			XX

To record direct labor costs incurred:

Manufacturing Wages	XX		
Direct Labor Price Variance	X	or	X
Wages Payable			XX

To assign direct labor to production:

Work in Process Inventory	XX		
Direct Labor Efficiency Variance	X	or	X
Manufacturing Wages			XX

To record actual overhead costs incurred:

Manufacturing Overhead	XX	
A/P, Accum. Dep., etc.		XX

To allocated overhead to production:

Work in Process Inventory	XX	
Manufacturing Overhead		XX

To record completion of units:

Finished Goods Inventory	XX	
Work in Process Inventory		XX

To record cost of sales:

Cost of Goods Sold	XX	
Finished Goods Inventory		XX

The overhead variances are recorded when the Manufacturing Overhead account is reduced to zero (closed). See Exhibit 24-18.

In all of these entries, credit variances are favorable, debits are unfavorable. At year-end, all variance accounts are closed with a reconciling net debit (or credit) to Income Summary.

A **standard cost income statement** lists cost of goods sold at standard cost followed by the specific variances for direct materials, direct labor, and manufacturing overhead. Remember, debit variances are unfavorable (and therefore added to the cost of goods sold amount) while credit variances are favorable (and therefore deducted from the cost of goods sold amount). This format shows management what needs to be improved or corrected. See Exhibit 24-19 in your text.

> Helpful Hint: Review the Decision Guidelines titled *Standard Costs and Variance Analysis.*

TEST YOURSELF

All the self-testing materials in this chapter focus on information and procedures that your instructor is likely to test in quizzes and examinations.

I. Matching   *Match each numbered term with its lettered definition.*

_____ 1. Price variance
_____ 2. Standard cost
_____ 3. Variance
_____ 4. Efficiency variance
_____ 5. Production volume variance
_____ 6. Bench marking

_____ 7. Sales volume variance
_____ 8. Static budget
_____ 9. Flexible budget
_____ 10. Flexible budget variance
_____ 11. Overhead flexible budget variance

A. A budget prepared for only one level of activity
B. The difference between an actual amount and the corresponding budgeted amount
C. The difference between the actual quantity of input used and the standard quantity of input allowed for actual output, multiplied by the standard unit price of input
D. Difference between an amount in the flexible budget and the actual results
E. Difference between a revenue, expense, or operating income in the flexible budget, and the revenue, expense, or operating income amount in the master budget
F. Difference between total actual overhead (fixed and variable) and the flexible budget overhead amount for actual production volume
G. Difference between the actual unit price of an input (materials and labor) and a standard unit price, multiplied by the actual quantity of inputs used
H. Difference between the flexible budget overhead for actual production and standard overhead applied to production
I. Predetermined cost that management believes the business should incur in producing an item
J. Set of budgets covering a range of volume rather than a single level of volume
K. Using standards based on "best practice" level of performance

II. Multiple Choice   *Circle the best answer.*

1. As volume decreases, which of the following is true?

   A. Total variable costs decrease
   B. Variable cost per unit decreases

   C. Fixed cost per unit decreases
   D. Total fixed costs increase

2. A budget covering a range of activity levels is a:

   A. Flexible budget
   B. Static budget

   C. Conversion budget
   D. Pliable budget

3. Flexible budgets can be used as:

   A. a planning tool.
   B. a control device.

   C. both a planning tool and a control device.
   D. neither a planning tool nor a control device.

4. One possible explanation for a favorable sales volume variance and an unfavorable flexible budget variance is:

A. higher than expected sales and costs.
B. higher than expected sales and lower than expected costs.
C. lower than expected sales and higher than expected costs.
D. lower than expected sales and costs.

5. The term standard cost usually refers to ___ cost. The term budgeted cost usually refers to ___ cost.

A. unit, unit   C. total, unit
B. unit, total   D. total, total

6. Price variances relate to:

A. direct materials only.   C. manufacturing overhead only.
B. direct labor only.   D. both direct materials and direct labor.

7. A production volume variance relates to:

A. direct materials only.   C. manufacturing overhead only.
B. direct labor only.   D. both direct materials and direct labor.

8. In a standard cost income statement, gross margin equals:

A. Net sales - cost of goods sold at standard cost
B. Net sales - operating expenses
C. Net sales - cost of goods sold at standard cost + unfavorable variances - favorable variances
D. Net sales - cost of goods sold at standard cost - unfavorable variances + favorable variances

9. At the end of the accounting period, variance account balances are:

A. carried forward to the next accounting period.
B. closed to cost of goods sold.
C. closed to Income Summary.
D. none of the above.

10. The difference between the actual overhead cost and the flexible budget overhead for actual production is the

A. production volume variance.   C. sales volume variance.
B. flexible budget variance.   D. overhead flexible budget variance.

III. Completion   *Complete each of the following statements.*

1. _____ are resources given up to achieve a specific objective.
2. Total _____ costs change proportionately with changes in volume or activity.
3. Total _____ costs do not change during a given time period over a wide range of volume.
4. A _____ cost has both variable and fixed components.
5. If rent expense is fixed at $1,000 per month and sales increase from 2,500 units to 10,000 units, the rent per unit is _____ percent of the original amount.
6. A(n) _____ variance for materials or labor measures whether the quantity of inputs used to make a product is within the budget.
7. A(n) _____ variance for materials or labor measures how well a business keeps unit prices of materials and labor within standards.
8. A budget prepared for only one level of volume is called a _____ budget.
9. A _____ refers to any group of individual items.
10 A _____ variance increases net income; while a _____ variance decreases net income.

IV. Daily Exercises

1. Nello's Delicatessen produces pasta sauce, which is sold in one-quart containers. The pasta is made in 10 gallon batches. Each 10 gallon batch requires the following:

Ingredients	Cost
90 pounds of tomatoes	25¢/lb
2 head of garlic	90¢ ea.
20 pounds of onions	15¢/lb
2 gallons red wine	$6.50/gallon
2 cups olive oil	20¢/ounce
8 ounces fresh herbs	10¢/ounce

In addition, the one quart container in which the sauce is sold costs the business 9¢. Calculate the standard cost to produce one quart of pasta sauce.

2. To produce a 2-pound loaf of sourdough bread, the San Francisco Bakery's standard material cost is 80¢ per loaf (40¢ per pound). During the first week of March, the San Francisco Bakery purchased 120,000 pounds of ingredients costing $47,400 and paid $1,200 for 60,000 sacks. The week's production was 59,550 loaves of bread. Compute the direct materials price, efficiency, and total materials variances. Assume all ingredients purchased and sacks purchased were used in production.

3. Review the information in Daily Exercise 2 above and journalize entries to record the materials variances.

4. Review the information in Daily Exercise 2 above. San Francisco Bakery's direct labor standard is .020 direct labor hours per unit of output, at a standard cost of $11.75 per hour . For the first week of March, production required 1,200 direct labor hours and the total direct labor cost was $14,700. Compute the direct labor price, efficiency, and total direct labor variances.

5. Review the information in Daily Exercise 4 above and journalize entries to record labor variances.

V. Exercises

1. If variable costs are $5.00 per unit, the relevant range is 6,000 to 15,000 units, and total costs were $60,000 for 8,000 units:

   A. How much were fixed costs?

   B. What is the flexible budget formula for total costs?

   C. At the 10,000 units level, what are total budgeted costs?

319

2.

Actual production	3,300	units
Actual cost (6,700 feet of direct materials)	$33,701	
Standard price	$ 4.75	per foot
Materials efficiency variance	$ 2,660	F

A. Compute the materials price variance.

B. Compute standard feet per unit.

3. Assuming 2,400 hours of direct labor were budgeted for actual output at a standard rate of $12.00 per hour and 2,500 hours were worked at a rate of $11.75 per hour.

A. Compute the labor price variance.

B. Compute the labor efficiency variance.

4. The Massimo Manufacturing Company hopes to produce 360,000 units of product during the next calendar year. Monthly production can range between 20,000 and 40,000 units. Per unit variable manufacturing cost have been budgeted as follows: direct materials, $2; direct labor, $2.50; and overhead, $1.25. Prepare a flexible budget for 20,000, 30,000, and 40,000 units of output.

VI. Beyond the Numbers

Refer to the information (and solution) for Exercise 4 above. During June, 30,000 units were manufactured. Costs incurred were as follows: $59,000 for direct materials, $77,250 for direct labor, and $37,300 for overhead. Were the costs controlled?

_____

_____

_____

_____

_____

VII. Demonstration Problems

Demonstration Problem #1

A flexible budget for Miyamoto, Inc., is presented below:

Miyamoto, Inc.
Flexible Budget
For the Year Ended December 31, 20X6

	Budget Formula per unit	Various Levels of Volume		
Units	-	40,000	48,000	56,000
Sales	$4.75	$190,000	$228,000	$266,000
Variable expenses	$2.20	88,000	105,600	123,200
Fixed expenses		56,000	56,000	56,000
Total expenses		144,000	161,600	179,200
Operating income		$ 46,000	$ 66,400	$ 86,800

The static (master) budget is based on a volume of 48,000 units. Actual operating results for 20X6 are as follows:

Sales (49,500 units)	$227,700
Variable expenses	106,920
Fixed expenses	57,570

Required:

1. Prepare an income statement performance report for 20X6.
2. Show that the total variances in operating income account for the net difference between actual operating income and the static (master) budget income.

Requirement 1 (income statement performance report)

Miyamoto, Inc.
Income Statement Performance Report
For the Year Ended December 31, 20X6

	(1)	(2) (1) - (3)	(3)	(4) (3) - (5)	(5)
	Actual Results at Actual Prices	Flexible Budget Variances	Flexible Budget for Actual Volume Achieved	Sales Volume Variances	Static (Master) Budget
Units					
Sales	$	$	$	$	$
Variable expenses					
Fixed expenses					
Total expenses					
Operating income	$	$	$	$	$

Requirement 2 (reconciling variances)

$_____

_____

$========

$_____

_____

$========

Demonstration Problem #2

Fun Fabric uses a standard cost system. They produce specially manufactured goods in large batches for catalogue companies featuring unusual decorative household items. They have just received an order for 10,000 units of a decorative wall hanging. Their standard cost for one wall hanging is:

Direct materials - 2.5 feet @ $2/ft	$ 5.00
Direct labor 1.5 hours @ $8/hr	12.00
Overhead 1.5 hours @ $6/hr	9.00
Standard cost/unit	$26.00

The normal capacity for the factory this period is 16,000 direct labor hours. Overhead costs are equally divided between variable and fixed expenses and are applied on the basis of direct labor hours. Janice Walters, the company president, has promised to have the wall hangings ready for shipment by the end of the month. The customer has agreed to pay $40 each.

During the month the following events occurred:

1. Purchased 27,500 feet of raw materials at $1.90/ft.
2. Received and placed into production 27,500 feet of raw materials.
3. Direct manufacturing wages incurred, 14,700 hours at $8.25/hr.
4. Assigned 15,000 direct labor hours to the job.
5. Recorded $91,600 of overhead costs.
6. Applied manufacturing overhead to the job.
7. The wall hangings were completed.
8. Shipped 10,000 units to the customer and billed the customer $400,000.

Requirements:

1. Journalize the transactions.
2. Post your transactions to the appropriate T-accounts.
3. Record the overhead variances.
4. Prepare a standard cost income statement.

Requirement 1 (journal entries)

Explanation	Debit	Credit

Requirement 2 (post to T-accounts)

Materials Inventory		Direct Materials Price Variance		Direct Materials Efficiency Variance

Manufacturing Wages		Direct Labor Price Variance		Direct Labor Efficiency Variance

Manufacturing Overhead

Work in Process Inventory		Finished Goods Inventory		Cost of Goods Sold

Requirement 3 (record overhead variances)

Explanation	Debit	Credit

Requirement 4

Fun Fabric
Standard Cost Income Statement

SOLUTIONS

I. Matching

1. G	3. B	5. H	7. E	9. J	11. F
2. I	4. C	6. K	8. A	10. D	

II. Multiple Choice

1.   A   Variable costs on a per unit basis are not affected by changes in volume (B). Fixed cost per unit increases as volume decreases (C). Total fixed costs do not change as a result of volume changes in the relevant range of production (D).

2.   A   A static budget is prepared for only one level of activity (B). Answers C and D have no meaning.

3.   C   All budgets are used for planning. Since the flexible budget is prepared for the actual level of activity achieved, it provides for precise control.

4.   A   The sales volume variance measures differences between the static budget and the flexible budget for actual volume achieved. The flexible budget variance measures differences between actual results and the flexible budget for actual volume achieved. Accordingly, higher than expected sales could be expected to give a favorable sales volume variance, and actual costs above flexible budget costs could be expected to give an unfavorable flexible budget variance.

5.   B   A standard cost is a carefully predetermined cost that is usually expressed on a per-unit basis. It is a target cost, a cost that should be attained. Budgeted costs are total costs. Think of a standard variable cost as a budget for a single unit.

6.   D   Price variances relate to materials and labor.

7.   C   Production volume variances relate to overhead. The variances relating to direct materials and direct labor are the price and efficiency variances.

8.   C   Unfavorable variances are added to cost of goods sold and favorable variances are deducted.

9.   C   Because the variances relate to only the current period, they are closed out to Income Summary at the end.

10.   D   Overhead flexible budget variance, which is the difference between the actual overhead cost and the flexible budget overhead for the actual number of outputs.

III. Completion

1. Costs
2. variable
3. fixed
4. mixed
5. 25 percent (2,500 units / 10,000 units)
6. efficiency
7. price
8. static
9. cost pool
10. favorable; unfavorable

IV. Daily Exercises

1.

Tomatoes	90 lbs × 25¢/lb	=	$22.50
Garlic	2 heads × 90¢ ea.	=	1.80
Onions	20 lbs × 15¢/lb	=	3.00
Wine	2 gallons × $6.50 ea.	=	13.00
Olive Oil	16 oz. × 20¢/oz.	=	3.20
Herbs	8 oz. × 10¢/oz	=	.80
Total			$44.30

$44.30 / 40 quarts =	$1.1075
Container	.09
Total	$1.1975

2.

Actual cost (120,000 lbs @ $0.395)	$47,400
Less: Budgeted unit cost × actual inputs	
(120,000 lbs × $0.40)	48,000
Materials price variance	$ 600 F

Budgeted costs for actual inputs (see above)	$48,000
Less: Standard cost for actual production	
((59,550 × 2 lbs) × $0.40)	47,640 (rounded)
Materials efficiency variance	$ 360 U

Total flexible budget variance = Materials price variance + Materials efficiency variance
= 600 F + 360 U
= $ 240 F

3.

Materials Inventory (120,000 lbs × $0.40)	48,000	
Direct Materials Price Variance		600
Accounts Payable (120,000 lbs × $0.395)		47,400
Work in Progress Inventory (119,100 lbs × $0.40)	47,640	
Direct Materials Efficiency Variance	360	
Materials Inventory (120,000 lbs × $0.40)		48,000

4. Actual cost (1,200 hours @ $12.25) $14,700
    Less: Budgeted unit cost × actual usage
            (1,200 × $11.75)   14,100
            Labor price variance $ 600 U

    Budgeted costs for actual hours (see above) $14,100
    Less: Standard cost for actual production
            (1,191 × $11.75)   13,994 (rounded)
            Labor efficiency variance $ 106 U

    Total flexible budget variance = Labor price variance + Labor efficiency variance
                     = 600 U + 106 U
                     =$ 706 U

5.

Manufacturing Wages (1,200 × $11.75)	14,100	
Direct Labor Price Variance	600	
Wages Payable (1,200 × $12.25)		14,700
Work In Process Inventory (1,191 × $11.75)	13,994	
Direct Labor Efficiency Variance	106	
Manufacturing Wages		14,100

V. Exercises

1. A. Total costs = Fixed costs + Variable costs
         $60,000 = X + ($5 × 8,000)
          60,000 = X + $40,000
         $20,000 = X

         Fixed costs were $20,000

    B. Total budgeted costs = ($5 × # of units produced) + $20,000

C. Total budgeted costs = ($5 × 10,000) + $20,000 = $70,000

2. A. Actual cost $33,701
  Less: Budgeted unit cost x actual usage
     ($4.75 x 6,700)   31,825
    Materials price variance $ 1,876 U

  B. $2,660 F = (6,700 feet - X) × $4.75
   X = 7,260 feet = inputs that should have been used
   7,260 feet / 3,300 units = 2.2 standard feet

3. A. Actual cost (2,500 hours @ $11.75) $29,375
  Less: Budgeted unit cost × actual usage
     (2,500 × $12.00)   30,000
    Labor price variance $ 625 F

  B. Budgeted costs for actual hours (see above) $30,000
   Less: Standard cost for actual production
     (2,400 × $12.00)   28,800
    Labor efficiency variance $ 1,200 U

4.

Massimo Manufacturing Company
Monthly Flexible Budget Report

Output	20,000	30,000	40,000
Variable costs			
Direct materials ($2)	$ 40,000	$ 60,000	$ 80,000
Direct labor ($2.50)	50,000	75,000	100,000
Overhead ($1.25)	25,000	37,500	50,000
	$115,000	$172,500	$230,000

VI. Beyond the Numbers

To answer the question we need to compare actual results with the budget.

Massimo Manufacturing Company
Budget Report
For the Month Ended June 30, 20XX

	Actual	Budget	Variance
Units	30,000	30,000	0
Variable costs			
Direct materials	$ 59,000	$ 60,000	$1,000 F
Direct labor	77,250	75,000	2,250 U
Overhead	37,300	37,500	200 F

Totals	$173,550	$172,500	$1,050 U

Overall, costs were controlled. The unfavorable variance for total variable costs was less than 1% of the budgeted amount (1,050 / 172,500). However, this overall result has been adversely affected by a 3% (2,250 / 75,000) unfavorable variance in direct labor costs while both direct materials and overhead show favorable variances.

VII. Demonstration Problems

Demonstration Problem #1 Solved and Explained

Requirement 1 (income statement performance report)

Miyamoto, Inc.
Income Statement Performance Report
For the Year Ended December 31, 20X6

	(1) Actual Results at Actual Prices	(2) (1) - (3) Flexible Budget Variances		(3) Flexible Budget for Actual Volume Achieved	(4) (3) - (5) Sales Volume Variances		(5) Static (Master) Budget
Units	49,500	0		49,500	1,500	F	48,000
Sales	$227,700	$7,425	U	$235,125	$7,125	F	$228,000
Variable expenses	106,920	1,980	F	108,900	3,300	U	105,600
Fixed expenses	57,570	1,570	U	56,000	-		56,000
Total expenses	164,490	410	F	164,900	3,300	U	161,600
Operating income	$ 63,210	$7,015	U	$ 70,225	$3,825	F	$ 66,400

Explanations:

Column 1 contains actual results that were presented in the problem statement.

Column 3

Column 3 contains the flexible budget for the volume actually sold. Actual sales were 49,500 units. Budgeted revenue is $235,125 ($4.75 per unit × 49,500). Budgeted variable expenses are $108,900 ($2.20 per unit × 49,500). Budgeted revenue and budgeted variable expenses may be calculated by multiplying units actually sold by the budget formula amounts in the flexible budget. Note that fixed expenses of $56,000 are constant at all the production levels presented in the flexible budget.

Column 5

The amounts in column 5 are the static, or master budget amounts. The problem notes that the static budget is based on 48,000 units, a volume level also found in the flexible budget.

Column 2

The flexible budget variances are the differences between actual results (column 1) and flexible budget amounts (column 3).

For example, the flexible budget variance for sales is $7,425 U (actual sales were less than the flexible budget amount).

For example, the flexible budget variance for variable expenses is $1,980 F (actual variable expenses were less than the flexible budget amount.) It may help to remember that spending less than planned is favorable, while spending more is unfavorable.

<u>Column 4</u>

Sales volume variances are the differences between flexible budget amounts for actual sales and static budget amounts. Note that no sales volume variance exists for fixed expenses, since fixed are constant within the relevant range. The criteria to determine whether the variances are favorable or unfavorable are the same as detailed in the explanation for column 2.

Requirement 2 (reconciling variances)

Static (master) budget operating income $66,400
Actual operating income at actual prices   63,210
    Total difference to account for $ 3,190 U

Sales volume variance $3,825 F
Flexible budget variance   7,015 U
    Total net variance $3,190 U

Since the unfavorable flexible budget variance is greater than the favorable sales volume variance, the overall net variance is unfavorable.

Demonstration Problem #2 Solved and Explained

Requirement 1 (journal entries)

1)	Materials Inventory (27,500 × $2)	55,000	
	Direct Materials Price Variance (27,500 × $.10)		2,750
	Accounts Payable (27,500 × $1.90)		52,250
2)	Work in Process Inventory (25,000 × $2)	50,000	
	Materials Efficiency Variance (2,500 × $2)	5,000	
	Materials Inventory		55,000

3)	Manufacturing Wages (14,700 × $8)	117,600	
	Direct Labor Price Variance (14,700 × $.25)	3,675	
	Wages Payable (14,700 × $8.25)		121,275
4)	Work in Process Inventory (15,000 × $8)	120,000	
	Direct Labor Efficiency Variance (300 × $8)		2,400
	Manufacturing Wages		117,600
5)	Manufacturing Overhead	91,600	
	Various accounts		91,600
6)	Work in Process (15,000 × $6)	90,000	
	Manufacturing Overhead		90,000
7)	Finished Goods Inventory (10,000 × $26)	260,000	
	Work in Process		260,000
8)	Cost of Goods Sold	260,000	
	Finished Goods Inventory		260,000
	Accounts Receivable	400,000	
	Sales		400,000

Requirement 2 (post to T-accounts)

Materials Inventory	
(1) 55,000	(2) 55,000

Direct Materials Price Variance	
	(1) 2,750

Direct Materials Efficiency Variance	
(2) 5,000	

Manufacturing Wages	
(3) 117,600	(4) 117,600

Direct Labor Price Variance	
(3) 3,675	

Direct Labor Efficiency Variance	
	(4) 2,400

Manufacturing Overhead	
(5) 91,600	(6) 90,000

334

Work in Process Inventory		Finished Goods Inventory		Cost of Goods Sold	
(2) 50,000	(7) 260,000	(7) 260,000	(8) 260,000	(8) 260,000	
(4) 120,000					
(6) 90,000					

Requirement 3 (record overhead variances)

Explanation	Debit	Credit
Production Volume Variance (1)	3,000	
Overhead Flexible Budget Variance (2)		1,400
Manufacturing Overhead (3)		1,600

(1) the fixed portion of overhead costs ($3) times the difference between normal capacity and budgeted or, $3 × 1,000 hour = $3,000.

(2) the difference between actual overhead ($91,600) and the sum of the budgeted variable ($3 × 15,000) and normal fixed ($3 × 16,000) or, $45,000 + $48,000 = $93,000 - $91,600 = $1,400

(3) the balance in the manufacturing overhead account

Requirement 4

Fun Fabrics
Standard Cost Income Statement

Sales revenue		$400,000
Cost of goods sold at standard cost	$260,000	
Manufacturing cost variances:		
Direct materials price variance	(2,750)	
Direct materials efficiency variance	5,000	
Direct labor price variance	3,675	
Direct labor efficiency variance	(2,400)	
Overhead flexible budget variance	(1,400)	
Production volume variance	3,000	
Cost of goods sold at actual cost		265,125
Gross margin		$134,875

Study Tips: The standard cost income statement reports cost of goods sold at standard cost, then modifies this amount by the variances for direct materials, direct labor and overhead. Debit variances reflect additions to cost of goods sold while credit variances are deductions. The standard cost income statement is for internal purposes only.

Chapter 25 - Activity-Based Costing and Other Cost Management Tools

CHAPTER OVERVIEW

As businesses attempt to remain competitive in an international environment they strive for competitive advantages. Some of these involve better management of costs, efforts to deliver higher quality products to the customer, and the introduction of systems that allow management to effectively plan for future operations. While we have been investigating a variety of topics concerning "costs" in recent chapters, we now turn our attention to some of the issues at the forefront of cost management. The learning objectives for this chapter are to

1. Develop activity-based costs (ABC).
2. Use activity-based management (ABM) to make business decisions, including achieving target costs.
3. Decide when ABC is most likely to pass the cost-benefit test.
4. Describe how a just-in-time (JIT) production system works and record its manufacturing costs.
5. Contrast the four types of quality costs and use these costs to make decisions.

CHAPTER REVIEW

Objective 1 – Develop activity-based costs (ABC).

Activity-based costing (ABC) is the result of the need by companies for more accurate information concerning product costs thereby allowing managers to make decisions based on accurate information. **ABC** is a system that focuses on activities as the fundamental cost objects. The costs of those activities become the building blocks for compiling the indirect costs of products, services, and customers. Companies that use ABC continue to trace direct costs (direct materials and direct labor) to cost objects in the same way as you learned in Chapter 20. The challenge addressed by ABC costing is to equitably allocate the indirect costs, both manufacturing and non-manufacturing to the products, services, or customers that caused those costs. ABC recognizes that frequently multiple cost drivers exist. When this occurs, applying costs on the basis of a single cost driver results in distorted product costs. Organizing cost information by activity provides detailed information not available using a single application rate. Applying ABC to products requires these seven steps:

1. Identify the activities.
2. Estimate the total indirect cost of each activity.
3. Identify the allocation base for each activity's indirect costs.
4. Estimate the total quantity of each allocation base.
5. Compute the cost allocation rate for each activity:

Allocation rate	**=**	**Estimated total indirect costs of activity (Step 2)**
for activity		**Estimated total quantity of cost allocation base (Step 4)**

6. Obtain the actual quantity of each allocation base used by the cost object
7. Allocate the costs to the cost object:

   Allocated activity cost = Allocation rate for activity (step 5) × Quantity of allocation base used by the cost object (step 6)

Objective 2 - Use activity-based management (ABM) to make business decisions, including achieving target costs.

Activity-based management (ABM) refers to using activity-based cost information to make more accurate decisions that both increase profits while satisfying customer needs. Once the product pricing has been determined, other decisions based on product pricing can be made with accuracy. For instance, deciding whether to produce something or simply purchase it from a supplier can now be more accurately determined. In addition, ABC may highlight issues regarding production levels, product mix and selling price.

Value engineering is used to reevaluate activities to reduce costs while satisfying customer needs. To accomplish this requires companies to use cross-functional teams so representatives from marketing, production, design, and accounting analyze the product to estimate how proposed changes will affect costs.

The traditional way to determine a product's selling price was to accumulate costs from the entire value chain and then add an amount for profit. Target pricing uses a completely different approach. With target pricing, the sales price is determined first, based on the amount that customers are willing to pay for the product or service. This target price is then reduced by the profit with the resulting difference being the target cost for the product. See Exhibit 25-10.

Target sale price – Desired profit = Target cost

With the target cost available, managers are now able to re-examine the results of value engineering and attempt to identify appropriate cost reduction strategies. If there is a larger variance between the re-calculated costs and target cost, then, the need exists for additional value engineering analysis to reduce costs further. If costs cannot be reduced further, then the difference will affect the amount of profit realized by the company. See Exhibit 25-11.

Objective 3 – Decide when ABC costing is most likely to pass the cost-benefit test.

While the concept behind ABC is simple--products cause activities, and activities consume resources--, ABC systems can be extremely complex and therefore costly. To implement ABC successfully, the benefits should exceed the costs. Generally, companies in competitive markets are more likely to benefit from ABC. In addition, companies with high indirect costs, multiple product lines using varying resources, and companies with varying production levels for those product lines are likely to benefit.

Existing cost systems may need revision when management cannot explain changes in profits, when bids are lost (or won) unexpectedly, when competitors under-price the company but remain profitable, when employees "don't believe the numbers," where a single-allocation-based-system exists and when production has been re-engineered but the accounting system has not.

Study Tip: Carefully review the ABC Decision Guidelines in your text so you become familiar with ABC costing.

Objective 4 - Describe how a just-in-time (JIT) production system works and record its manufacturing costs.

In a **traditional production system,** large inventories of raw materials, work in process, and finished goods are maintained. However, maintaining large inventories is a problem since inventory ties up cash that could be used for other purposes. In addition, large amounts of inventory may result in problems caused by inferior quality, obsolescence, and could cause production bottlenecks to be overlooked.

The actual manufacturing processes in a traditional production system can also result in inefficiencies. The actual physical movement of goods in process can be quite long resulting in further inefficiencies. **Throughput time** is a term used to describe the time between the receipt of raw materials and the completion of a finished good. As an equation it is expressed as follows:

Throughput time   =   Processing time + waiting time + moving time + inspection time + reworking time

Whereas processing time adds value to a product, the other elements in the equation are **non-value-added** activities and considered waste.

Just-in-time (JIT) production systems (introduced in Chapter 19) are designed to eliminate the waste found in a traditional system. Underlying JIT systems are the following four concepts:

1. **Arrange production activities in self-contained cells**- processes are arranged so production is continuous without interruption or work in process inventories.
2. **Short setup times** - JIT minimizes the amount of time required for setup on machines used for more than one product.
3. **Broad employee roles** - in a traditional system, employees are trained to complete one specific task. Under JIT, employees are crossed-trained to do more than operate a single machine. This promotes greater flexibility, boosts morale and lowers costs.
4. **Small batches produced just-in-time** - under JIT businesses schedule production in small batches *just in time* to satisfy needs. Production does not begin until an order is received. This is referred to as a "**demand-pull**" system because the customer's order (the demand) "pulls" the product through the manufacturing process. In turn, the product acts as a "demand" to "pull" raw materials into the manufacturing process.

Review Exhibit 25-13 in your text for a comparison of a traditional system with a JIT system.

Under JIT costing, a backflush costing system is used. Backflush costing is a standard costing system that starts with output completed and works backwards to apply manufacturing costs to units sold and to inventories. Backflush costing takes less time and is less expensive to use than the traditional standard costing.

338

In a JIT system, no distinction is made between raw materials inventory and work in process. Instead they are combined into one account, Raw and in Process (RIP).

When materials are acquired:

RIP Inventory	XX	
Accounts Payable		XX

Recorded at actual amounts

As conversion costs are incurred:

Conversion Costs	XX	
Various Accounts		XX

Recorded at actual costs

When the number of units of finished product is known:

Finished Goods Inventory	XX	
RIP Inventory		XX
Conversion Costs		XX

The amount for each account above is based on standard costs.

When goods are sold:

Cost of Goods Sold	XX	
Finished Goods Inventory		XX

Recorded at standard amounts

Price variances are recorded at the time materials are acquired while efficiency variances are not recorded until goods have been completed. Over/underallocated conversion costs are transferred to Cost of Goods Sold.

Objective 5 - Contrast the four types of quality costs and use these costs to make decisions.

Quality is the conformance of the attributes of a product or service to a specific set of standards.

Four types of **quality costs** are:
- **Prevention costs** are incurred to *avoid* poor quality goods and services.
- **Appraisal costs** are incurred to *detect* poor quality goods and services.
- **Internal failure costs** are incurred when the company detects and corrects poor-quality goods or services *before* delivery to customers.
- **External failure costs** are incurred when the company does not detect poor-quality goods or services until *after* delivery to customers.

See Exhibit 25-15 in your text for examples of quality costs.

TEST YOURSELF

All the self-testing materials in this chapter focus on information and procedures that your instructor is likely to test in quizzes and examinations.

I. Matching   *Match each numbered term with its lettered definition.*

_____ 1. Internal failure costs
_____ 2. Activity-based costing
_____ 3. Prevention costs
_____ 4. Appraisal costs
_____ 5. Activity-based management
_____ 6. External failure costs

_____ 7. Just-in-time costing
_____ 8. Target price
_____ 9. Target cost
_____ 10. Backflush costing
_____ 11. Value-engineering

A. Systematically evaluating activities in an effort to reduce costs while satisfying customer needs
B. A system that focuses on activities as the fundamental cost objects and uses the costs of those activities as building blocks for compiling the costs of products and other cost objects
C. A standard costing system that starts with output completed and works backward to apply manufacturing cots to units sold and to inventories
D. Allowable cost to develop, produce, and deliver the product or service
E. What customers are willing to pay for the product or service
F. Costs incurred in detecting poor quality goods or services
G. Costs incurred to avoid poor quality goods or services
H. Using activity-based cost information to make decisions that increase profits while satisfying customers' needs
I. Another term for just-in-time costing
J. Costs incurred when poor quality goods or services are not detected until after delivery to customers
K. Cost incurred when poor quality goods or services are detected before delivery to customers

II. Multiple Choice   *Circle the best answer.*

1. In manufacturing, all the following are non-value-added activities except:

   A. inspection time.
   B. moving time.

   C. processing time.
   D. reworking time.

2. The first step in an ABC system is:

   A. estimate the total indirect costs.
   B. identify the allocation base.

   C. identify the activities.
   D. estimate the total quantity of each allocation base.

3. Raw Materials Inventory and Work in Process Inventory are combined in

   A. target costing.
   B. value engineering.

   C. activity based costing.
   D. a JIT costing system.

4. All of the following are characteristics of quality costs except:

A. use of benchmarking for evaluation   C. difficult to identify individual components
B. difficult to measure   D. types of financial performance measures

5. Which of the following are likely to use activity-based costing system?

A. Financial institutions   C. Textile manufacturer
B. Retailer   D. All of the above

6. Which of the following is an example of an external failure cost?

A. Reworking time   C. Training program costs
B. Cost to honor warranties   D. Inspection costs

7. All of the following are nonfinancial measures of quality except:

A. amount of machine "down" time.   C. unit failure.
B. return on sales.   D. training hours per employee per month.

8. Value engineering is most closely associated with:

A. just-in-time costing.   C. target costing.
B. activity-based management.   D. none of the above.

9. Backflush costing is most closely associated with:

A. target costing.   C. value engineering.
B. just-in-time system.   D. activity-based costing.

10. Cross-training employees is a feature of which of the following?

A. Target costing   C. Activity based costing
B. Just-in-time costing   D. Value engineering

III. Completion   *Complete each of the following.*

1. Four characteristics common to the just-in-time inventory are:
    1. _____
    2. _____
    3. _____
    4. _____
2. Combining raw materials and work in process inventories is a feature of a _____ system.

    Identify the following acronyms:
3. ABC _____
4. ABM_____
5. RIP_____
6. JIT_____
7. Quality costs are features of _____.
8. The four types of quality costs are: 1) _____,
    2)_____, 3) _____,
    and 4)_____.
9. Demand-pull refers to a production process where _____ triggers the manufacturing process.
10. Of the four types of quality costs, the one that is potentially the most devastating to a company is
    _____.

IV. Daily Exercises

1. Classify each of the following quality costs as a prevention cost, an internal failure cost, an appraisal cost, or an external failure cost.

    a. Direct materials and direct labor costs incurred to repair defective products returned by customers
    b. A training class for customer service representatives to teach them techniques for completing customer orders quickly, efficiently and correctly
    c. Salary of a technician who randomly selects goods from the warehouse and tests them for conformance to company specifications
    d. Time and materials costs incurred to rework those items determined by the testing technician as below standard
    e. $28,000 balance in Sales Returns for the return of defective products
    f. Fee paid to pick up and dispose of rejected products from production area

    a. _____
    b. _____
    c. _____
    d. _____
    e. _____
    f. _____

2. List the following ABC system steps in correct order (use 1 through 7):

_____ A. Identify the allocation base for each activity's indirect costs.
_____ B. Identify the activities
_____ C. Obtain the actual quantity of each allocation base used by the cost object
_____ D. Estimate the total quantity of each allocation base
_____ E. Estimate total indirect costs of each activity
_____ F. Allocate the costs to the cost object
_____ G. Compute the cost allocation rate for each activity

3. Zollner Tool and Die has collected the following information on overhead costs:

ACTIVITY	AMOUNT	COST DRIVER
Machine setups	$90,000	Number of setups
Machining	325,000	Number of machine hours
Inspecting	42,000	Number of inspections

During the period, Zollner estimates they will have 675 machine setups, 15,000 machine hours and a total of 1,350 inspections. Calculate the overhead rate for machine setups, machining and inspecting.

4. Totally Tees manufactures specialty T-shirts sold at music festivals and uses a JIT costing system. The standard cost for their basic model is $4.50 for raw materials and $1.10 for conversion costs. For a recently completed order of 12,000 shirts, the following costs were incurred:

Raw material purchases $54,000
Conversion costs   12,480

Prepare journal entries for this order using JIT costing.

V. Exercises

1. Trendy Trunks Manufacturing Co. uses activity-based costing to account for its manufacturing process. The direct materials for each trunk cost $3,700. Each trunk includes 60 parts, and finishing requires 15 hours of direct labor time. Each trunk requires 225 welds. The manufacture of 10 Trendy Trunks requires two machine setups.

Manufacturing Activity	Cost Driver Chosen as Application Base	Conversion Cost per Unit of Application Base
Materials handling	Number of parts	$ 5.00
Machine setup	Number of setups	$800.00
Welding of parts	Number of welds	$ 3.00
Finishing	Direct labor hours	$ 32.00

Compute the cost of each trunk.

2. Review the information in Daily Exercise #3, and assume the following additional information. Zollner manufactures one standard product (a drill bit used in furniture construction) and two specialty products, a gear and a corkscrew. Machine setups, machining hours, and inspections for the three products were:

Activity	Drill Bits	Gears	Corkscrews
Machine setups	520	90	65
Machine hours	8,900	3,200	2,900
Inspections	820	270	260

Calculate the total overhead costs for each of these three products.

3. Review the information in Daily Exercise #3, but assume Zollner uses a traditional cost allocation system for overhead. The allocation base is number of units produced, and during the current period Zollner's production was as follows:

Drill bits	520,000
Gears	90
Corkscrews	1,300
Total units	521,390

A. Calculate overhead costs assigned to each product based on production.

B. Compare your results with these in Exercise #2. Which method is more realistic, and why?

4. Fab's Fashions Company uses a JIT costing system, with trigger points at the time of direct materials purchase and the transfer of completed goods to finished goods. The company has received an order for 20,000 sweaters at $15 each. The standard direct materials cost is $6.50 per sweater and a standard conversion cost of $5.50 per sweater. Direct materials were purchased for $129,000 and conversion costs totaling $110,400 were incurred. 20,000 sweaters were produced and shipped to the customer.

Prepare journal entries for the above transactions.

Date	Accounts	Debit	Credit

VI. Beyond the Numbers

Clothing manufacturers typically produce 5% more units than called for in a contract. Called "overruns," these excess units are deemed necessary because of anticipated defects in some of the units produced. Usually, these defects are the result of faulty direct materials and/or workmanship. Part of the overrun cannot be reworked and is scrapped. Other parts can be reworked but are not needed to fill the order. A third part is simply excess. Many times, the excess that is not scrapped is sold to a factor that then resells the merchandise to an outlet store where it is sold as "seconds."

Analyze a typical 5% overrun with respect to quality costs—prevention, appraisal, internal failure, and external failure.

_____
_____
_____
_____
_____
_____
_____
_____
_____
_____
_____
_____
_____
_____

VII. Demonstration Problems

Demonstration Problem #1

Conor Cup Company manufactures environmentally friendly cups in two sizes for coffee bars offering carryout service. The company uses a traditional system for allocating manufacturing overhead costs. Last year, the following results were reported:

	8 oz. cups	12 oz. cups	Total
Direct materials	$1,350,000	$1,800,000	$ 3,150,000
Direct Labor	400,000	600,000	1,000,000
Overhead	2,400,000	3,600,000	6,000,000
Total	$4,150,000	$6,000,000	$10,150,000

Overhead costs were allocated on the basis of direct labor costs. Last year 510,000 cases of 8 oz. cups were manufactured (each case contains 500 cups) and 800,000 cases (each containing 300 cups) of 12 oz. cups were manufactured.

Requirement:

Calculate the cost per cup and the cost per case for each size.

Demonstration Problem #2

Refer to the information in Demonstration Problem #1.

You have been asked by the company controller to analyze the allocation of overhead costs to the two products using an activity-based costing system. You begin by analyzing the specific components of the $6,000,000 in overhead costs assigned last year. Your investigation determines the following:

Components	Cost
Indirect materials	$ 300,000
Supervisors' salaries	450,000
Equipment depreciation	3,150,000
Equipment conversion costs	1,500,000
Miscellaneous overhead	600,000
Total	$6,000,000

In consultation with the controller, the following decisions are made regarding costs and cost drivers:

Cost	Cost Driver
Indirect materials	Direct materials
Supervisors' salaries	Direct labor cost
Equipment depreciation	Hours of equipment use
Equipment conversion costs	Number of conversions
Miscellaneous overhead	Cases of output

Further investigation disclosed the following:

The equipment was used 70% for the 12 oz. cups and 30% for the 8 oz. cups. The equipment was converted a total of 120 times during the year, 90 times for the 12 oz. cups and 30 times for the 8 oz. cups.

Requirements:

1. Apply activity-based costing using the results of your investigation to allocate overhead to each size of cup.
2. Calculate the per-cup cost for each size of cup given your results in requirement 1.

Requirement 1

Requirement 2

SOLUTIONS

I. Matching

1. K	3. G	5. A	7. C	9. D	11. H
2. B	4. F	6. J	8. E	10. I	

II. Multiple Choice

1. **C** Non-value-added activities are those that do not add value to the product. Inspecting, · moving, and reworking are examples of non-value added activities. Processing costs are value-added activities.

2. **C**
   1. Identify the activities.
   2. Estimate the total indirect cost of each activity.
   3. Identify the allocation base for each activity's indirect costs.
   4. Estimate the total quantity of each allocation base.
   5. Compute the cost allocation rate for each activity:

      Allocation rate = $\dfrac{\text{Estimated total indirect costs of activity (Step 2)}}{\text{Estimated total quantity of cost allocation base (Step 4)}}$
      for activity
   6. Obtain the actual quantity of each allocation base used by the cost object
   6. Allocate the costs to the cost object:

      Allocated activity cost = Allocation rate for activity (step 5) × Quantity of allocation base used by the cost object (step 6)

3. **D** RIP (Raw and In Process) is a feature of just-in-time costing.

4. **D** Quality costs are nonfinancial performance items.

5. **D** Activity-based costing is a concept of accumulating costs using multiple cost drivers and is not specific to particular businesses or industries - it can be used by any organization.

6. **B** External failures are those that occur after the customer has received the product or service. Of the four options, the only one that would involve a customer is the cost of warranties.

7. **B** Return on sales is the only choice listed that can be expressed in financial terms.

8. **C** Value engineering refers to techniques used to reduce the cost of a product while maintaining its satisfaction to the customer. Value engineering is one way to achieve target costing.

9. **B** Target costing, value engineering and activity-based costing all relate to either cost measurement (ABC) or cost reduction (target costing and VE). Backflush costing is synonymous with just-in-time costing.

10. **B** Cross training is a prominent feature of just-in-time costing.

III. Completion

1. arrange production activities in self-contained cells, short setup times, broad employee roles, small batches produced just-in-time (order not important)
2. JIT costing
3. ABC = activity-based costing;
4. ABM = activity-based management
5. RIP = Raw and In Process
6. JIT = just-in-time
7. total quality management
8. prevention costs, appraisal costs, internal failure costs, external failure costs
9. the receipt of a customer order
10. external failure costs

IV. Daily Exercises

1. a. external failure cost
   b. prevention cost
   c. appraisal cost
   d. internal failure cost
   e. external failure cost
   f. internal failure cost

2.

3	A.
1	B.
6	C.
4	D.
2	E.
7	F.
5	G.

3. Machine setups = $90,000/675 = $133.33/setup
   Machining = $325,000/15,000 hrs = $21.67/hour
   Inspecting = $42,000/1,350 = $31.11/inspection

4.

RIP Inventory	54,000	
Accounts Payable		54,000
Conversion Costs	12,480	
Accounts Payable		12,480
Finished Goods Inventory	67,200	
RIP Inventory		54,000
Conversion Costs		13,200
Cost of Goods Sold	67,200	

Finished Goods Inventory		67,200
Conversion Costs	720	
Cost of Goods Sold		720

V. Exercises

1.

Direct materials	$3,700
Materials handling (60 parts @ $5.00)	300
Machine setup ($800 x 2 / 10)	160
Welding (225 x $3.00)	675
Finishing (15 x $32.00)	480
Total cost	$5,315

2.

Drill Bits

Activity	Number	Cost
Machine setups ($133.33)	520	$ 69,333 (rounded)
Machine hours ($21.67)	8900	192,833 (rounded)
Inspections ($31.11)	820	25,511 (rounded)
Total		$287,677

Gears

Activity	Number	Cost
Machine setups ($133.33)	90	$12,000
Machine hours ($21.67)	3200	69,333
Inspections ($31.11)	270	8,400
Total		$89,733

Corkscrews

Activity	Number	Cost
Machine setups ($133.33)	65	$ 8,667
Machine hours ($21.67)	2900	62,833
Inspections ($31.11)	260	8,089
Total		$79,589

3.

A. Total overhead costs = $ 90,000
                                                   325,000
                                                     42,000
                                                 $457,000

Drill bits = 520,000 / 521,390 × $457,000 = $455,782
Gears = 90 / 521,390 × $457,000 = $78.88
Corkscrews = 1,300 / 521,390 × $457,000 = $1,139

B. It is obvious a traditional costing system based on production drastically distorts the allocation of overhead. It would also be distorted if only one of the activities (setups, hours, or inspections)

353

were the allocation base. Granted, this is an extreme example but it does serve to illustrate the point that activity-based costing can result in a more realistic application of overhead.

> **Study Tip:** Remember, ABC relates only to overhead, not direct materials or direct labor.

4.

RIP Inventory	130,000	
Direct materials price variance		1,000
Accounts Payable		129,000
Conversion costs	110,400	
Various accounts		110,400
Finished Goods Inventory	240,000	
RIP Inventory		130,000
Conversion costs		110,000
[($6.50 + $5.50) × 20,000)]		
Cost of goods sold	240,000	
Finished Goods Inventory		240,000
Accounts Receivable	300,000	
Sales		300,000
Cost of goods sold	400	
Conversion costs		400
(To transfer underapplied overhead)		

VI. Beyond the Numbers

Ideally, a manufacturer should strive for zero defects. However, this is not always possible. To obtain defect-free material, the manufacturer needs to work closely with the supplier(s). This is a prevention cost. During the manufacturing process, appraisal costs are involved as a result of inspection costs. In addition, internal failure costs are incurred to both rework (when possible) and to dispose of units that can neither be reworked nor sold as seconds. If you analyze the situation carefully you will see that there are no external failure costs. The clothing manufacturer ships only goods that conform to the order. Any excess goods that can be sold are factored to an outlet store. As long as the costs associated with the excess are considered when they are sold, no external failure costs are involved. As stated above, zero defects is the ideal and something companies should strive to achieve. However, given the 5% excess, clothing manufacturers seem to have adjusted well enough to cover the costs incurred with the excess (one of the fastest growing segments in retailing are the "outlets").

VII. Demonstration Problems

Demonstration Problem #1 Solved and Explained

<u>8 oz. cups:</u>

Total cost	$4,150,000
Total cups (510,000 cases × 500 ea)	255,000,000
Cost per cup ($4,150,000 / 255,000,000)	$0.01627
Cost per case ($4,150,000 / 510,000)	$8.14

<u>12 oz. cups:</u>

Total cost	$6,000,000
Total cups (800,000 cases × $500 ea)	240,000,000
Cost per cup ($6,000,000 / 240,000,000)	$0.025
Cost per case ($6,000,000 / 800,000)	$7.50

Demonstration Problem #2 Solved and Explained

Requirement 1

Component	Cost	8 oz.	Calculations	12 oz.	Calculations
Indirect material	$300,000	$128,571	$\frac{\$1,350,000}{\$3,150,000} \times \$300,000$	$ 171,429	$\frac{\$1,800,000}{\$3,150,000} \times \$300,000$
Supervisor's salary	450,000	180,000	$\frac{\$400,000}{\$1,000,000} \times \$450,000$	270,000	$\frac{\$600,000}{\$1,000,000} \times \$450,000$
Equipment depreciation	3,150,000	945,000	30% × $3,150,000	2,205,000	70% × $3,150,000
Conversion costs	1,500,000	375,000	30/120 × $1,500,000	1,125,000	90/120 × $1,500,000
Miscellaneous	600,000	233,588	$\frac{\$510,000}{\$1,310,000} \times \$600,000$	366,412	$\frac{\$800,000}{\$1,310,000} \times \$600,000$
Total		$1,862,159		$4,137,841	

Requirement 2

<u>8 oz. cups</u>

	$1,350,000	(Direct materials)
	400,000	(Direct labor)
	1,862,159	(Overhead - from Requirement 2)
Total cost	$3,612,159	

or $3,612,159 / 255,000,000   = $0.0142 per cup

<u>12 oz. cups</u>

	$1,800,000	(Direct materials)
	600,000	(Direct labor)
	4,137,841	(Overhead - from Requirement 2)
Total cost	$6,537,841	

or $6,537,841 / 240,000,000   = $0.027 per cup

Chapter 26 - Special Business Decisions and Capital Budgeting

CHAPTER OVERVIEW

In recent chapters you have learned about a variety of issues all related to the topic of "costs." Most of these issues looked at costs (and behavior) in the short run. When costs are correctly recorded and carefully analyzed, a business is in a better position to plan for future operations. We now turn our attention to some special decisions businesses frequently must make and to issues concerning the acquisition of long-term (capital) assets. The learning objectives for this chapter are to

1. Identify the relevant information for a special business decision.
2. Make five types of short-term special business decisions.
3. Use payback and accounting rate of return models to make longer-term capital budgeting decisions.
4. Use discounted cash flow models to make longer-term capital budgeting decisions.
5. Compare and contrast the four capital budgeting methods.

CHAPTER REVIEW

Objective 1 – Identify the relevant information for a special business decision.

To achieve business goals, managers must develop strategies by choosing among alternative courses of action. Managers make decisions by:

- Defining business goals
- Identifying alternative courses of action
- Gathering and analyzing relevant information to compare alternatives
- Choosing the best alternative to achieve goals.

The key in choosing the best alternative is focusing on information that is *relevant*. Relevant information is expected future data that differs among alternatives. Information that does not differ is irrelevant and will not change a business decision. See Exhibit 26-1 and 26-2 in your text.

Objective 2 – Make five types of short-term special business decisions.

One approach to short-term decision-making is called the **relevant information approach** (also called the incremental analysis approach). This approach focuses on two factors for making short-term special decisions:

1. Focus on *relevant* revenues, costs, and profits
2. Use a *contribution margin approach* that separates variable costs from fixed costs

Now, let's take a look at five types of short-term decisions. Each of these short-term decisions is evaluated by comparing the expected increase in revenues to the expected increase in expenses. If there is no change in fixed expenses, then they are not relevant to the decision-making process and are ignored. Thus, the decision will be based on comparing the expected increase in revenues to the expected increase in *variable* expenses. Review Exhibits 26-4 and 26-5.

Correctly analyzing a business decision requires you to ignore **irrelevant costs**. A cost that is the same for all decision alternatives is NOT relevant and must be ignored. You should consider only those costs and revenues that change between alternatives.

1. **Special sales order.** The example in your text that analyzes whether to accept the special sales order of oil filters is an excellent example of a special sales order. Using the conventional income statement as the basis for the decision is not the correct approach because of the nature of fixed costs. However, when the question is analyzed using the contribution margin format, the irrelevant costs (fixed expenses) are ignored and a better decision results.

2. **Dropping products, departments, and territories.** When considering when to drop products, departments, or territories, with *no change* in fixed costs, the only relevant information is the expected decreases in revenues and variable costs, which together show the contribution margin and change in operating income. Study Exhibit 26-7 in your text. When considering when to drop products, departments, or territories with *a change* in fixed costs, the analysis must include the change in fixed costs as well as changes in variable costs and revenues. Refer to Exhibit 26-8 for an example. The key to deciding whether to drop products, departments or territories is to compare the lost revenue against the costs that can be saved from dropping them. If the lost revenues from dropping a product, department or territory exceed the cost savings from dropping them, then do not drop them. If the cost savings exceed the lost revenues from dropping a product, department, or territory, then drop them.

3. **Product mix.** When deciding which product to emphasize, it is necessary to determine whether a constraint or limiting factor exists. A **constraint** is a factor that restricts production or sales of a product. Constraints may be stated in terms of labor hours, machine hours, materials, or storage space. To maximize profits, the decision rule to follow when deciding which product to emphasize is to emphasize the product with the highest contribution margin per unit of the constraint. Exhibit 26-9 in your text presents an example of how to maximize the contribution margin per machine hour.

4. **Outsourcing (make or buy).** The outsourcing decision is one where managers decide whether to buy a component product or service or to produce it in-house. The heart of these decisions is *how best to use available facilities.* The relevant information for the make analysis includes: 1) direct materials, 2) direct labor, 3) variable overhead, and 4) fixed overhead. The relevant information for the buy analysis is: 1) the fixed overhead that will continue whether the part is made or bought and 2) the purchase price to buy the part. The decision rule to follow when deciding whether to outsource is if the incremental costs of making exceed the incremental costs of outsourcing, then outsource; if the incremental costs of making are less than the incremental costs of outsourcing, then do not outsource. This analysis shows whether it is cheaper to make the part or to buy the part. Review Exhibit 26-10 in your text. The analysis in Exhibit 26-10 assumes there is no other use for the facilities freed up. Sometimes facilities can be used to make other products if the product currently produced is purchased from an outside supplier. In the make or buy decision, the alternatives become: 1) make, 2) buy and leave the facilities idle, and

3) buy and use the facilities for other products. When the facilities could be used for some other purpose, then the opportunity cost of the alternative not chosen must be considered. An **opportunity cost** is the benefit foregone by not choosing an alternative course of action. An opportunity cost is not a business transaction and is therefore not recorded in the accounting records. It is only used as a consideration in making a decision between alternatives. As indicated in Exhibit 26-11 the alternative with the lowest net cost is the *best use of the facilities.*

5. **Selling as is or processing further.** The sell as is or process further decision rule to follow is if extra revenue (from processing further) exceeds the extra cost of processing further, then process further. If the extra revenue (from processing further) is less than the extra cost of processing further, then do not process further. Exhibit 26-13 illustrates the sell as is or process further decision. Note that past historical costs of inventory are **sunk costs**—they cannot make a difference to the decision; the sunk costs are irrelevant because they are present under both alternatives.

Study Tip: Review the Decision Guidelines title *Short-Term Special Business Decisions* in your text.

Objective 3 – Use payback and accounting rate of return models to make longer-term capital budgeting decisions.

Capital budgeting refers to budgeting for the acquisition of capital assets—assets used for a long period of time. There are four popular capital budgeting decision models presented in this chapter. They help managers evaluate and choose among alternatives. Whether the acquisition of a capital asset is desirable depends on its ability to generate net cash inflows—that is inflows in excess of outflows—over the asset's useful life.

1) **Payback** is the length of time it takes to recover, in net cash inflows, the dollars invested in a capital outlay. The payback model measures how quickly managers expect to recover their investment dollars.

If annual net cash inflows are equal each year, then:

$$\text{PAYBACK PERIOD} = \frac{\text{AMOUNT INVESTED}}{\text{EXPECTED ANNUAL NET CASH INFLOWS}}$$

The decision rule is to invest only if payback period is shorter than the asset's useful life. Investments with shorter payback periods are more desirable, *only if all other factors are the same.* However, investment decisions should not be made based on payback period alone because the payback period only highlights the length of time required to recover an investment, and does not consider profitability. See Exhibit 26-14 for an illustration of the payback model where net cash inflows are equal each year.

2) The **accounting rate of return** measures the operating income an asset generates.

$$\text{ACCOUNTING RATE OF RETURN} = \frac{\text{AVERAGE ANNUAL OPERATING INCOME}}{\text{AVERAGE AMOUNT INVESTED IN THE ASSET}}$$

AVERAGE ANNUAL OPERATING INCOME FROM ASSET	=	AVERAGE ANNUAL NET CASH INFLOW FROM ASSET	-	ANNUAL DEPRECIATION ON ASSET

$$\text{AVERAGE AMOUNT INVESTED} = \frac{\text{AMOUNT INVESTED} + \text{RESIDUAL VALUE}}{2}$$

See Exhibit 26-15 for an example of this calculation. Companies that use the accounting rate of return model set a minimum required rate of return. The decision rule is if the expected accounting rate of return exceeds the required rate of return, then invest; if it does not, then do not invest.

Although the accounting rate of return measures profitability, it ignores the time value of money, a topic you were introduced to in Chapter 15.

Objective 4. – Use discounted cash flow models to make longer-term capital budgeting decisions.

The following two models consider the timing of the cash outlay for the investment and the timing of the net cash inflows that result. These models are the most commonly used in capital budgeting.

3) **Net present value** is a decision model that brings cash inflows and outflows back to a common time period by discounting these expected future cash flows to their present value, using a minimum desired rate of return. The **minimum desired rate of return** used to calculate present value is called the **discount rate** (also called the hurdle rate, required rate of return, cost of capital, and target rate). Exhibit 26-17 in your text illustrates present value analysis in which the annual cash inflows are equal (an annuity) and Exhibit 26-19 illustrates the same analysis in which the annual cash inflows are different. Note that when the annual cash inflows are equal, you use Exhibit 26-16, Present Value of an Annuity of $1, to find the present value factor. When the cash inflows are not equal, you use Exhibit 26-18, Present Value of $1, to find the present value factor for each year you have cash inflows.

The steps to determine the net present value of a project are:

1. Find the present value of annual cash inflows.
2. Find the present value of the residual, if any.
3. Add (1) and (2) to obtain the present value of the net cash inflows.
4. Subtract the investment (which is already in present value terms) from the present value of the net cash inflows (3) to obtain the net present value of the project.

The net present value method is based on cash flows and considers both profitability and the time value of money. The decision rule is to only invest in capital assets if the net present value is positive.

4) **Internal rate of return** is another discounted cash flow model. The internal rate of return (IRR) is the rate of return that a company can expect to earn by investing in the project; the higher the IRR, the more desirable the project. The IRR is the discount rate that makes the net present value of an investment project equal to zero. There are three steps in calculating the internal rate of return:

1. Identify the expected net cash inflows.

2. Find the discount rate that makes the present value of the total cash inflows equal to the present value of the cash outflows. Work backwards to find the discount rate that makes the present value of the annuity of cash inflows equal to the amount of the investment by solving the following equation for the annuity present value (PV) factor:

Investment = Expected annual net cash inflow × Annuity PV factor

$$\text{Annuity PV factor} = \frac{\text{Investment}}{\text{Expected annual net cash inflow}}$$

3. Turn to the Present Value of an annuity of $1 (Exhibit 26-17) and scan the row corresponding to the project's expected life and choose the column with the number closest to the annuity PV factor that was calculated in Step 2. to find the interest rate that reflects the IRR.

4. Compare the IRR determined in Step 3 with the minimum desired rate of return. The decision rule is to invest in capital assets if the IRR exceeds the required rate of return. See Exhibit 26-20 in your text.

Objective 5. – Compare and contrast the four capital budgeting methods.

Exhibit 26-21 summarizes some of the strengths and weaknesses of the four capital budgeting models described above. The two discounted cash flow models (net present value and internal rate of return) are favored because they consider both profitability and the time value of money whereas the payback model ignores both while the accounting rate of return considers only profitability.

Study Tip: Review the Decision Guidelines titled *Capital Budgeting* at the end of the chapter.

TEST YOURSELF

All the self-testing materials in this chapter focus on information and procedures that your instructor is likely to test in quizzes and examinations.

I. Matching   *Match each numbered term with its lettered definition.*

_____1. Accounting rate of return
_____2. Capital budgeting
_____3. Decision model
_____4. Time value of money
_____5. Opportunity cost
_____6. Relevant information
_____7. Annuity

_____8. Constraint
_____9. Discount rate
_____10. Net present value
_____11. Payback period
_____12. Sunk cost
_____13. Internal rate of return

A. A method or technique for evaluating and choosing among alternative courses of action
B. Actual outlay incurred in the past and present under all alternative courses of action; irrelevant because it makes no difference to a current decision
C. Expected future data that differs between alternative courses of action
D. Formal means of making long-range decisions for investments such as plant locations, equipment purchases, additions of product lines, and territorial expansions
E. Item that restricts production or sales
F. Calculated as average annual net cash inflow from asset minus annual depreciation on asset, divided by average amount invested
G. Length of time it will take to recover, in net cash inflows from operations, the dollars of a capital outlay
H. Management's minimum desired rate of return on an investment, used in a present value computation
I. The benefit that can be obtained from the next best course of action in a decision
J. Method of computing the expected net monetary gain or loss from a project by discounting all expected cash flows to their present value and deducting the cost of the investment, using a desired rate of return
K. Stream of equal periodic amounts
L. The fact that one can earn income by investing money for a period of time
M. The rate of return on a project that makes the net present value equal to zero

II. Multiple Choice   *Circle the best answer.*

1. Relevant information:

   A. is expected future data.
   B. differs among alternative courses of action.
   C. does not include sunk costs.
   D. all of the above.

2. The standard income statement categorizes expenses:

   A. into cost of goods sold and selling and administrative expenses.
   B. into variable expenses and fixed expenses.
   C. both A and B.
   D. neither A nor B .

3. The contribution margin income statement categorizes expenses:

    A. into cost of goods sold and selling and administrative expenses.
    B. into variable expenses and fixed expenses.
    C. both A and B.
    D. neither A nor B .

4. Select the correct statement concerning the payback period.

    A. The longer the payback period, the less attractive the asset.
    B. The shorter the payback period, the less attractive the asset.
    C. The longer the payback period, the more attractive the asset.
    D. Both B and C are correct.

5. The accounting rate of return considers:

    A. the timing of cash flows.   C. profitability.
    B. the time value of money.   D. all of these.

6. The net present value method of capital budgeting considers:

    A. only cash flows.
    B. only the time value of money.
    C. both cash flows and the time value of money.
    D. the length of time to recoup the initial investment.

7. If a potential investment has a negative net present value:

    A. it should be accepted in all situations
    B. it should be rejected in all situations
    C. it should be accepted if payback is less than five years
    D. it should be rejected if the accounting rate of return is less than 16%

8. The internal rate of return (IRR) method, while similar to the net present value (NPV) method, differs from it in the following respect(s):

    A. IRR identifies expected future cash flows.
    B. IRR identifies the excess of the project's present value over its investment cost.
    C. IRR identifies a specific rate of return for the investment.
    D. all of the above

9. Which of the following capital budgeting decision models is based on profitability?

    A. Payback   C. Net present value
    B. Accounting rate of return   D. Internal rate of return

10. In deciding whether to take a year off from college and work full-time or continue in school and work part-time, the opportunity cost is:

   A. the amount of money already invested in your education.
   B. the amount saved from college expenses by working full-time.
   C. the amount of earnings foregone by selecting one option over the other.
   D. the difference between the projected total income of the two options.

III. Completion   *Complete each of the following.*

1. A(n) _____ income statement is more useful for special decision analysis than the standard income statement.
2. The item that restricts production or sales is called a _____ .
3. Fixed costs are only relevant to a special decision if _____ _____ .
4. A(n) _____ is the cost of the foregone next best alternative, or profit given up, by selecting one alternative over another one.
5. _____ costs are not formally recorded in the accounting records.
6. The major weakness of the payback is that it _____ _____ .
7. An investment should be rejected if its net present value is _____ .
8. A project's internal rate of return (IRR) is that rate of interest that makes the present value of the project's cash inflows and cash outflows _____ .
9. The _____ refers to earning income by investing money for a period of time.
10. Generally accepted accounting principles are based on accrual accounting whereas capital budgeting is based on _____ .

IV. Daily Exercises

1. Place the following in correct sequence (1 through 4):

    _____a. Define business goals
    _____b. Gather and analyze relevant information to compare alternatives
    _____c. Identify alternative courses of action
    _____d. Choose the best alternative to achieve the goals

2. Compute the payback period given the following information:

Cost of new machinery	$450,000
Useful life	9 years
Annual depreciation	$50,000
Annual net cash inflow attributed to new machinery	$18,000

3. Continental Manufacturing produces a component that sells for $62. The manufacturing cost per component is $38. Variable manufacturing costs are $29 and fixed manufacturing costs are $9 per unit. Continental has received an offer for 8,000 components; however, the components will have to be slightly modified to conform to metric measurements. Modifying each component will cost 50¢. The buyer is willing to pay $33 for each component. Assuming Continental has excess capacity, identify the relevant and irrelevant factors in deciding to accept the offer.

4. Using the information in Daily Exercise #3 above, decide whether Continental should accept the offer.

5. Molinari, Inc., is planning to construct a new facility at a total cost of $25,000,000. The project will have a 20-year life at the end of which it will be abandoned. It is expected to generate net income of $3,750,000. Calculate the accounting rate of return of the new facility.

6. Review the information in Daily Exercise #5 above and consider the following additional information. Net cash inflows from the new facility are expected to be $5,000,000 annually for 20 years. Calculate the cash payback period.

7. Review the information in Daily Exercises #5 and #6 above and consider the following additional information. Molinari has a 12% minimum rate of return on investment. Calculate the net present value of the investment, using the discounted cash flows. (Hint: you'll need the present value tables in your text.)

V. Exercises

1. A clothing wholesaler has offered to pay $20 per unit for 2,500 hats. This offer would put idle manufacturing capacity in use and not affect regular sales. Total fixed costs will not change. There will be only half the normal variable selling and administrative costs on this special order.

Normal selling price per hat	$25.00
Variable costs per hat:	
Manufacturing	14.00
Selling and Administrative	3.00
Fixed costs per hat:	
Manufacturing	2.00
Selling and Administrative	2.50

A. What is the relevant information associated with this special order?

B. What difference would accepting this special order have on company profits?

366

2. Braden, a bright young CPA, has provided you with the following information:

Salary at current position	$40,000
Revenues expected by opening his own office	125,000
Expenses expected for the new office	100,000

A. What is the opportunity cost associated with working at his current position?

B. What is the opportunity cost associated with starting his own business?

C. From purely a quantitative standpoint, what should he do?

3. Eric's Nursery is concerned that operating income is low, and is considering dropping its garden implements department. The following information is available:

	Total	Plants & Fertilizers	Garden Implements
Sales	$425,000	$225,000	$200,000
Variable expenses	239,500	91,500	148,000
Contribution margin	185,500	133,500	52,000
Fixed expenses	153,000	81,000	72,000
Operating income (loss)	$ 32,500	$ 52,500	($ 20,000)

Eric can avoid $48,000 of his nursery's fixed expenses by dropping the Garden Implements division.

Determine whether Eric should drop the Garden Implements department.

VI. Beyond the Numbers

Review the information in Exercise #2 and list additional considerations (both quantitative and qualitative) that might influence Braden's decision.

_____
_____
_____
_____
_____

VII. Demonstration Problems

Demonstration Problem #1

A. S&L Inc., produces two products, S and L, with the following per unit data:

	Product	
	S	L
Selling price	$50	$24
Variable expenses	30	15
Units that can be produced each hour	4	8

The company has 8,000 hours of capacity available. Which product should the company emphasize?

B. Body Works, Inc., has the following manufacturing costs for 4,000 of its natural bath sponges:

Direct materials	$ 6,000
Direct labor	3,000
Variable overhead	2,000
Fixed overhead	5,000
Total	$16,000

Another manufacturer has offered to sell Body Works similar sponges for $3.25 each. By purchasing the sponges outside, Body Works can save $2,000 of fixed overhead cost. The released facilities can be devoted to the manufacture of other products that will contribute $2,000 to profits. What is Body Works' best decision?

| | Alternatives | | |
	Make	Buy and leave facilities idle	Buy and use facilities for other products

Decision:

Demonstration Problem #2

The data for a piece of equipment follows:

Cost	$40,000
Estimated annual net cash inflows:	
Year 1	12,000
Year 2	12,000
Year 3	12,000
Year 4	12,000
Residual value	8,000
Estimated useful life	4 years
Annual rate of return required	12%

The present value of an amount of $1 at 12% is:

Year	1	2	3	4
Interest factor	0.893	0.797	0.712	0.636

The present value of an annuity of $1 at 12% is:

Year	1	2	3	4
Interest factor	0.893	1.690	2.402	3.037

Required:

1. What is the payback period for the equipment?
2. What is the accounting rate of return for the equipment?
3. What is the net present value of the equipment?
4. Indicate whether each decision model leads to purchase or rejection of this investment. Would you decide to buy the equipment? Give your reason.

Requirement 1 (payback period)

Requirement 2 (accounting rate of return)

Requirement 3 (net present value analysis)

Requirement 4 (decision)

SOLUTIONS

I. Matching

1. F	3. A	5. I	7. K	9. H	11. G	13. M
2. D	4. L	6. C	8. E	10. J	12. B	

II. Multiple Choice

1. D   Relevant information is the expected future data that differ between alternative courses of action. A sunk cost is an actual outlay that has been incurred in the past and is present under all alternatives. Sunk costs are irrelevant.

2. A   Answer B describes the contribution margin format income statement.

3. B   Answer A describes the "standard" income statement format.

4. A   Payback is the length of time it will take to recover, in net cash flow from operations, the dollars of a capital outlay. The shorter the payback the better. The longer it is, the less attractive.

5. C   The accounting rate of return is calculated by:
Average Annual Operating Income ÷ Average amount invested.
By looking at the numerator, answer C can be seen to be the best.

6. C   The net present value method computes the present value of expected future net cash flows and compares that present value to the initial investment. Answer C covers this approach.

7. B   The initial investment is subtracted from the present value of the investment's expected future cash flows. If negative, the investment does not recover its cost. If positive, the investment generates a return above the minimum required. Only projects with zero or positive net present value should be considered.

8. C   Both the NPV and IRR methods make use of expected future cash flows (answer A). Answer B is not correct because it describes only NPV. Only the IRR method (and not NPV) generates a specific rate of return for the project.

9. B   The accounting rate of return model is based on profitability; the other three models are based on net cash flows.

10. C   The opportunity cost is the benefit obtained from the next best course of action, so if the decision is to remain in school, the opportunity cost is the full-time wages not earned, whereas if the decision is to work full-time, the opportunity cost is the foregone part-time income.

III. Completion

1. contribution margin (The contribution margin format highlights how costs and income are affected by decisions.)
2. limiting factor, constraint (Such things as the size of the factory labor force, available storage space, availability of raw materials, available machine time, or market share can act as constraints.)
3. fixed cost differs among alternatives (Recall: a cost is relevant only if it differs between alternatives. A cost can differ between alternatives and still be fixed for each alternative.)
4. opportunity cost (It is not the usual outlay (cash disbursement) cost. If you quit your job to start your own business, the salary from the job you gave up is the opportunity cost of starting your own business.)
5. Opportunity (Since these costs do not involve giving up an asset or incurring a liability, they are not recorded.)
6. ignores profitability and the time value of money (Because of these shortcomings, the payback period can lead to unwise decisions.)
7. negative (If negative, the investment does not recover its cost. If positive, the investment generates an acceptable rate of return. Only projects with zero or positive net present value should be considered.)
8. equal
9. time value of money
10. cash flows

IV. Daily Exercises

1.

1	A.
3	B.
2	C.
4	D.

2. $450,000 / $18,000 = 25$ years

3.

Relevant
Variable manufacturing costs ($29)
Additional 50¢ cost/component
Continental has excess capacity
The $33 selling price

Irrelevant
The $62 selling price
$9.00 fixed costs

4. If the offer is accepted

Sales (8,000 × $33)	$264,000
Less: Variable Costs (8,000 × $29)	232,000
Additional Variable Costs (8,000 × 50¢)	4,000
Increase in Net Income	$28,000

5.

$$\text{Accounting rate of return} \quad = \quad \frac{\text{Average annual operating income}}{\text{Average amount of investment in asset}}$$

$$= \quad \frac{\$3,750,000}{(\$25,000,000/2)}$$

$$= \quad 30\%$$

6.

$$\text{Cash payback period} \quad = \quad \frac{\text{Amount invested}}{\text{Net cash inflows}}$$

$$= \quad \frac{\$25,000,000}{\$5,000,000}$$

$$= \quad 5 \text{ years}$$

7.

	Present Value at 12%	Net Cash Inflow	Total Present Value
Present value of equal annual net cash inflows for 20 years	7.469	$5,000,000	37,345,000
Investment			25,000,000
Net present value of new facility			$12,345,000

V. Exercises

1. A. The relevant information is the special order price of $20 per unit, the variable manufacturing cost of $14 per unit, and one-half the normal variable selling and administrative expenses which amount to $1.50 per unit ($3 × 1/2).

    B. Additional revenues from special order (2,500 × $20) $50,000
       Less: Variable manufacturing cost (2,500 × $14)   (35,000)
       Less: Variable selling and admin. cost (2,500 × $1.50)   (3,750)
       Increase in profits $11,250

2. A. The opportunity cost is the net revenue given up by keeping the existing position: $125,000 revenue - $100,000 expense = $25,000.

    B. The opportunity cost is the cost of giving up the existing position: $40,000.

    C. The current position pays $40,000. Going into business will net $25,000. Keeping the present position makes Braden $15,000 better off.

3. The relevant information is the contribution margin that would be lost if the garden implements department is eliminated and the fixed costs that would be eliminated. The nursery would lose the $52,000 contribution margin if the department is closed and would reduce fixed costs by $48,000. The lost contribution margin is $4,000 greater than the reduction in fixed costs ($52,000 contribution margin lost - $48,000 fixed costs eliminated), so the department should not be closed. The nursery is $4,000 better off by keeping it.

VI. Beyond the Numbers

Probably the most significant quantitative consideration is the potential increase in salary compared with the potential increase in income from the business. For instance, if salary increases are likely to average 10% over the foreseeable future while the business growth potential is 20% annually, in a few years the income from the business will surpass the salary. An important qualitative consideration is being an employee versus your own boss. Frequently, it is the intangible costs and benefits that cloud the issue and make decision-making so complex.

VII. Demonstration Problems

Demonstration Problem #1 Solved and Explained

A. Product to Emphasize

	Product	
	S	**L**
(1) Units that can be produced each hour	4	8
(2) Contribution margin per unit*	$20	$9
(3) Contribution margin per hour (1) × (2)	80	72
Capacity: Number of hours	× 8,000	× 8,000
Total contribution margin for capacity	$640,000	$576,000

* Contribution margins: S: $50 - $30 = $20; L: $24 - $15 = $9

Decision: The Company should emphasize Product S because its contribution margin at capacity is greater by $64,000.

Explanation:

When a constraint exists, such as the number of hours available, we must conduct our profit analysis in terms of the constraint. Since only 8,000 hours are available, our profit will be greatest if we produce the products that offer the highest contribution margin per hour. To compute the contribution margin per hour for each product, multiply the contribution margin per unit of each product times the number of units of each product that can be produced per hour.

Study Tip: The product with the highest contribution margin per hour will provide the highest profit.

B. Make or Buy

	Make	Buy and leave facilities idle	Buy and use facilities for other products
		Alternatives	
Direct materials	$ 6,000	-	
Direct labor	3,000	-	
Variable overhead	2,000	-	
Fixed overhead	5,000	$ 3,000	$ 3,000
Purchase price from outsider	-	13,000	13,000
Total cost of obtaining sponges	16,000	16,000	16,000
Profit contribution from other products	-	-	(2,000)
Net cost of obtaining 4,000 sponges	$16,000	$16,000	$14,000

Decision: The Company should buy the sponges and use the facilities for other products.

Explanation

Continuing to make the sponges will cost the same $16,000 that it currently costs. The current cost to produce is relevant because it will change if the sponges are purchased. If the sponges are purchased, the relevant information is the purchase price and the amount of fixed overhead that *will continue.* The problem tells us that $2,000 of fixed overhead will be saved. Since total fixed overhead is $5,000, $3,000 ($5,000 - $2,000) of fixed overhead will continue, and the sponges will cost $16,000. If the facilities are used to earned an additional $2,000 profit, the net cost of the sponges is $14,000 ($16,000 - $2,000). For this alternative, the additional relevant information is the profit from the other product that could be produced.

Study Tip: Relevant information differs among alternative courses of action.

Demonstration Problem #2 Solved and Explained

Requirement 1 (payback period)

When the annual net cash flows are constant, the payback period is equal to the amount of the investment divided by the annual net cash flows.

$$\$40,000 \div \$12,000 = 3.3 \text{ years}$$

Requirement 2 (accounting rate of return)

The accounting rate of return is average annual operating income from the investment divided by the average amount invested. Average annual operating income is equal to net cash inflows from operations (0) minus annual depreciation (D). Average amount invested is the sum of the investment (I) plus residual value (RV) divided by 2.

$R = (O - D) \div [(I + RV) \div 2] = (\$12,000 - \$8,000*) \div [(\$40,000 + \$8,000) \div 2] = 0.167 = 16.7\%$
* $D = (\$40,000 - \$8,000) \div 4 \text{ years} = \$8,000$

Requirement 3 (net present value analysis)

The steps to determine the net present value of a project are:

Present value of net equal annual cash inflows ($12,000 × 3.037)	$ 36,444
Present value of residual value ($8,000 × 0.636)	5,088
Present value of the equipment	41,532
Investment	40,000
Net present value	$ 1,532

Explanations:

Since the annual cash flow is the same amount, $12,000, it is an annuity. Multiply the annual amount, $12,000, by the present value of an annuity for 4 years. The present value of the cash inflows is $12,000 × 3.037, or $36,444.

The residual value of $8,000 is discounted to its present value ($8,000 × 0.636 = $5,088).

The present value of the equipment is $41,532 ($36,444 + $5,088).

The investment is $40,000.

The net present value of the investment is the present value of the equipment minus the investment.

NPV of Equipment = $41,532 - $40,000 = $1,532

Requirement 4 (decision)

The payback period is less than the useful life of the equipment. The accounting rate of return is higher than the 12% required return. Both methods indicate that the equipment should be purchased. The net present value is positive, which indicates that the rate of return exceeds the 12% required return. This decision model also indicates that the equipment should be purchased. Since the net present value considers both profitability and the time value of money (and the preferred decision model), and is positive in this instance, the equipment should be purchased.